LOWERING
NONTARIFF
BARRIERS

STANLEY D. METZGER

LOWERING
NONTARIFF
BARRIERS

U.S. Law, Practice, and Negotiating Objectives

THE BROOKINGS INSTITUTION
Washington, D.C.

Library of Congress Cataloging in Publication Data:

Metzger, Stanley D
  Lowering nontariff barriers.
  Includes bibliographical references.
  1. Foreign trade regulation—United States.
I Title.
KF1976.M38   343′.73′087   73-19767
ISBN 0-8157-5686-0

THE BROOKINGS INSTITUTION is an independent organization devoted to nonpartisan research, education, and publication in economics, government, foreign policy, and the social sciences generally. Its principal purposes are to aid in the development of sound public policies and to promote public understanding of issues of national importance.

The Institution was founded on December 8, 1927, to merge the activities of the Institute for Government Research, founded in 1916, the Institute of Economics, founded in 1922, and the Robert Brookings Graduate School of Economics and Government, founded in 1924.

The Board of Trustees is responsible for the general administration of the Institution, while the immediate direction of the policies, program, and staff is vested in the President, assisted by an advisory committee of the officers and staff. The by-laws of the Institution state, "It is the function of the Trustees to make possible the conduct of scientific research, and publication, under the most favorable conditions, and to safeguard the independence of the research staff in the pursuit of their studies and in the publication of the results of such studies. It is not a part of their function to determine, control, or influence the conduct of particular investigations or the conclusions reached."

The President bears final responsibility for the decision to publish a manuscript as a Brookings book or staff paper. In reaching his judgment on the competence, accuracy, and objectivity of each study, the President is advised by the director of the appropriate research program and weighs the views of a panel of expert outside readers who report to him in confidence on the quality of the work. Publication of a work signifies that it is deemed to be a competent treatment worthy of public consideration; such publication does not imply endorsement of conclusions or recommendations contained in the study.

The Institution maintains its position of neutrality on issues of public policy in order to safeguard the intellectual freedom of the staff. Hence interpretations or conclusions in Brookings publications should be understood to be solely those of the author or authors and should not be attributed to the Institution, to its trustees, officers, or other staff members, or to the organizations that support its research.

74- 01305

Foreword

AS INTERNATIONAL EFFORTS to liberalize trade have brought about a steady reduction in tariffs, other obstacles to trade have become more prominent. Some nontariff restrictions are specifically intended to protect national industries; others, intended primarily to protect the environment, discourage deceptive practices, or otherwise promote public welfare, can also have trade-distorting effects.

The impact of nontariff barriers on trade has not been quantified beyond the broadest kind of surmise. Yet some barriers are so obviously important that their susceptibility to elimination or reduction at the international bargaining table is an important issue even in the absence of precise measurement of their restrictive effects.

A group of U.S., European, and Japanese trade experts that met in 1969 to define a program of studies on nontariff barrier reduction pronounced six classes of such restrictions so "clearly significant" as to warrant thorough analysis. They are: quantitative restrictions on imports (including voluntary restraints affecting exports); buy-national laws and policies giving domestic or local goods preference over imported goods; antidumping regulations and countervailing duties; customs valuation methods and procedures; industrial standards affecting imported products; and government aids to industry that give domestic products an advantage over imports. The group decided not to deal with the effects of nontariff restrictions on agricultural products, since to do so adequately would require an approach far broader than that needed to analyze the effects of nontariff barriers on other products.

In this study Stanley D. Metzger analyzes the operation and relative importance of the six kinds of barriers within the United States, discusses the domestic legal and political factors that will affect the possibility of negotiating reductions, identifies the barriers most likely to be negotiable, and suggests the method best suited to reducing or removing each one.

Mr. Metzger is professor of law at Georgetown University Law Center. During the preparation of this study he was a senior fellow in the Brookings Foreign Policy Studies program. From 1967 to 1969 he served as Chairman of the U.S. Tariff Commission and earlier participated actively in the formulation of trade legislation and in trade negotiations as a State Department legal adviser.

Other studies growing out of the 1969 discussions are under way in Holland, Canada, Japan, the United Kingdom, West Germany, Australia, Italy, and the European Community. Among the cooperating organizations are the John F. Kennedy Institute of the University of Tilburg (Holland), the Private Planning Association of Canada, the Japanese Economic Research Center, the U.K. Trade Policy Research Center, and the Institut für Weltwirtschaft of Kiel. The several studies will concentrate on the factors in each country or region that will affect negotiation on nontariff barriers. It is hoped eventually to publish a synthesis of these related studies.

Among those who assisted the author in preparing this study were his research assistants William T. Adams, Alfred Eichenlaub, and Andrew DeCicco at the Georgetown University Law Center and his students Peter Williams and Savery McD. Gradoville. Helpful comments were made by several members of the Brookings Foreign Policy Studies staff: Henry Owen, director of the Foreign Policy Studies program, Edward R. Fried, Philip H. Trezise, C. Fred Bergsten, and Robert E. Asher. John M. Leddy read the manuscript carefully and made numerous useful suggestions. The author wishes to record his gratitude to all of them. Alice M. Carroll edited the manuscript and Patricia P. B. Wells prepared the index.

The Institution is indebted to the Ford Foundation for partial support of the study. As in all Brookings books, the views expressed here are those of the author, and should not be ascribed to the Ford Foundation or to the trustees, officers, or other staff members of the Brookings Institution.

KERMIT GORDON
President

October 1973
Washington, D.C.

Contents

Index   242

Tables

CHAPTER ONE

The Negotiating Problem

SINCE THE END of World War II, the major trading nations of the world have been actively engaged in lowering the high tariff barriers they had established against each other's goods during the 1920s and the Depression of the 1930s. Six negotiations, beginning in 1947 and culminating in the highly successful Kennedy Round of June 1967, achieved a remarkable diminution of tariff levels—average rates of duty on imports have been reduced to something less than 10 percent for the major participants in international trade.[1] These deep reductions have contributed to extraordinary increases in the levels of international trade over the low point of the early 1930s, and for the people of the participating nations to historically high living standards during a period of sustained economic development.

Progress toward freer international trade, with its concomitant economic benefits, has also widened the areas of peaceful cooperation, as nations have curtailed sharply the use of economic weapons reminiscent of earlier years and begun trading more with each other. Tariff reductions were not the only benefits achieved through this cooperative venture in dismantling barriers to trade. A group of trade rules is now embodied in the General Agreement on Tariffs and Trade (GATT), the same agreement that contained the results of the tariff negotiating sessions. Going beyond the objective of merely protecting the tariff concessions from nullification and impairment, the GATT constitutes a comprehensive charter of fair trading rules: unconditional most-favored-nation treatment on

1. See Ernest H. Preeg, *Traders and Diplomats* (Brookings Institution, 1970), Chap. 13 and App. A.

duties and other charges on the importation of goods, national treatment of those goods once they have passed through the customs house, a ban on quantitative restrictions (subject to important exceptions). They point to an international trading system in which every form of protectionist device except the tariff itself would eventually be eliminated, and tariff levels would eventually be bargained down to a point where they would no longer seriously impede international trade based on comparative economic advantage in the production of goods.

But while very substantial progress has been made in securing reciprocal cuts in tariffs and the elimination of balance of payments restrictions during the postwar years, progress has been slow indeed in getting rid of the deeply entrenched nontariff barriers which had built up over the latter half of the nineteenth and the first third of the twentieth centuries.

Tremendous variety, substantial complexity, and consequent tenacity are characteristic of nontariff barriers.[2] Whether the issue is preferential government purchasing of domestically produced articles, or the terms of antidumping and countervailing duty legislation and their administration, or customs valuation techniques that have built-in protectionist biases, or the myriad other domestic practices aimed specifically at benefiting domestic industry, each has in varying degree become part of the warp and woof of the society in which it is found. Each has its own constituency, the special interest group that called the barrier into being and is alert to any effort to tamper with it in a manner that would lessen its efficacy as a protective device.

These constraints were perfectly obvious in 1947, when the GATT was negotiated; even so, many of the trade rules written into the agreement were inconsistent with particular pieces of domestic legislation in many of the signatory countries. For example, Canada's antidumping law did not require an injury determination before antidumping duties could be levied—mere sales at less than the goods brought in home markets were sufficient. The countervailing duty law of the United States likewise had no injury test—mere subsidization of dutiable imports to the U.S. market

2. See Robert E. Baldwin, *Nontariff Distortions of International Trade* (Brookings Institution, 1970), for an analysis and informal catalog of the major nontariff barriers erected by the major trading nations of the world. See also Harald B. Malmgren, *Trade Wars or Trade Negotiations? Nontariff Barriers and Economic Peacekeeping* (Washington: Atlantic Council of the United States, 1971); and Gerard Curzon and Victoria Curzon, *Hidden Barriers to International Trade,* Thames Essay No. 1 (London: Trade Policy Research Centre, 1970).

triggered the added duty to offset the subsidy. Yet GATT Article VI requires an injury test in both cases.

The problem could have been solved by requiring countries to conform their laws with GATT rules before becoming contracting parties. This possibility was quickly rejected in the GATT negotiations because such a requirement would have prevented a number of important countries' becoming parties to the agreement for an indefinite period. In some, executive branches could adopt and attempt to effectuate liberal trade policies, but legislatures were notoriously more recalcitrant; in others the government was not prepared to run the political hazards of changing laws.

The method adopted was to permit the continued application of inconsistent domestic legislation existing at the time the country became a contracting party, but not to permit any intensification of the inconsistency, or the creation of any new inconsistencies. This freeze principle was also applied to the derogations from the most-favored-nation principle, such as British Commonwealth, French Union, and the U.S.-Cuban and U.S.-Philippines tariff preference arrangements.

As a consequence of this solution, all of the pre-GATT domestic legislation of each of the twenty-three original (by 1973, eighty-three) signatories that required the imposition of nontariff barriers to international trade was protected by a grandfather clause from being considered in violation of GATT.

There can be little doubt that a price was paid for this solution of the dilemma. For by taking the pressure off inconsistent domestic laws, it further entrenched the nontariff barriers created by them, and indeed emboldened those benefited by the barriers to believe that somehow they had been legitimized. This made their removal or amelioration the more difficult over the years, as the old inconsistent laws continued to work their will. The GATT rules with which they were inconsistent looked more and more ineffectual because so long out of tune with actual state practice. Indeed, the weakness of the GATT rules arising from the grandfather clause has contributed greatly to the widely held belief that those rules affecting nontariff barriers function more as a brooding omnipresence influencing the conduct of nations than as a code of law binding their actions.[3]

3. See Robert E. Hudec, "The GATT Legal System: A Diplomat's Jurisprudence," *Journal of World Trade Law*, Vol. 4 (1970), p. 615, on the actual operation of the GATT code of rules, indicating the manner in which they influence conduct

In addition to the nontariff barriers that the GATT rules legislated against but nonetheless protected by the grandfather clause, there were numerous nontariff barriers that were not even dealt with by the GATT. Private restrictive business practices having an adverse effect on international trade—territorial division of markets and price fixing, the deliberate use of industrial specifications to favor domestic producers, for example— were not even made the subject of GATT rules (they were to have been dealt with in the International Trade Organization charter), and could only be dealt with, if at all, as measures impairing the value of trade concessions for which compensation could, on proof of damage, be demanded.[4]

The weakness of GATT's regulation of nontariff barriers is most glaring in the agricultural and raw material field. Article XVI fails to establish specific rules against subsidization of exports of these materials while nonetheless permitting countries to countervail such imports. The no-quota rule of Article XI specifically excepts important agricultural products, and the 1955 waiver given the United States allows import quotas on agricultural products even where there are no domestic production or marketing controls on the price-supported domestic product. This latter action set the stage for the European Economic Community's common agricultural policy which utilizes variable import levies and ancillary devices limiting imports to a greater extent than had ever been practiced hitherto.

The first serious effort, other than GATT itself, to deal with nontariff barriers was the Kennedy Round of Tariff Negotiations, which began in 1963. Unfortunately, the relatively haphazard method of selecting the barriers, the limited number dealt with, the unevenness of their impact, and the sorry aftermath of the agreements concluded brought into sharp

---

and yet have a far less effectively binding quality than most systems of law are thought to possess.

4. Under Article XXIII of the General Agreement on Tariffs and Trade (GATT) a contracting party may withdraw concessions granted in return for those "nullified or impaired" by action of another contracting party. That action can consist of a violation of the GATT, or the application of a measure that may or may not conflict with GATT, or impairment of the expectations of the concession-granting party caused by "the existence of any other situation." See Stanley D. Metzger, *Law of International Trade: Documents and Readings* (Lerner Law Book, 1966), Vol. 1, pp. 575–76.

relief the serious problems presented for future significant and successful negotiations on nontariff barriers.

The principles and procedures for conducting the Kennedy Round negotiations were established in "a very difficult and at times rancorous" negotiation in May 1963.[5] The United States desired to see a deep-cutting, straight tariff negotiation on industrial goods, with nontariff barriers and the agricultural sector treated separately from tariffs. The European Economic Community desired to see a much thinner negotiation—less than 50 percent across-the-board tariff cuts. The six-country group wanted negotiations on certain nontariff barriers (those the United States habitually employed) linked closely with tariff negotiations, so that they could use any failure to lower nontariff barriers to offset the tariff cuts desired by the United States.

The compromise Ministerial Conference Resolution governing the Kennedy Round required that the negotiations deal with nontariff barriers as well as with tariffs; that there be equal "substantial linear tariff reductions" (later refined to a working hypothesis of 50 percent reductions subject to a minimum of exceptions); and that it be open to each country to "request additional trade concessions or to modify its own offers"—which in context meant to reduce them—where this "is necessary to obtain a balance of advantages between it and the other participating countries."[6]

The importance of the nontariff barrier negotiations and the barriers selected was perhaps most graphically put in a joint statement of French and Italian business leaders:

As a rule negotiations cover only tariffs; but obviously when it is anticipated that the entire set of customs tariffs is to be substantially reduced, steps must also be taken to abolish or standardise non-tariff barriers, lest the latter jeopardize or nullify the value of the tariff reductions.

It is well known that sometimes non-tariff measures hit merchandise more heavily than tariffs and plunge economic agents into a state of uncertainty in determining prices. There is as yet no catalogue of non-tariff trade barriers, but we do know that they are more numerous on the American side than on the Community side.

We shall simply recall the following:

Customs appraisal of value, i.e., the American selling price. This method

5. Stanley D. Metzger, "The Prospects for the Kennedy Round," in Dennis Cameron Thompson (ed.), *The Expansion of World Trade: Legal Problems and Techniques* (London: Stevens & Sons for British Institute of International and Comparative Law, 1965), p. 17.

6. Ibid.

contrasts with GATT rules and results in extremely high levies (sometimes 100 percent of the price on the original invoice), which creates a factor of doubt prejudicial to the development of sales to the United States;

The Buy American Act, under which the American Government can, in certain cases, award preference tenders to American goods despite their higher prices;

The Antidumping Act, with procedure lasting two to three years which, improperly invoked, stops all the imports involved;

Customs tariff classification, etc.

In regard to this angle of the negotiations, the parties are likewise at variance over the procedure to be followed, as the Americans want to handle it separately, while the EEC has no desire to see it removed from the tariff aspects.[7]

The difficulties of negotiating on nontariff barriers were as well known to European businessmen as to the EEC itself. As one observer pointed out in mid-1964:

Many of them, such as anti-dumping procedures, for example, are laid down in domestic laws and regulations which are very hard to change. Often, substantive determinations under these procedures, such as whether "material injury" to a domestic "industry" has occurred in consequence of sales at less than fair value, are committed to the judgment of independent and bipartisan regulatory commissions. With respect to others, such as the American selling price method of customs valuation for certain chemical products, there may be doubts concerning the bare legal authority to negotiate changes without new legislation, as well as the familiar problem of deciding to change a forty-year-old practice without submitting the matter to the legislative process for judgment even if the legal question is answered satisfactorily.

Concerning other types of non-tariff barriers, such as the Buy American Act, where preferences are given to domestic suppliers in governmental purchases despite higher prices, the high preference currently being given may have been imposed for balance of payments reasons, which do not necessarily right themselves in time for tariff bargaining sessions.[8]

Unfortunately, the lugubrious prediction inherent in that appraisal was only too well borne out. The aftermath of the nontariff agreements signed in Geneva on June 30, 1967—the Antidumping Code and the separate agreement on American selling price (ASP)—was most unhappy. Finding that the Antidumping Code trammeled the Tariff Commission's ability to read loosely the injury requirement of U.S. law, the Congress authorized the commission to continue to do so, in direct contravention of the

7. Comité Europeen pour le Progrés Economique et Social (CEPES), quoted in ibid., pp. 24–25.
8. Ibid., pp. 23–24.

code. The ASP agreement, made subject to congressional consent, has simply not been adopted, despite the efforts of successive administrations to secure its acceptance.

Thus, after a quarter century of substantial progress in lowering the tariff barriers to increased international trade, the trading nations were faced with practically all of the nontariff barriers that had always beset them in their efforts to trade with each other.

Nontariff barriers can of course present definitional problems. Is an antidumping or countervailing duty a nontariff barrier? Is the American selling price system of valuation for tariff purposes a nontariff barrier? Are regulations that are imposed for benign reasons of avoiding deception of the public—such as marking of origin of goods or grading of agricultural products—but that are capable of being used for protectionist purposes, barriers to trade? These classification problems exist, but they are not really serious in international trade terms. For there are so many generally acknowledged, unproblematical nontariff barriers to trade that have an important adverse effect on the volume and quality of the world's trade as to dwarf those on which there may be some disputation. For example, it is clear that preferences for local products in governmental procurement are a potent barrier to international trade. So, too, are quantitative restrictions of imported products, agricultural, mineral, or industrial, such as governmental quotas on wheat, cotton, and oil and oil products, as well as voluntary restraints imposed by exporting countries at the instance of importing countries over such products as steel exports to the United States, or Japanese textile products to the United States, Canada, and European countries. In general, all regulations of trade other than ordinary rates of duty imposed on ordinary classifications of articles valued according to customary methods can be considered nontariff barriers to the extent that they can be, and often are, used to interdict trade for protectionist purposes—to protect, in added degree, domestic industry against competitive imports.

Unlike tariff barriers, however, nontariff barriers to trade are often extremely difficult to quantify in trade terms and are embedded in a wide variety of domestic legislation and practice whose application may be slight or substantial. Successful negotiation of these barriers is a far more complex question than that of tariffs. In the case of tariffs, the question is comparatively simple—if the President of the United States, or the European Commission, secures 50 percent tariff-cutting negotiating authority from the Congress (as in the Trade Expansion Act of 1962), or from the Council of Ministers, that is the limit to which an international agreement may go, but no approval is needed for the resulting agreement, which will be effective as internal law automatically following proclamation by the President, or semiautomatically in the case of the European Community.

The variety and complexity of nontariff barriers seriously condition the means that can be employed to reduce or eliminate these obstacles to increased international trade. Four methods are legally feasible in the United States for dealing with these barriers.

The normal trade-agreements technique is to secure advance authorization from Congress to enter into an agreement, proclaim it, and thereby change domestic law with which it is inconsistent. But a key congressional committee, the Senate Finance Committee, went out of its way during the Kennedy Round negotiations to signify strong disapproval of any such technique in the antidumping and ASP cases, and there is no reason to believe that Congress would authorize agreements in this area generally that could be made domestic law without further reference to the Congress, particularly when arguably they work a change in existing domestic law. Such was indeed the case with the International Antidumping Code of 1968 (see Chapter 4).

It is possible of course to secure a congressional resolution stating a general policy on negotiating nontariff barriers. But this kind of resolution, suggested by successive administrations in recent years as a desirable mechanism, is a dubious venture. Even if a clean resolution were procured, how much good would it do when an agreement reducing the protective qualities of such barriers came back for congressional approval? Congress is obviously not bound to approve a particularized agreement adversely affecting some constituent's interests in virtue of a generalized approval of the President's decision to "go out and negotiate." And, of course, the chances of securing a clean resolution cannot be rated favorable. For, viewed realistically, it would be surprising if any legislative resolution would emerge without a number of specific exceptions, such as antidumping and countervailing duties, and perhaps even buy-American and others, which organized interest groups have expended resources to protect from erosion. Moreover, even if some important nontariff barriers escaped statutory exception, this would not obviate separate indications by the administration that it would refrain from or limit severely any negotiation of them in order to avoid a statutory exception. In the course of discussions in the Organization for Economic Cooperation and Development and elsewhere on tariff preferences for the manufactured products of less developed countries, the United States has indicated that it would exclude textiles, shoes, and petroleum products despite their trade importance for the developing countries, no doubt in the belief that an unsuccessful struggle would ensue to keep them from being specifically excepted by Congress.

A third method is negotiation without any advance authorization by Congress but with submission of the result for approval. Again, the recent ASP experience, where just that technique was employed, is hardly a happy augury for the future. Negotiating partners of the United States, aware of this failure of Congress to approve the supplemental ASP agreement, may be expected to be extremely reluctant to proceed on that basis in any future negotiation.

The ASP method of post-agreement approval called for legislative change implementing the agreement, which change was not forthcoming. Another way to request approval is to lay the negotiated agreement on the table for a period, say, sixty days, during which one or both houses of Congress could veto it. If such a veto did not occur, the agreement would be effective internationally and would also change inconsistent prior federal legislation, as well as state law. This technique would require legislative authorization of the method itself, at least in the overriding of federal legislation. While Congress has authorized such a technique in the past, principally in the Reorganization Acts, it is at least doubtful that it would do so in the nontariff barrier area for reasons quite similar to those that make the advance authorization technique a dubious venture. Even were that considerable obstacle to be overcome, the checkered history of presidential reorganization plans, with many rejected, particularly in recent years, does not augur well for congressional abstinence from exercising its veto in the nontariff barrier area.

Finally, there is the method actually utilized in the Antidumping Code case, presidential negotiation within the confines of a fair and reasonable construction of an existing federal statute, not necessitating subsequent approval by Congress. The errors in that case were the ignoring of the Senate Finance Committee's warning against tampering with the U.S. Antidumping Act, and stretching to its utmost limits the construction of the act. Obviously, great caution is called for in using this method. But if care is taken that the agreement is well within the leeway of existing federal legislation, the fact that this method was unsuccessful in the antidumping case should not be given crucial weight.

Nor are these legal and political obstacles to the successful negotiation of nontariff barriers peculiar to the United States. While legal problems of the European Community and countries under a parliamentary system are not nearly so formidable as those of the United States, their political problems are serious; while the European Commission can negotiate on nontariff barriers, the Council of Ministers instructs it as to the scope of negotiations and the lengths to which it can go. The Council, in turn, reflects national attitudes, each of which has its own political and legal constraints.

Any serious negotiation on nontariff barriers must come to grips with these negotiating problems as a first order of business, for they are at least as important as the substance of negotiations, with which, indeed, they are inextricably intertwined. Which of the multifarious barriers to deal with initially, and in what modes, must be analyzed both in terms of the feasible methods of amelioration and in terms of the kinds of amelioration that are desirable. Those barriers that appear unlikely to be dealt with successfully may well be consigned for handling in other ways or in the distant future.

CHAPTER TWO

The Legal Framework for U.S. Negotiations

THE CONSTITUTION of the United States, as interpreted by the courts, defines and limits the roles played by the President, the Congress, the states, and the courts themselves in the making and effectuation of international agreements. Partly because the limitations are often unclear, tensions have developed over the years between the principal actors—the President and the Congress—significantly affecting decisions as to which nontariff barriers the United States can reasonably expect to negotiate upon at a particular time, what the U.S. position on a particular barrier can reasonably be expected to be, what form an international agreement should take, and how that agreement's effectuation as domestic law in the United States should be sought.

Constitutional Powers over Foreign Affairs

Article II, Section 1 of the Constitution vests the executive power of the United States in the President; Section 2 designates him commander-in-chief of the armed forces and authorizes him to nominate and, with the advice and consent of the Senate, appoint ambassadors and to receive those of foreign states. Those provisions have been construed as giving the President a general power to conduct the foreign relations of the United

States[1] to the extent that it is necessary for it to act as a state.[2] Article II, Section 2 also gives the President the exclusive power to make treaties "by and with the advice and consent of the Senate . . . provided two thirds of the Senators present concur."

The Congress's powers in foreign affairs exist only to the extent that they are specifically enumerated in the Constitution. Article I, Section 8 provides that "the Congress shall have power to lay and collect taxes, duties, imposts and excises . . . to regulate commerce with foreign nations . . . [and] to declare war." In addition, the Congress has a number of powers dealing with primarily domestic matters, such as appropriations, that in fact give it a considerable decision-making voice in the foreign affairs area.[3] The Senate's role in approving treaties that are negotiated by the President prior to their ratification by the United States, added to Congress's specific authority, make it clear that the sum of congressional power to affect foreign affairs is very substantial.

The states are expressly denied the authority to enter into international agreements without the consent of Congress by Article I, Section 10 of the Constitution. Nevertheless, in areas where the Constitution does not grant powers to the federal government and in areas where the powers granted are not exercised,[4] the states have room for action that can affect foreign relations and they sometimes do play a significant role in curtailing the free flow of foreign commerce.

No power granted to the United States by the Constitution is unlimited; the power to make international agreements is no exception to this rule. Despite the President's or the Congress's power to deal with matters by international agreement, the constitutional limitations on action by any

1. *Penhallow v. Doane,* 3 U.S. (3 Dall.) 54, 80–81 (1795); *United States v. Curtiss-Wright Export Corp.,* 299 U.S. 304 (1936).

2. One limitation on the scope of the President's authority to make executive agreements is the requirement that the subject matter of the agreement be of legitimate international concern. *Missouri v. Holland,* 252 U.S. 416 (1920). See American Law Institute, *Restatement (Second) of the Foreign Relations Law of the United States* (1965), sec. 117.

3. See generally Louis Henkin, "The Constitution, Treaties and International Human Rights," *University of Pennsylvania Law Review,* Vol. 116 (1968), p. 1012.

4. Such powers may be exercised by the states only if they do not unreasonably interfere with the exercise of the congressional power and Congress did not intend to preempt an area where it had the power to do so. Compare *Skiriotes v. Florida,* 313 U.S. 69 (1941) (no conflict with federal legislation prevents Florida from regulating sponge fishing by its citizens) with *United States v. California,* 332 U.S. 19 (1947) (only the United States has power to regulate exploitation of resources under territorial waters even though no federal legislation has been enacted).

government in the United States may prohibit the making or the effectuation of the agreement. For example, an international agreement that would derogate from the rights guaranteed by the Bill of Rights would be set aside to the extent to which it so derogated.[5]

Self-executing and Non-self-executing Agreements

An elaborate yet often ill-defined body of law and practice has evolved in the making and effectuation of international agreements. One of the significant distinctions in this law and practice is between self-executing and non-self-executing international agreements. These characterizations determine whether, when, and how the provisions of an agreement become effective as domestic law in the United States.

Whether an international agreement is self-executing is determined in the first instance by the executive, and in the last analysis by courts of the United States through interpretation of the agreement's language, its context, and its negotiating history, and other interpretive aids.[6] If these guidelines indicate that the signatories intended that the agreement should have effect as domestic law within their respective states concurrent with the agreement becoming binding on them internationally, the agreement—or one or more of its provisions—is said to be "self-executing." For example, a treaty providing that nationals of each party "shall be free" to carry on trade in the territory of the other on the same conditions as its own citizens has been held self-executing—that is, not requiring subsequent translation into domestic law by a legislative act. On the other hand, if the language and other interpretative aids indicate that the signatories intended that the agreement should have effect within their respective states at some future time—after it has become effective internationally *and* after a subsequent legislative act—then the agreement, or the specific provision, is non-self-executing. For example, a treaty providing that the parties "will seek legislation implementing the provisions of the agreement" is clearly non-self-executing. The distinction is not always an easy one to make, and ambiguous language can evoke differing judicial interpretations.[7]

5. See *Reid v. Covert,* 354 U.S. 1 (1957); see generally *Restatement,* sec. 117.

6. See generally *Restatement,* secs. 141, 147, 154.

7. Compare *Foster v. Neilsen,* 27 U.S. (2 Pet.) 253 (1829) (1819 Spanish Treaty held non-self-executing) with *United States v. Percheman,* 32 U.S. (7 Pet.) 51 (1833) (same treaty held self-executing). The Spanish-language version of the treaty was called to the Court's attention in the second case and proved to be decisive.

Once an agreement or a provision of an agreement has been characterized as self-executing, several consequences normally can be predicted. Assuming there are no constitutional restraints on the scope or validity of the agreement, it immediately overrides prior, and precludes future, inconsistent legislation (and constitutional provisions) of state and local governments within the United States.[8] It overrides prior inconsistent federal legislation if the agreement is a treaty in the U.S. constitutional sense, although it may not override such legislation if it is an executive agreement. If the agreement is determined to be non-self-executing, further action of some kind, normally by state or federal legislatures, is necessary in order to make the provisions of the agreement binding as domestic law—regardless of whether it is a treaty or an executive agreement.

Treaties and Executive Agreements

The term *international agreements* includes both executive agreements and treaties; the distinction between them is made under U.S. domestic law but not under international law. Under U.S. domestic law, the two differ in the manner in which they are made and in some respects in their effect on domestic law.

Their most distinguishing characteristic is the method by which they become effective as international obligations of the United States. Under the Constitution, once a treaty is signed, it must be submitted to the Senate for advice and consent by a two-thirds majority of those present and voting, then returned to the President. If he decides to exchange ratifications with the treaty partner of the United States, and does so, the process is complete and the United States is bound by the terms of the treaty, including its effective date. No constitutional provision requires that executive agreements be submitted to Congress for approval. Thus, if there are no other restraints on the exercise of his constitutional powers, the President need only sign an executive agreement for it to become binding in accordance with its terms, including the effective date specified therein.[9]

The name given an agreement is only indicative, not dispositive, of whether it is a treaty in the constitutional sense. Thus, the Universal Postal

8. See *Restatement,* secs. 141–45.
9. Ibid., secs. 130, 131.

Convention, the International Wheat Agreement, and the U.S.-Japan Security Treaty are all treaties in the constitutional sense—because the executive considered that it was important, for varying reasons, that they be submitted to the special U.S. treaty-making process involving the advice and consent of the Senate.

All agreements other than those submitted to the special treaty-making process are termed, generically, "executive agreements." They may be classified into three types, depending on the degree of congressional participation in their making or effectuation: those authorized by congressional act; those authorized by a treaty; and those based on the President's authority to act on his own, without congressional participation.

A classic example of an executive agreement specifically authorized in advance by Congress is the Trade Agreements Act of 1934 and its extensions, including the Trade Expansion Act of 1962. This act authorized the President to "enter into foreign trade agreements," reducing therein U.S. duties in exchange for reciprocal concessions, within certain specified limits. The President was further authorized by the legislation to "proclaim" such "modification of existing duties and other import restrictions" as were "required or appropriate to carry out any foreign trade agreement" that he had entered. This proclamation had effect as domestic law, that is, changing ad valorem duties on imports without referral of the agreement to Congress for its approval.

Somewhat similar are the Bretton Woods Agreements—the Articles of Agreement of the International Monetary Fund and of the International Bank for Reconstruction and Development which were negotiated by a delegation of representatives of the President, including members of Congress. Following the negotiation, a joint resolution authorizing the President to accept the agreement was introduced into both houses, the draft articles of agreement were presented, hearings held, and the resolution passed. In that instance, however, no proclaiming authority was granted; consequential changes in domestic law were enacted at the same time that the resolution was legislated.

An executive agreement authorized in advance by a treaty is exemplified in the U.S.-Japanese administrative agreement on bases, troops, and related dispositions, including the status of forces. A specific article in the U.S.-Japanese Security Treaty of 1951, to which the Senate had given its advice and consent, authorized the agreement.

The classic case of an executive agreement pursuant to the President's constitutional authority, acting without congressional participation, is an armistice agreement, or the U.S.-U.K. destroyers-for-bases agreement of 1940, in which the United States transferred fifty over-aged destroyers to the United Kingdom in exchange for long-term leases on bases in Bermuda and elsewhere.[10]

The legal consequences flowing from the particular categorization of an agreement may differ significantly. Self-executing treaties and executive agreements involving substantial congressional participation override prior and future inconsistent state laws and constitutions, and prior inconsistent federal law. An executive agreement arrived at by the President acting on his authority alone also overrides prior and future inconsistent state laws and constitutions if it is self-executing,[11] but it does not, according to the dominant legal opinion in the United States, override prior inconsistent federal law.[12]

Making International Agreements

Only the President, or a person acting under his authority, may enter into international agreements.[13] This exclusive authority, based on his constitutional role as chief executive and head of state, gives him broad discretion in deciding whether to treat an international arrangement as an executive agreement or as a treaty, and therefore to control legally, in degree, the process by which it becomes binding on the United States. Unless the President rests his authority for entering into an agreement on an act of Congress that requires him to submit the agreement to the Congress for its approval before it becomes effective (which is relatively infrequent), he is free to make an executive agreement. He also has broad

10. September 2, 1940, The Hull-Lothian Agreement, *State Department Bulletin,* Sept. 7, 1940, pp. 199–200.

11. See *Restatement,* sec. 144; *United States v. Belmont,* 301 U.S. 324 (1937); *United States v. Pink,* 315 U.S. 203 (1942).

12. *Restatement,* sec. 144(1)(b). The Supreme Court has not ruled on the question, declining a clear opportunity to do so in *United States v. Guy W. Capps, Inc.,* 348 U.S. 296 (1955), which it decided on grounds other than those of the Court of Appeals, which had ruled that an existing congressional enactment was not affected by a later executive agreement where the President was acting solely on his own constitutional authority, 204 F. 2d 655 (4th Cir. 1953).

13. *Restatement,* sec. 132.

discretion as to what form the agreement will take and thus can decide whether to employ self-executing or non-self-executing language.

The primary legal limitations on this power to make agreements that bind the United States internationally are those that regulate the scope of any agreement the President may choose to make. The subject matter of the agreement must be of international concern. The agreement must not contravene any of the limitations of the Constitution applicable to all powers of the United States.[14]

The requirement that the matter be of international concern has not been a significant stumbling block to the President's power to make valid agreements. The fact that an international agreement has significant domestic effects does not detract from the President's power. For example, a treaty specifying closed seasons and other measures for the protection of migratory birds—areas traditionally regulated by individual states—was upheld because the birds flew over or lived in both Canada and the United States.[15] In today's interdependent world it is difficult to conceive of areas likely to be the subject of international agreement that are not matters of international concern, at least as long as that term continues to be broadly construed.

The other limitation on the scope of presidential treaty-making powers retains a good deal of vitality, in part because it is open-ended—any new interpretation of the Constitution may expand or detract from current limitations. Thus, a Supreme Court holding that the right to trial by jury could not be overridden by the exercise of any power to make international agreements or treaties rendered unenforceable a provision of the status of forces agreement with the United Kingdom that subjected accompanying wives of servicemen to military courts under certain circumstances.[16]

By all odds the most important limitation on the President's ability to make an effective agreement acting solely on his own authority is the need to stay consistent with existing federal legislation. In a field so fraught with existing federal legislation as trade and commerce, he must secure congressional consent—advance authorization or subsequent approval—before entering an international agreement that will clearly alter domestic law. Where domestic law will not be altered, he can make an agreement relying on his own constitutional authority. But the fact that substantial

14. Ibid., sec. 117.
15. *Missouri v. Holland,* 252 U.S. 416 (1920).
16. *Reid v. Covert,* 354 U.S. 1 (1957).

disputes can arise as to whether an agreement does in fact change domestic law threatens the distinct possibility of a debate, perhaps a major one, concerning the propriety of the agreement.

Despite this limitation, the trend toward the use of the executive agreement is undeniable, as these figures show:[17]

Years	Treaties	Executive agreements
1789–1839	60	27
1839–1889	215	238
1889–1939	524	917
1939–1951	109	1,107

Furthermore, executive agreements have increasingly dealt with important matters, and recently they have been based more often on the President's independent powers in important matters than in the past.

Why has this movement away from use of the treaty form occurred? Primarily because use of the executive agreement avoids the necessity of acquiring the concurrence of a two-thirds majority of the Senate. Even though an executive agreement may require congressional approval, more than a simple majority is not necessary. The tensions and pressures between Congress and the President in the trade and commerce area, which often heighten in dealing with nontariff barriers—since they tend to impinge essentially on domestic interests—will undoubtedly continue to make avoidance of congressional approval, either before or after an international agreement is reached, appear desirable from time to time.

Presidential-Congressional Relations and Tensions

While Congress is expressly given the power to regulate interstate and foreign commerce by the Constitution, the President's independent, general responsibility for foreign affairs interferes with that power, directly or indirectly. If Congress exercises its power by directing the President to negotiate agreements relating to foreign commerce, the President is not bound to comply with the directive, though he may in fact decide that it is wise to negotiate an agreement independently on his constitutional powers.

17. Data for the first three periods are from Wallace McClure, *International Executive Agreements* (Columbia University Press, 1941); those for the last period are from an analysis by Charles Bevans, assistant legal adviser for treaty affairs, Department of State, of registers of treaties and other international agreements signed and acceded to or ratified during that period.

The President, on the one hand, has exclusive power to make international agreements, but Congress on the other hand often has exclusive power that is essential to the implementation of agreements. Congress, wishing to reach an international agreement on a subject that is within its power to regulate, such as foreign commerce, must rely on the President; it is powerless to act in his place. But Congress has powers that can provide the leverage necessary to encourage the President to carry out its wishes, one of the most effective being its power over appropriations. Another is the ability to pass legislation over a presidential veto, and thereby, for example, cut off foreign aid to any country that trades with North Vietnam.

A President's decision to make an agreement that avoids the necessity of congressional approval may create considerable tension. If presidential and congressional powers are concurrent, and Congress has not exercised its power with respect to a particular area, then action by the President is less likely to generate congressional opposition than a contravention of congressional action. But presidential negotiations independent of the approval of Congress and subsequent to legislation in the area can create great tension between the two arms of government. The controversy may be a direct one, regarding the consistency of the presidential agreement with existing legislation, or Congress may view the executive action as an intention to influence the application of existing legislation in a way it does not approve. The latter precisely describes Congress's reaction to the negotiation of the International Antidumping Code (see Chapter 4).

The virtually infinite number of products and industries that can be, and are, regulated makes product-by-product legislation of controls impossible. No attempt to so regulate tariffs has been made since the debacle of the Smoot-Hawley Tariff Act of 1930. In that act, what started as an effort to afford additional protection to agricultural products mushroomed into a highly protectionist bill that boosted tariffs for thousands of items, as legislative log-rolling occurred in earnest.

The same kinds of pressures make it difficult for Congress to achieve significant substantive changes in already enacted trade legislation—particularly if the legislation protects the interests of politically powerful industrial, agricultural, or labor groups. These groups often feel that movement from existing legislation would harm their position. Legislators, in consequence, know that any changes in legislation will necessitate lengthy political haggling and they will seek to avoid such confrontations whenever possible. For example, the last general U.S. tariff act, the Smoot-Hawley, was enacted in 1930, the Antidumping Act has remained virtually unchanged since 1921, and the countervailing duty statute and the Sherman Antitrust Act have remained fundamentally unchanged since their enactment in the 1890s.

The difficulties of Congress in dealing legislatively on a product-by-product or industry-by-industry basis in the international trade area do not similarly inhibit the executive branch. The relative remoteness of the executive from constituents' product pressures permits it to view the trade and commerce area from a national vantage point and base its policy on all factors contributing to the nation's well-being; where it has acted in response to constituent pressures, the response has usually been in consequence of strong congressional pressure. From an administrative standpoint, the ability to deal with trade and commerce problems without concentrated and direct political responsibilities, through specialized agencies and adequate manpower, permits the executive branch to make decisions relatively unhampered by political trade-offs or allegiances. The fact that it does so through interpreting, applying, and implementing basic congressional policy choices exemplified in existing law no doubt assists it greatly in this task. From the standpoint of flexibility, the President, having the capacity to negotiate with other nations within a range of choice afforded by congressionally established policy, is in a much stronger position than Congress to adjust the implementation of trade policies to those followed by the United States' trading partners.

Alternative Methods of Negotiating

A broad delegation of authority to the President, coupled with some standards, policy guidance, and limitations, is in the eyes of many the best means the Congress has of exercising its constitutional powers to regulate interstate and foreign commerce. Once legislation is passed, congressional control over the President's administration of an act normally is restricted to reporting requirements, a brief review during annual appropriations hearings, and the threat of amendment or repeal if the act or its administration appears to be grossly inadequate to Congress or the groups to which it is responsive. The President assembles the staff necessary to administer the act, interprets it through executive order and regulation, and administers it on a case-by-case basis.

Congressional Authorization of Agreements

Advance authorization to negotiate, as in the Trade Agreements legislation of 1934 and ensuing years through 1962, is becoming extremely difficult to secure, even in the relatively well-charted area of pure tariff-bargaining. Increased protectionist sentiment, rising sharply from 1967, the end of the Kennedy Round, to the present, has made it highly problematical whether such authorization can be forthcoming from the Congress in the nontariff barrier area in the next several years. Nothing in recent history gives aid and comfort to those who envision a broad grant of authority to the President to negotiate the lowering of nontariff barriers. The substantial decline and then the elimination of the surplus on the trade account of the American balance of payments, followed by a substantial deficit in recent years, the necessity twice to revalue the dollar, and the persistently high unemployment rate in the United States have tended to sustain and even expand protectionist sentiment. In many quarters it is believed that these matters will not turn round definitively for at least several years. The domestic political atmosphere seems unlikely to be conducive to the securing of broad congressional authority to negotiate the reduction or elimination of protectionist nontariff barriers. Though advance congressional authority is the best solution for presidential negotiating problems, it is likely to be unattainable.

Congressional Approval of Treaties

If congressional authorization in advance of negotiation of agreements to reduce nontariff barriers is unobtainable, what about the treaty method, involving advance negotiation and subsequent congressional approval? History suggests that this method is quite infeasible.

Just how formidable the obstacle of two-thirds senatorial approval can become is classically illustrated in the fate of the Kasson treaties. Section 4 of the Dingley Tariff Act of 1897 authorized the President to "enter into" commercial treaties with respect to a number of goods, but treaty concessions would not become effective until "such treaty shall have been duly ratified by the Senate."[18] Accordingly, President McKinley's agent, John A. Kasson, between 1897 and 1899 negotiated seven treaties that made substantial concessions from tariff rates contained in the 1897 act. Major interest groups—domestic producers who feared foreign competition and

18. *Tariff Act of 1897,* chap. 11, 30 Stat. 205.

those who saw the treaties as an undesirable infringement of the principle of protection—opposed ratification of the treaties. Despite President McKinley's strong support, no action was taken in 1900 or 1901 by the Senate Foreign Relations Committee to report them out. Kasson resigned, disheartened; President McKinley continued his support, as did his successor, Theodore Roosevelt, to no avail. Finally, in 1903, action on the treaties was abandoned, and they remained pigeonholed in the Senate Committee on Foreign Relations.

This episode was alluded to by President Hoover in 1932 when he vetoed a bill amending the Tariff Act of 1930 that would have authorized the President to negotiate reciprocal trade agreements subject to subsequent approval by a two-thirds senatorial majority. While President Hoover's veto was based primarily on his disapproval of lowering tariffs and encouraging imports during the Great Depression, he noted that

the futility of the Executive negotiating such treaties as reciprocal tariffs has been often demonstrated in our past. Before we definitely adopted the policy of equal treatment to all nations the Congress had from time to time authorized such treaties. Out of some 22 such treaties providing for reciprocal tariff concessions, the Congress either refused to confirm or failed to act in 16, and 2 of the remaining 6 failed of confirmation by other governments.[19]

In stark contrast to these difficulties were the relative successes of agreements negotiated under Section 3 of the Dingley Act and under the Trade Agreements Act of 1934 and its successors in which effectuation was not conditioned on subsequent approval by the Congress as a whole or by a two-thirds majority in the Senate. Under the Dingley Act the main control retained by Congress was the possibility of terminating the agreements upon notice; this power was exercised once.[20] Eight agreements were negotiated under this authority, however, that resulted in immediate concessions on a limited number of products. Under the Trade Agreements Acts a short time limit on the authority of the President to enter into foreign trade agreements (three years in the 1934 act, and periods varying from one to five years in succeeding acts) was the principal congressional control. A much larger number of agreements, resulting in concessions on a broad variety of products which took immediate effect, were negotiated under this legislation. Unfortunately, this solution is unlikely to be attainable in the next several years for use in nontariff barrier negotiations.

19. Press release, White House, Weekly Issue No. 137, May 14, 1932, p. 481.
20. See U.S. Tariff Commission, *Reciprocity and Commercial Treaties* (1919), pp. 28–29.

Congressional Approval of Agreements

The Agreement on Automotive Products between the United States and Canada, concluded in 1965, contained provisions that the United States would "seek enactment of legislation authorizing duty-free treatment of imports of the products of Canada"; that after enactment of such legislation "the United States shall accord duty-free treatment" to such products; and that the agreement would not enter into force definitively until "notes are exchanged between the two Governments giving notice that appropriate action in their respective legislatures has been completed."[21] Shortly after the completion of negotiations, and following some debate over whether the President had the constitutional authority to use this method to avoid the necessity of getting a two-thirds majority of the Senate to advise and consent to the agreement,[22] a majority of both houses of Congress enacted implementing legislation. The prime controls retained by Congress were a requirement that the President periodically report on the operation of the agreement to Congress and the possibility of repeal or amendment.

While this is one of the more remarkable accommodations between Congress and the President, the two having exercised their concurrent powers with respect to the regulation of foreign trade and commerce, many congressional voices were raised in protest against Congress being presented with a fait accompli, which they must approve on pain of repudiating a negotiation.

Debate over the President's authority to negotiate the General Agreement on Tariffs and Trade (GATT) in 1947 and the International Antidumping Code in 1968, as well as debate over their domestic effect, was more intense than that over the Automotive Products Agreement—primarily because these two agreements, while not self-executing, nonetheless were not contingent on congressional approval for their implementation.

The GATT, signed by President Truman in 1947, has never been submitted to the Senate for ratification as a treaty or to the Congress as a

21. Jan. 16, 1965, 17 U.S.T. 1372, T.I.A.S. No. 6093.
22. See, for example, remarks of Senator Gore (Democrat of Tennessee) in *To Provide for the Implementation of the Agreement Concerning Automotive Products between the Government of the United States of America and the Government of Canada, and For Other Purposes,* Hearings before the Senate Committee on Finance, 89 Cong. 1 sess. (1965), pp. 85–87; and remarks of Representative Curtis (Republican of Missouri) in *Congressional Record,* Vol. 111, 89 Cong. 1 sess. (1965), p. 22374.

whole for approval, the executive considering that it was authorized by the Trade Agreements Act. While certain of its provisions have been held in lower court cases to overrule prior domestic law,[23] the decisions do not appear to appreciate that both Article XXIV, Section 12 and the Protocol of Provisional Application of the GATT indicate its non-self-executing character. At all events, congressional hostility to the President's failure to secure congressional review has been marked. The Trade Agreements Extension Acts of 1951, 1953, 1954, 1955, and 1958 include the biting statement that "the enactment of this Act shall not be construed to determine or indicate the approval or disapproval by the Congress of the Executive Agreement known as the General Agreement on Tariffs and Trade."[24]

Congressional hostility to executive agreements of the self-executing variety was epitomized in the 1954 George Amendment to the Bricker Amendment to the Constitution. The George Amendment would have required that an executive agreement be submitted to the Senate for its advice and consent by a two-thirds majority before it became effective as domestic law. It received a large majority of the votes in the Senate, but, ironically, failed by one vote (60–31) to obtain the requisite two-thirds support required for a constitutional amendment.[25] Hostility to non-self-executing executive agreements that could nonetheless have some effect on domestic law surfaced again after the negotiation of the Antidumping Code of 1968.

Agreements Not Requiring Congressional Action

It seems clear that if any progress is to be made in the near future in the area of international agreements reducing or eliminating nontariff barriers to international trade, the only methods in fact available are advance negotiation and subsequent congressional approval or failure to disapprove, or negotiation on the President's constitutional authority, with no congressional reference.

The former, utilized in the 1965 Agreement on Automotive Products between the United States and Canada, must be used whenever the agree-

23. See John H. Jackson, "The GATT in U.S. Domestic Law," *Michigan Law Review,* Vol. 66 (1967), p. 249.

24. See sec. 10 of *Trade Agreement Act of 1951,* 65 Stat. 72.

25. *Congressional Record,* Vol. 100, 83 Cong. 2 sess. (1954), p. 2358.

ment is inconsistent with existing federal legislation, whether the agreement is self-executing or not. If self-executing, it is a legal necessity; if not, Congress must be asked to pass implementing legislation. Though coordination in advance of the agreement so as to assure congressional support and some of the other difficulties involved present problems in this fait accompli method, it remains, despite its difficulties, one of the two realistically available methods.

The other practical means of negotiating international agreements is the presidential agreement, kept within the confines of existing congressional legislation. The Antidumping Code of 1968 is an example of this method, though a poor one. The difficulty in that case arose from the fact that it was an arguably close case whether the agreement in some of its aspects was inconsistent with the U.S. Antidumping Act of 1921.

If it is clear that the existing legislation and the agreement are consistent, as is the case with legislation that grants the President wide leeway in implementation, and the agreement's provisions are well within the leeway, then this method of making and effectuating international agreements in the trade field is fully available. The importance of this method is apparent in the buy-national procurement field (see Chapter 3).

The constitutional limits on the scope of the President's negotiating authority and other practical factors must weigh heavily in any decision as to whether the negotiation and effectuation of an international agreement on a particular nontariff distortion of trade is possible and, if so, how best to proceed. This weighing must take place on a case-by-case basis, and a specific judgment must be made as to the modality by which agreement is to be effectuated with respect to each nontariff barrier proposed as a subject of negotiation. That judgment will be at least as important as the provisions of the substantive agreement itself.

CHAPTER THREE

Buy-National Laws
and Policies

WITH AN ANNUAL BUDGET exceeding $200 billion, the federal government is the nation's most important consumer of goods and services, and the high level and wide variety of governmental expenditures offer a potential source of profit for almost any business. In general, any enterprise or individual may compete for a government contract and the lowest bidder, if a responsible business capable of fulfilling contract specifications, will win the contract. The government's obligation to award to the lowest bidder is limited, however, by the Buy American Act and other restrictive legislation.

Government Contracting Practices

The federal law pertaining to government contracts is applied through the Armed Services Procurement Regulations (ASPR)[1] for Department of Defense contracts, and the Federal Procurement Regulations (FPR)[2] for the majority of nondefense purchases (a number of independent agencies have their own rules for contract procedures). The decisions of fed-

1. 32 C.F.R. secs. 1–39 (1970), implementing the Armed Services Procurement Act of 1947.
2. 41 C.F.R. sec. 1 (1970), implementing the Federal Property and Services Act of 1949.

eral district courts and the Court of Claims are an important additional source of law. The comptroller general, in overseeing the nation's accounts, and several administrative boards and agencies—for example, the Armed Services Board of Contract Appeals—also participate in the formulation of government contract principles.

The most common method of government contracting is through solicitation and acceptance of bids. The initial step is advertisement of the need for supplies or services. These advertisements, sent to contractors who have expressed interest in receiving government contracts, contain all information necessary for the contractor to formulate a realistic bid, that is, a description of the supplies or services desired, specification of the quality and quantity required, and the time and procedure for submitting a bid.

The federal statutes call for use of the advertising procedure whenever possible but allow direct negotiation in exceptional circumstances. The exceptions are numerous enough that a large number of contracts, involving a high percentage in dollar value, are reached through negotiation.

In general, all businesses, whether or not foreign owned, are treated alike under U.S. law. In procurement by the Department of Defense, however, preferences in awarding contracts are given to domestically owned enterprises. The other agencies also apply preferences to domestically produced goods and services. Preferences can cause problems for both foreign and domestically owned businesses that sell goods made in whole or in part outside the United States.

The major impediment to the use of foreign goods in contracts with the U.S. government is the Buy American Act,[3] which was enacted in 1933 in an effort to curb high unemployment caused by the Depression and, additionally, to retaliate against other nations' policies of exclusive domestic purchases.[4] Other federal statutes also work preferences among suppliers. The Small Business Act seeks to ensure that a fair proportion of government contracts are received by small-business concerns; it requires inclusion of small businesses on lists of bidders, wide publicity of purchasing practices, and allowance of ample time for preparation of bids,

3. 41 U.S.C. sec. 10a–10d (1964).
4. Paul H. Gantt and William H. Speck, "Domestic v. Foreign Trade Problems in Federal Government Contracting: Buy American Act and Executive Order," *Journal of Public Law,* Vol. 75 (1958), pp. 378, 379; this valuable article has been utilized liberally in this chapter. Laurence A. Knapp, "The Buy American Act: A Review and Assessment," *Columbia Law Review,* Vol. 61 (1961), p. 430, has also been a very useful source.

and, in some cases, it requires that a small business receive the contract. The procurement regulations of federal agencies also attempt to aid labor surplus areas through policies designed to encourage businesses there to participate in the government contracting process.

Department of Defense

The Department of Defense is the government's largest procurer of goods and services. Appropriations for 1970, for example, exceeded $70 billion and were spent on items ranging from electronic components to office supplies.[5] While the Army, Navy, and Air Force procure special items, such as particular major weapons systems, for their own use, general supplies are purchased by the Defense Supply Agency (DSA). The DSA in 1969 procured more than $5 billion in goods and services and administered contracts valued at $54 billion.[6]

Among the restrictions on procurement by the Department of Defense that may discriminate against foreigners or foreign goods and services is the Buy American Act. The Armed Services Procurement Regulations make only one major addition to the act's general restrictions: the price differential applicable to foreign bids. Either 6 percent of the product's price inclusive of duty or 50 percent of its price exclusive of duty, whichever is higher, must be added to all foreign bids. This restriction has been imposed since 1959 for balance of payments reasons.

For several years defense appropriations bills have contained a provision restricting purchase of food, clothing, wool, and certain other agricultural products to domestic suppliers. Goods that cannot be purchased in sufficient quantity at U.S. market price are excepted.

The Department of Defense prohibits purchases of supplies originating from the USSR and Soviet-controlled areas, except those specified under import security controls. The regulations list countries considered to be Soviet-controlled areas.

Finally, security regulations may operate against foreign-owned businesses. The Defense Department's industrial security regulations (ISR) require that contracts involving classified information be given only to

5. *Defense Appropriations Act of 1970,* 83 Stat. 465, Pub. L. No. 91-170 (1969); and *Military Construction Act,* 83 Stat. 469, Pub. L. No. 91-171 (1969).
6. U.S. Department of Defense, Supply Agency, *An Introduction: Defense Supply Agency* (1970).

contractors or subcontractors who have had security clearances. In general, the regulations provide that a contractor under foreign ownership, control, or influence shall be ineligible for security clearance. In the determination of foreign influence, ultimately the issue is whether the foreign enterprise has sufficient interest in the contracting business to control corporate policies and employees or to have access to classified information.[7]

Other Federal Agencies

Discrimination against foreign goods and services in procurement by other federal agencies, such as the General Services Administration, the Department of Health, Education, and Welfare, the Atomic Energy Commission, and the National Aeronautics and Space Administration, is guided primarily by the Buy American Act, without special regulations, and in some instances through security precautions against foreign personnel, as in the Department of Defense.

State and Local Governments

State and municipal contracting and bidding procedures are generally similar to those of the federal government. At least one-third of the states restrict their governmental purchases of foreign goods, either by statute or through administrative purchasing procedures. Substantively, state buy-American statutes are broadly similar to the federal act. California's statute, for example, calls for the purchase of only materials manufactured "substantially all" from articles made in the United States, as does the federal statute.

At both the state and federal level, contracts are awarded to the lowest bidder for tender of goods in the United States after passing through customs. Foreign producers must therefore estimate the U.S. duty before making their bids. The complexities of tariff classification and valuation

7. Factors used in determining foreign influence include: distribution of voting rights; corporate structure of the company; control by foreign interests of the appointment and tenure of officers, directors, and other employees; concentration of aliens employed by the facility; foreign owners, officers, and other employees who may have access to classified information; financial backing by a foreign interest; practices of the business regarding licensing and related patent agreements, and so forth.

(discussed in Chapter 6, below) place a number of foreign-origin products at a serious disadvantage in the bidding procedure.

Federal Buy-American Policies

Mr. President, I may want to offer some amendments to this proposition myself. I may wish to offer amendments providing that no State shall buy anything that is not produced within the State, and that no county shall buy anything that is produced outside the county, and that no farmer shall be allowed to buy anything at all or sell anything that grows on his farm, and also to offer a motion that the American eagle shall be displaced as the emblem of the Republic and a terrapin be substituted in its stead—a terrapin closed up in its shell and hermetically sealed. If trade is a curse let us stop it.[8]

With this hyperbole, Senator Gore (Democrat of Oklahoma) in 1933 greeted a proposal that the so-called buy-American bill be added as a floor amendment to the Treasury and Post Office appropriation bill for the fiscal year 1934. In less florid terms, he argued that a proposal to compel American taxpayers to pay more for domestic goods than for imported goods, after the imported goods had scaled high tariff walls, would not be an economy measure; that the proposal invited combinations among American manufacturers, since imports were banned at any price; and that the imports were paid for with American exports, which were produced with American labor.[9] But other arguments won the day.

Senator Vandenberg (Republican of Michigan) described the legislation as "primarily . . . an employment measure conceived in the notion that American tax money should maintain American labor in a moment of American crisis and exigency," and added the emotional appeal:

It occurs to me that in a time like this, when we are beset upon all sides with an almost inescapable and unavoidable responsibility to provide employment for unemployed American people, we have a right to draw the line . . . in defense of American industry and American employment, when we are spending American tax funds. Why have an American make-work program which makes work in Europe or in Asia? I am not blind to the need for export trade. I am speaking solely of government funds and their expenditure. Mr. President, the American Treasury is not the world's community chest.[10]

8. *Congressional Record,* Vol. 76, 73 Cong. 1 sess (1933), p. 2868.
9. Ibid., p. 3268.
10. Ibid., p. 3254.

Senator Davis (Republican of Pennsylvania) agreed:

Why we permit these competitive imports or products from other lands to be dumped unto the United States while our own workmen are in the bread-lines is beyond my comprehension. As long as we maintain the American standard of living there is not the slightest hope of America's competing with the cheap labor of Europe and Asia unless we give ample protection to American industry and agriculture.

Our Government, through contractors, is buying foreign products while our workers are idle. It is bad enough for us to refuse legislation which will bar these products, but when it comes to the Government of the United States' levying a tax on the American people and using that tax money to buy foreign-made products while its own are idle, I have not words to describe my opposition to it.[11]

Other supporters of the measure were responding to the protests of domestic bidders against possible foreign competition for the purchase of heavy electrical equipment for the Hoover (Boulder) Dam. Earlier, in the purchase of turbines for the Madden Dam for the Panama Canal, a German firm had been the apparent low bidder, "but . . . consideration of other factors in addition to the price, which would affect the final cost of the United States, resulted in award to the second low bidder."[12] For the Hoover Dam, however, Secretary of the Interior Wilbur warned on February 10, 1933:

Under the law now applicable to the Interior Department, award must be made to the low bidder, whether American or foreign, provided the requirements of the specification are met. Until and unless Congress passes legislation similar to that applicable to the War departments, a German manufacturer can bid on the turbines and if the bid is low the foreign concern must be awarded the contract.[13]

Secretary Wilbur's statement followed by one week introduction of buy-American legislation by Senator Hiram Johnson (Republican of California). Bid opening for the furnishing of hydraulic apparatus for the Hoover power plant had been scheduled for February 3, but was postponed until March 10. So short was the notice of the postponement that several bidders were already on the way to Denver for the bid opening. The Treasury and Post Office Appropriation Act, 1934, containing the

11. Ibid., p. 2985.
12. Letter from Secretary of the Interior Wilbur to Senator D. A. Reed (Republican of Pennsylvania), Feb. 10, 1933, in Gantt and Speck, "Domestic v. Foreign Trade Problems," p. 380.
13. Ibid.

buy-American provisions, was signed by President Hoover on his last day in office, March 3. When bids were opened for the hydraulic apparatus on March 10, none of the six bids was submitted by a foreign manufacturer. The contract was awarded to a domestic firm.

Another of Senator Johnson's aims was to retaliate against the actions of other governments. The British, he pointed out, had since 1930 required that all supplies for assisted public works be of British origin. They did so, without legislation, by the simple assertion in contracts for public construction and for public road construction that "all materials required for the assisted work will be of British origin, and all manufactured articles of British manufacture."[14] Senator Hiram Bingham (Republican of Connecticut) agreed with Senator Johnson that the United States should impose similar restrictions:

I am informed, the powers that be in Great Britain put an embargo on goods coming from the colonies—namely and specifically, from Canada—which contain more than 50 percent of goods not originating in the colony itself. This movement, known as the "buy British" movement, is spreading rapidly, and is a direct threat at much of our own industry. *There is only one way to meet a perfectly reasonable national movement of that kind and that is the so-called "buy American" movement.*[15]

The legislation was also designed to close a loophole in the previous year's appropriation act that had allowed the Post Office Department to buy twine manufactured in the United States of Indian jute. The act allowed the procurement of articles of the "growth, production *or* manufacture" of the United States.[16] Senator Byrnes (Democrat of South Carolina) charged that "the Postmaster General had wrongfully interpreted the law as not requiring him to exercise his discretion in favor of American cotton,"[17] and several senators urged that the legislation be amended to assure that articles bought be of the "growth, production *and* manufacture" of the United States.[18]

14. *Congressional Record,* Vol. 76, 73 Cong. 1 sess. (1933), p. 3254. The clause is from British Treasury Minutes of Sept. 11, 1929, instructions to the advisory committee in charge of grants under the Development Act of 1929. It was limited only by "such exceptions as the committee may regard as necessary or desirable in any particular case, having regard to all the circumstances, including the comparative prices of British and foreign articles."

15. Ibid., p. 3175. Italics added.

16. 47 Stat. 580, 604 (1932).

17. *Congressional Record,* Vol. 76, 73 Cong. 1 sess. (1933), p. 3255.

18. *Post Office Appropriations Bill, 1934,* Hearings before the Subcommittee of the House Committee on Appropriations, 72 Cong. 2 sess. (1932), pp. 23–24.

The combined circumstances favoring a domestic preference for government procurement proved to be effective in 1933. The Buy American Act passed that year has remained in force ever since.[19]

The Buy American Act

The first section of the act, dealing with supply contracts, permits government agencies to purchase for the public use only goods produced in the United States "substantially all" from domestic articles. Since the statute focuses on the final product, items are considered to have been produced "substantially all" from American goods if 50 percent or more of their total cost is allocable to domestic products used in the finished article.

Foreign purchases are not prohibited absolutely. Goods produced abroad may be purchased if they are to be used outside the United States or if they are unavailable in sufficient quantity or quality in the United States. Both of these stipulations appear to be conceptually clear. A third exception that allows the head of an agency to substitute foreign for domestic goods he finds unreasonably costly or the acquisition of which is considered inconsistent with the public interest is more complex. Normally, the cost of foreign goods is deemed reasonable if the offered price plus 6 percent is less than the price of the competing domestic product (a rarely used alternative permits the offered price exclusive of applicable duty and all costs after arrival in the United States plus 10 percent to be compared to the American cost). The 6 percent preference was established in 1954 by executive order of President Eisenhower following a twenty-year history of a 25 percent buy-American preference.

All three exceptions are limited, however, by additional preferences for American products contained in regulations issued under the act. For example, the 6 percent price differential may be raised to 12 percent if the low American bidder is a small business concern or is located in a labor surplus area. And any otherwise acceptable low bid may be rejected if such action is considered necessary for the national security.

The second section of the act, covering construction contracts, is the logical corollary of the supply provision. By requiring contractors (and subcontractors) to use raw materials produced in the United States and manufactured articles substantially all of which have been manufactured

19. See Appendix A for the text of the act.

in the United States, it ensures that the United States does not purchase indirectly those articles it does not buy directly. As with supply contracts, exceptions are allowed for unavailable materials and when the purchase of domestic materials would be unreasonably costly or inconsistent with the national interest.

Executive Order 10582

During World War II the Buy American Act was expressly waived by Executive Order 9001. The postwar slogan "trade not aid" revealed the act's part in preventing friendly foreign nations from paying their own way and thereby diminishing their need for grants and loans. Dissatisfaction with the buy-American policy coincided with an increase of bidding by foreign firms on government contracts, particularly during 1952–54. The devaluation of sterling in 1949 had stimulated British exports of heavy electrical equipment to the United States; even before the "trade not aid" policy was announced, officials of the Mutual Security Administration had encouraged British firms to bid on government contracts: "In effect, they were told 'if you blighters want dollars, come over and earn them.' "[20]

Officials charged with setting government procurement policy, and contracting officers, found themselves in an uncomfortable position. For more than twenty years they had interpreted the Buy American Act as an almost absolute prohibition on the purchase of foreign goods and materials despite its relatively flexible terms; the Treasury Department's 25 percent preference regulation was generally applied by all government procurement officials. Now an increasing number of official and semiofficial reports clamored for repeal of the Buy American Act or for the liberalization of the buy-American policies.

The Gray Commission, the first of many postwar presidential commissions on foreign economic policy, found the buy-American principle "in direct conflict with the basic foreign economic policies of the United States."[21] In 1953 the Bell Commission charged that "Buy-American restrictions result in higher Government costs and establish a 'super tariff' on goods used by the Government."[22]

20. Percy Wells Bidwell, *What the Tariff Means to American Industries* (Harper for Council on Foreign Relations, 1956), p. 230.

21. *Report to the President on Foreign Economic Policies,* 81 Cong. 2 sess. (1950), p. 84.

22. U.S. Public Advisory Board for Mutual Security, *A Trade and Tariff Policy in the National Interest,* 83 Cong. 1 sess. (1953), p. 5.

The staff papers that accompanied the 1954 report of the Randall Commission cited some "spectacular illustrations of the effect which increased foreign competition might have on government costs. . . . In one case, the competition of a foreign firm to supply microscopes to the Defense Department led the American firms which had previously preempted the field to reduce their offering prices by 20 percent. In another case, an American firm which was facing foreign competition in the supply of heavy electrical equipment dropped its bid by about 13 percent, representing a saving of over $600,000."[23] The staff papers contained an estimate, "subject to only the roughest sort of approximation" and "subject to extremely wide margins of error," that the United States government might be able to save up to $100 million annually through lower prices and to increase customs revenue by $100 million if the buy-American principle were eliminated.[24]

The Randall Report recommended:

The Buy-American Act and legislative provisions of other acts containing the Buy-American principle should be amended to give authority to the President to exempt from the provisions of such legislation the bidders from other nations that treat our bidders on an equal basis with their own nationals. Pending such amendment, the President by Executive Order should direct procurement agencies in the public interest to consider foreign bids which satisfy all other considerations on substantially the same price basis as domestic bids.[25]

An accompanying minority report pointed to the desirability of insuring to the United States basic industries and services essential in both peace and war: "This corollary effect, resulting from the Buy-American Act, should be recognized as an essential goal and function of any new policy."[26] The minority believed that the act should "be applied to protect the industrial basis essential to the national security and sound economy of the United States."[27]

On December 17, 1954, President Eisenhower issued Executive Order 10582 in an attempt to meet the demands for enlargement of international trade in a manner consistent with a sound domestic economy.[28] The order was designed to make the application of the Buy American Act uniform

23. U.S. Commission on Foreign Economic Policy, *Staff Papers* (1954), pp. 317–18.
24. Ibid., p. 318.
25. U.S. Commission on Foreign Economic Policy, *Report to the President and the Congress* (1954).
26. Ibid., p. 19.
27. Ibid., p. 8.
28. Press release, James C. Hagerty, Dec. 17, 1954.

within the executive branch. It classifies supplies as foreign if the cost of their foreign components constitutes 50 percent or more of the costs of all their component products, and declares a domestic bid price is unreasonable and purchase at that price inconsistent with the public interest if the domestic price exceeds the foreign price including duty by 6 percent.[29] The 6 percent differential may be set aside for reasons of national interest, to assist domestic small business firms, to promote production in an area of substantial unemployment, to protect essential national security interests, or whenever the head of the agency considers the domestic price to be reasonable, or domestic production to be in the public interest.

These exceptions as a group are not quite as formidable in operation as they would appear. The first is a catch-all provision designed to meet unforeseeable situations, as is the last, which is intended to avoid legal attacks on the validity of agency procurement decisions. Since a small business must normally possess fewer than 500 employees to qualify for preference in government procurement, this exception is seldom applied.

Furthermore, application of the exceptions is not mandatory; department heads have discretion to accept or reject a domestic bid coming within one of the exceptions. This discretion has, however, exposed the departments to the pressure of political forces, with the result that the unemployment exception, for example, has assumed a mandatory rather than a discretionary character.

THE UNEMPLOYMENT EXCEPTION

The mandatory application of the unemployment exception resulted from the third Chief Joseph case, which involved the procurement, in 1955, of the last generators and transformers for a hydroelectric project. The low bidder was the same British firm, English Electric, whose low bids had been rejected in the 1953 and 1954 Chief Joseph cases. This fact and the tension that the two earlier cases had created were emphasized by the press, which hailed the case as a test of the liberal buy-American policy expressed in the President's 1954 message to Congress and the executive order that had just been issued.[30] In the 1955 case involving generators, a differential of about 18 percent existed in favor of the British bid, which was some $900,000 less than the domestic bid, and, considering import

29. See Appendix B for the text of the order.
30. *Electrical World*, Feb. 21, 1955, p. 89; *Journal of Commerce* (New York), Feb. 3, 1955, p. 1.

duties payable, offered the U.S. Treasury a total combined saving of about $1.4 million. On transformers the differential was approximately 17 percent and the total saving about $130,000. Thus the British bids, totaling about $6 million, offered an aggregate saving of over $1.5 million.

Consideration of the case extended over some seven months, under the personal supervision of Secretary of Defense Charles Wilson, a former head of General Motors. Other cabinet departments and White House officials were also concerned with the disposition of the case, as were various members of the congressional delegation from Pennsylvania, acting at the instance of the domestic bidders.

First, the case was referred to the director of the Office of Defense Mobilization for advice; he ruled that rejection of the British bids was not necessary under the national security exception of the executive order. Meantime, the secretary of labor had designated the Pittsburgh area, where the plants of both domestic bidders were located, as falling within the unemployment exception. Unemployment there stood at about 9 percent when the generator bids were opened in February. By July, however, it had fallen to 6.1 percent and by September to 5.2 percent.[31] Due to the time-lag between collection of data and promulgation of corresponding area reclassifications, it still was listed in the category of those to which the unemployment exception was applicable when Secretary Wilson's decision was announced on August 27, 1955.

Secretary Wilson had been made fully aware that it was within his discretion not to apply the unemployment exception. His attention had also been called to the sharply declining unemployment in the Pittsburgh area, to the President's declaration in his 1954 message that the unemployment exception should apply only to areas of persistent as well as substantial unemployment, to the fact that the focus of the 1954–55 unemployment in Pittsburgh had been in the steel and associated metals industries, and not the electrical industry, and to the great savings offered by the British bids. He nonetheless directed that the British bids be rejected on the basis of the unemployment exception.[32]

The decision was the subject of sharp criticism.[33] The British government instructed Foreign Secretary Macmillan to register with the United

31. Pennsylvania State Employment Service, *Pittsburgh Labor Market Letter,* monthly issues, January–December 1955.

32. Press release, Department of Defense, No. 806-55, Aug. 27, 1955.

33. The *Washington Post and Times Herald,* under the heading "Platitudes for

States government its "grave concern" over the decisions.[34] In Europe, criticism of the decision was coupled with an attack on the contemporaneous action of President Eisenhower raising the duties on bicycles, which had also caused storms of protest from Britain and the other seven European countries affected.[35]

As a consequence of the decisions and the ensuing protests, discretion in the application of the unemployment exception was eliminated. In November 1955 the government agencies concerned agreed that the differential favoring the domestic bidder should be doubled to 12 percent whenever the unemployment exception was applicable, a formula since embodied in their procurement regulations. This mathematical formula completely eliminated the exercise of discretion in individual cases and has since been applied routinely regardless of political intercessions for domestic bidders.

THE NATIONAL SECURITY EXCEPTION

A few months after the last Chief Joseph case, representatives of the hydraulic equipment section of the U.S. electrical industry filed an application with the director of the Office of Defense Mobilization (ODM) seeking a complete ban on all foreign hydroturbine imports under the national security exception of the executive order. Though Executive Order 10582 contemplated only that other agencies refer individual procurement cases to the director, Director Flemming entertained the application nonetheless.

While this petition was under consideration, the Department of the Interior referred low bids submitted by an Austrian firm on two procure-

---

Sale," stated that "in the first major application of the liberalized Buy American Act the Administration has deliberately fallen flat on its face. . . . Is it not time to end this hypocrisy? . . . The whole affair is sickening." (Aug. 30, 1955.) The *Wall Street Journal,* in an editorial entitled "Rigging the Rules," asserted that "the Government should [not] pretend to a competitive bidding policy and then squeeze out the low bidder just because it is a foreign firm. . . . We make what is, presumably, a bona fide request for bids. A foreign firm makes a bona fide bid that is the lowest of the lot. But come award day the foreign entry finds he's playing under a movable handicap. This newspaper has never thought that a protectionist policy was, in the long run, a wise one. But if we are going to have one, let it at least be forthright." (Aug. 31, 1955.) *Fortune* said, "The decision comes pretty close to an exhibition of bad faith on the part of the U.S. Government." (October 1955, p. 108.)

34. *New York Herald Tribune,* Aug. 29, 1955.
35. See *Time,* Sept. 12, 1955, p. 27.

ments of turbines to ODM for advice. Director Flemming concluded in the first matter that the situation did not appear to justify his recommending that all hydroturbine contracts should be limited to U.S. suppliers. He recommended that decisions continue to be made on a case-by-case basis, but gave assurances that, in the light of the importance of the domestic industry's skills and tools, the impact of imports on further developments in the industry would be kept under close study by ODM and its advisory interagency task force.[36]

In the case of the two Austrian bids, however, Director Flemming advised the Department of the Interior that it would be justified in awarding these contracts to the domestic low bidder on national security grounds. He based his advice on the insufficiency of supply in the United States of certain types of machine tools possessed by the domestic low bidder, and on the latter's low production level and insecure financial position. He also referred to the small business status of the domestic bidder and the fact that it was located in an unemployment exception area, but acknowledged that these factors "may have" no bearing on the national security question.[37] The Department of the Interior awarded the contracts to the domestic bidder.

In 1958 and early 1959, individual companies and the domestic electrical industry association again petitioned for a full ban not only on foreign purchase of hydraulic turbines but on all imports of power equipment, under the national security provision of the 1955 and 1958 Trade Agreements Acts. The newly named Office of Civil and Defense Mobilization (OCDM) divided the petitions into two cases; the case dealing solely with steam-turbine generators became known as the "main Section 8" case. While these cases were pending, the celebrated Greer's Ferry case, involving an Army Engineer procurement of hydraulic turbines, reached OCDM.

The low bidder in this procurement, by a margin substantially in excess

36. Letter from Director Flemming to Mr. Rheingan of National Electrical Manufacturers Association, March 8, 1957, in Gantt and Speck, "Domestic v. Foreign Trade Problems," p. 380.

37. Letter from Director Flemming to Assistant Secretary of the Interior Aandahl, March 12, 1957, in ibid. Mr. Flemming's reference to the small business and unemployment exceptions was uncalled for since they are within the jurisdiction of the secretary of the interior. The secretary mentioned these gratuitous observations while resting his decision to reject the foreign bid primarily on the national security advice given him.

of the requisite 6 percent, was English Electric, the British firm involved in all the Chief Joseph cases. Responding to a Department of Defense request for advice, the director of OCDM formally advised the department (and informally affirmed to interested agencies and parties) that he would suspend his determination until his decision on the main Section 8 case, the issues in the two proceedings being the same. Ten days thereafter, however, he advised the Department of Defense to award the contract to the competing domestic bidder on national security grounds. His letter stated that the delay in determining the general industry petitions would be greater than he had anticipated, and should not interfere with procurement of the Greer's Ferry turbines. Though he admitted that the issues presented were part of "the large and complex national security problem," the director disposed of the merits of the Greer's Ferry case in four sentences:

This procurement will require the use of elephant tools which are available in relatively few domestic plants. If the present procurement is not awarded to the domestic producer, there is reason to believe that domestic productive capacity in this category will be reduced to a level inadequate for emergency requirements. We have been consistently striving to maintain and augment domestic elephant tool capacity by such means as have been available to us. Plants of this type together with the skilled manpower for their operation are vital segments of the national mobilization base.[38]

Before reaching these conclusions, the director had been informed that the order board of the domestic producers of large hydraulic turbines, composed of four companies, stood at an all-time high; the impact of foreign competition was insignificant, there having been one instance of foreign turbine procurement in history, with ten of the eleven federal turbine awards in the period from 1956 to mid-1958 having been to domestic bidders; and that a large volume of hydraulic turbine business was in view due to the continuing large-scale development of hydroelectric power projects by federal, state, and private agencies.

Another fact may be added. In his 1958 senatorial campaign speeches, Hugh Scott (Republican of Pennsylvania) had made statements to the effect that, as a result of his prior intercession at the White House, he had been assured that the contracts would be awarded to the Philadelphia

38. Letter from Director Hoegh to the assistant secretary of defense, Jan. 16, 1959, in ibid.

Baldwin-Lima-Hamilton Corporation, the low domestic bidder. As he later put it to a reporter, "I got the contract."[39]

The implication that the case had been determined long before reference of the national security question to the director, himself a member of the White House establishment, combined with the trade policy implications of the result reached, gave rise to an avalanche of criticism and protest far out-distancing that in the Chief Joseph cases. In addition to the broad press coverage and uniformly critical editorials, members of Congress individually and jointly severely criticized the administration and threatened an investigation of the case. In Britain the decision was received with bitter official and public ridicule and with demands that Britain "fight back." The British ambassador, after lodging a protest with the secretary of state, told reporters that it taxed British credulity to believe "that the entire national security of the United States were imperiled if two turbines were built by her ally, Britain."[40] What infuriated the British even more was their discovery that Britain, including the British government itself, had been purchasing millions of dollars worth of heavy engineering equipment from the Baldwin firm.[41]

The furor engendered by the decision finally abated when President Eisenhower, after concluding discussions of "recent restrictive United States trade actions" with Prime Minister Macmillan, stated their belief in "the principle of interdependence. We believe that you cannot keep a coalition of free countries . . . unless we adopt cooperative measures that do promote the interests of all. . . . I think the greatest need is to look at the long-term benefits of the whole group, because with that group, our own fortunes are tied up."[42]

Five months after his Greer's Ferry advice, the OCDM director issued a memorandum of decision on the main Section 8 case, stating that the equipment in question was not being "imported in such quantities or under such circumstances as to threaten to impair the national security."[43]

39. *Time,* Feb. 2, 1959, p. 64.
40. Quoted in *New York World Telegram & Sun,* Jan. 24, 1959.
41. *New York Times,* Jan. 25, 1959, p. E2.
42. Ibid., Mar. 26, 1959, p. 12.
43. Office of Civil and Defense Mobilization, *Memorandum of Decision in the Matter of the Petitions of General Electric Company, National Electric Manufacturers Association and Others Under Section 8 of the Trade Agreements Act Extension, 1958,* June 12, 1959.

He concluded that failures of foreign equipment in operation would not result in significant power interruptions; that necessary maintenance and repair could, in the event of national emergency, be performed by U.S. facilities;[44] that the national security was not threatened by the possibility of interference with deliveries of foreign equipment by wartime blockade; and that import competition had had a negligible impact on the economic position of the domestic electrical industry. Giving hydraulic turbines special consideration, he concluded that domestic capacity was so substantial, and the ratio of imports so small, that imports did not threaten national security. He expressed his readiness, however, to reexamine this conclusion should imports substantially preempt U.S. requirements.[45]

The decision was widely reported and applauded in the domestic and British press, although with cynical references to the director's contrary conclusion in Greer's Ferry, of fresh and vivid memory.

Another national security case that coincided with the Greer's Ferry case involved the Tennessee Valley Authority. It had awarded a steam generator contract to a British firm, whose bid of about $13 million was some $6.3 million less than the lowest domestic bid. Immediately, the domestic industry appealed to the OCDM director to require TVA to cancel the award. In a lengthy public statement, the TVA pointed out that it had invited foreign bids because of disturbingly large increases in the bids by the three domestic producers of steam-turbine generators; that the large difference between the foreign and domestic bids in this instance could not be accounted for by wage cost differences; and that, for a number of reasons, including budgetary savings and the need to strengthen the economies of our allies, it had concluded that the foreign award served, rather than prejudiced, the national security of the United States.[46] The director of OCDM is reported to have advised the domestic industry that this procurement decision lay in TVA's discretion.[47]

The director's memorandum of decision on the second part of the electrical industry's petition was issued on November 18, 1960. Noting that

44. Ibid., p. 13. The director also found that it was not established that foreign equipment was of inferior quality and prone to breakdowns, as alleged by the domestic industry.

45. Ibid., p. 6.

46. *TVA Statement on Purchase of Turbogenerator from C. C. Parsons & Co., Ltd., England*, Feb. 27, 1959.

47. See *Journal of Commerce* (New York), March 2, 1959, p. 11.

the volume of foreign equipment in this category supplied or on order was significant, and that the domestic producers of steam turbines were able to meet whatever mobilization requirements they might be called upon to assume, he rejected the industry's claims of national security threat and its challenge to the year-and-one-half-old TVA foreign award. In purchases of foreign equipment since then, TVA has not sought the director's advice and the domestic industry has not made further appeals under Section 8 of the Trade Agreements Act.

Another case raising the national security issue involved procurement of towing locomotives and associated equipment by the Panama Canal Company, a dependency of the Department of the Army. A Japanese firm was the low bidder by 16 percent. The Army, reportedly at the behest of the Ohio congressional delegation, sought to obtain advice from the congressional appropriations committees to counter strong support of the foreign bid from Senator Holland (Democrat of Florida), a member of the Senate Appropriations Committee, and from the Department of State.[48] The Army referred the case to OCDM; it awarded the contract to the Japanese firm after being advised by the director that impairment, rather than enhancement, of the U.S. national security would result if the Japanese bid were rejected.[49]

THE PUBLIC INTEREST EXCEPTION

As the balance of payments position of the United States continued to post deficits in the late 1950s and 1960s, the Department of Defense, relying on Section 5 of Executive Order 10582, in 1962 instituted as an interim measure a gold flow factor. This factor provided on foreign bids an upward adjustment of either 6 percent including duty or 50 percent not including duty, "whichever results in the *greater* valuated price."[50] The Department of Defense in 1970 stated that it intended to continue the practice until "the United States balance of payments deficit is corrected,"[51] which has not yet occurred.

48. Ibid., April 15, 1960, p. 1. Miami, in Senator Holland's home state, was constructing a large international trade center and was otherwise basing its growth drive substantially on foreign trade development.

49. Ibid., May 12, 1960, p. 1.

50. *Armed Services Procurement Regulations,* sec. 6-104.4(6). Italics added.

51. Ibid., sec. 6-102.2(a).

Other Buy-National Practices

Since 1954 a rider—the Berry amendment—has been attached to Department of Defense appropriations acts requiring the service departments to procure certain food, clothing, and cloth supplies entirely from domestic sources, even when purchased for use overseas. Department of Defense requests that Congress remove this rider, leaving such procurements subject to the normal Buy American Act requirements, have been of no avail.

In April 1959 the Department of Commerce instructed regional offices of its Bureau of Roads that states could not limit the use of foreign materials in federal road programs to any greater extent than permitted by the Buy American Act and the 1954 executive order implementing it.[52] Many state agencies denied foreign suppliers even the opportunity to bid on materials needed for roads constructed with the aid of federal funds. Opposition from the states caused the Department of Commerce first to postpone and later, in effect, to withdraw its instructions, leaving the states free to discriminate against foreign supplies in accord with their general laws. The Department of Justice has failed to advise Commerce on its question whether it can require state compliance with federal standards.[53]

In contrast, the Rural Electrification Administration requires its local and state procurement authorities to enforce the Buy American Act and Executive Order 10582.

In October 1958 the Post Office Department issued instructions banning the purchase of foreign-produced office equipment. While the accompanying press reports indicated some conflict concerning what had stimulated this directive, it was plainly contrary to the Buy American Act, the executive order, and the administration's procurement policy. After repeated protests by foreign suppliers and their diplomatic representatives, the Post Office Department issued new instructions in July 1959, recognizing that its procurement is subject to the provisions of the act and the executive order.

In 1960 the Bureau of Reclamation, an agency of the Department of the Interior, opened bids on hydraulic turbines for four unrelated projects. In all cases the foreign bids were low by adequate differentials. In three cases a Japanese supplier submitted the low bid, and in the fourth the

52. *Journal of Commerce* (New York), April 23, 1959, p. 2.
53. Ibid., Sept. 7, 1960, p. 2.

British firm involved in the Chief Joseph and Greer's Ferry cases was the low bidder. Neither foreign manufacturer had previously supplied turbines to other users in the United States, but the British bidder had on two occasions supplied turbines to the Army Engineers and it had many turbines in operation in Canada.

The Department of the Interior made one award each to the Japanese and British firms, and the other two to the lowest U.S. bidders. The bureau did not wish to award more than one contract to a producer, foreign or domestic, who had not previously manufactured turbines for the bureau;[54] since all domestic manufacturers could satisfy this requirement, this ruling operated as a restriction only against foreign suppliers.

In response to the protest of a dissatisfied domestic bidder, the comptroller general issued a ruling that the reasons given for restricting the awards were incompatible with the requirements of federal advertised bidding, and that all three cases in which the Japanese firm was the low bidder should have been awarded to that firm.[55] Federal procurement laws require bidders to furnish proof of their competence by listing equipment of equivalent technical characteristics previously manufactured and in operation and by providing further proof of their financial standing and ability to complete the work. Both foreign bidders had satisfied these requirements and examination of the British bidder's turbines in actual operation was feasible both in the United States and in Canada.

Enforcement of the Buy American Act

At the outset, enforcement of the Buy American Act seems to have been accomplished generally by requiring a certification of domestic origin on vouchers for payment; the statute was deemed to be applicable regardless of whether the contract gave any notice of buy-American requirements. In a relatively short time, however, departments began to insert a buy-American clause in contracts, thus creating a consensual obligation on those supplying the government to comply with the act. The contract clause furnished little guidance beyond a reading of the statute itself. A 1955 holding of the comptroller general that an invitation for bids did not adequately permit determination of the proportion of foreign components

54. Press release, U.S. Department of the Interior, Aug. 12, 1960.
55. 40 Comp. Gen. 339 (1960).

and must be readvertised caused the agencies thereafter to set forth the percentage of materials of foreign origin permitted under a contract.[56]

The derivation of the buy-American prohibition from an appropriations act and the early requirement for certification of compliance in the voucher for payment point up its principal means of enforcement. A contractor who does not furnish domestic products simply cannot and will not be paid by the government, at least under the contract; and recovery of the value of his products may be doubtful and in any event entails a difficult claims procedure. In addition, with a buy-American contract clause, goods of foreign origin may be rejected and the contract terminated for default in performance. Finally, when bidders are obliged to certify the percentage of foreign materials in the products they intend to furnish, that percentage or the actual percentage determined after investigation may show a violation of the act and lead to rejection of the bid.

These sanctions presuppose that the government is dealing directly with the supplier and can accept or reject, and pay for or not pay for, the goods in question. They are inapplicable to construction contracts where the requirement is that the contractor shall use, in performance of the work, only domestic goods. Section 3 of the Buy American Act requires that all contracts for construction, alteration, or repair of any public building or work must include a provision for debarment from award of government contracts in case of violation.

Failure to comply with the buy-American requirements is determined by the head of an executive agency. No construction contract may be awarded to debarred persons or firms in the United States or elsewhere "within a period of three years after such finding is made public." However, the language does not apply to supply contracts, so that such persons and firms may be solicited for bids or proposals and awarded contracts for other work.

In view of the difficulties of understanding the application of the act and the ease with which foreign materials can be incorporated in construction materials, the debarment sanction is severe. However, in a case where an insignificant amount of foreign material was incorporated in a public building by good faith mistake and without intent to violate the act, the comptroller general held that the sanction need not be applied and that the building need not be torn down to remove the foreign material.[57]

56. 35 Comp. Gen. 7 (1955).
57. 36 Comp. Gen. 718 (1957).

Impact of the Buy American Act

In 1960, procurement in compliance with the 1954 executive order in ten federal agencies was surveyed. Awards in excess of $10,000 to foreign producers during 1958 constituted about $10 million of a total of $21 *billion* of purchases surveyed and during 1959 constituted about $39 million of a total of about $32 *billion;* foreign awards were concentrated in a few articles and commodities, electric power equipment being the leader in both years. The direct and indirect savings resulting from foreign competition, according to that partial survey of government purchases, were considerable.

As little as 0.25 percent of the federal government's 1958 purchases of nonagricultural tradable commodities (excluding ordnance) that were subject to the Buy American Act is estimated to have been from foreign sources.[58] In 1960 only 0.15 percent and in 1962 only 0.11 percent of such federal procurement (other than goods not available in the United States) was from foreign sources; if the buy-American restriction had not existed, foreign procurement in 1958 might have been $231 million rather than the $37 million it was.[59] In view of the consistently low levels of foreign procurement and the downward trend since 1954, it is clear that despite the liberalization sought in the executive order, the original intention of the Buy American Act to restrict governmental procurement to U.S. suppliers was being achieved.

The decline in foreign sales to federal agencies in the face of a trade expansion effort can be accounted for in part by the existence of competitive domestic goods in many industries and by the reluctance of foreign suppliers to cope with the complexities and intricacies of the governmental procurement process. Perhaps an equal or greater cause is the antiforeign face of the act and the application of Executive Order 10582 to deny foreign awards in cases attracting wide international attention. Moreover, neither at the time of its issuance nor later was any announcement made to the public or to the thousands of federal procurement officers scattered over the United States and abroad that the executive order was designed to *promote* expansion of imports by reducing the previous barriers to federal purchases from foreign sources. From various importer reports, it

58. Robert E. Baldwin, *Nontariff Distortions of International Trade* (Brookings Institution, 1970), p. 72.
59. Ibid., p. 74.

seems likely that many federal procurement officers remain imbued with the antiforeign mandate they had followed for years, consider application of the exceptions a distracting venture into unfamiliar territory, and therefore view overtures by foreign suppliers with hesitance and concern, if not resistance. In any case, buy-American rides on.

To the question whether the act is desirable, the response of official study groups and editorial opinion has been a repeated, uniform, and sometimes resounding "no," with consequent recommendations for repeal of the act. In conflict with the essentials of long-standing U.S. trade policies, saddling the government with extra costs, and conducive to international embarrassment and strain, the act has been declared wrong in principle and deleterious in effect.

State Buy-American Policies

Among the many elements that must be considered part of U.S. tariff and trade policy are state buy-American policies. How great should a state's sovereignty be in establishing its governmental purchasing program? What is the nature and extent of U.S. treaty obligations in trade matters? Does the power to regulate foreign commerce lie exclusively with Congress? Does congressional control of interstate and foreign commerce impose an affirmative duty on the national government to seek to remove state burdens on interstate and foreign commerce?

Understanding of any state buy-American policy is impeded by the fact that such policy is manifest in the state constitution, statutes, ordinances, and informal policy; it is practiced by state purchasing officials, municipalities, and private action groups; and it may appear in such diverse garbs as outright prohibition or seemingly innocuous, yet equally prohibitive, licensing, labeling, bidding, and inspection requirements.

A 1963 survey revealed that fourteen of forty states responding restricted their governmental purchasing of foreign goods by statute or policy.[60] Only six admitted that prices were increased thereby, and only one of these applied preferences in favor of domestic bidders through the

60. National Association of State Purchasing Officials, Committee on Competition in Governmental Purchasing, "1963 Survey on In-State Preference Practices, Domestic or Foreign Purchases" (Chicago: NASPO, 1963; processed).

differential price mechanism used by the federal government. This would indicate that in the other states the reduction in the number of bidders was an independent factor in price increases. A 1967 survey indicated that more than twenty states and many local governments discriminated in their purchasing policies against foreign products and producers, but by 1969 only seventeen did so.[61]

The degree of restrictive purchasing demonstrated in the 1963 survey may be understated. Two of the country's most industrialized states, New York and Ohio, for example, failed to reply to the questionnaire. Yet, an Ohio finance department spokesman admitted, "We have been purchasing only domestic goods for the past two or three years," even though bills designed to make buy-American an affirmative state policy failed to pass the Ohio legislature.[62] An assistant to the New York State commissioner of general services reported, "We're pressured to buy only New York products."[63]

In some states where preferential pricing is not authorized, the risk of criminal penalties for failure to select local products where prices are comparable may effectively create preferences. Iowa, which has not been characterized as strongly protectionist, has no price preferences in favor of in-state bidders or products, nor does it restrict foreign purchases. The state's code provides that every purchasing agent "shall use only those products and provisions grown and coal produced within the state of Iowa, when they are found in marketable quantities in the state and are of a quality reasonably suited to the purpose intended, and can be secured without additional cost over foreign products or products of other states."[64] Requests and bids must assert that preference. Contracts must contain a preference provision for Iowa domestic labor, and offenders shall be guilty of a misdemeanor.

What criteria are to be applied in determining whether or not in-state procurement constitutes additional cost? Faced with the knowledge that local producers may invoke these code provisions, will a state-employed

61. See United States–Japan Trade Council, *State "Buy American" Policy* (Washington: U.S.–Japan Trade Council, 1967), and *State Buy American Restrictions: A Current State by State Summary* (Washington: U.S.–Japan Trade Council, 1969).

62. *Wall Street Journal,* Oct. 2, 1962, p. 1.

63. Ibid., p. 20.

64. Iowa Code sec. 73.1 (1962); other relevant provisions are found in secs. 73.2–10.

purchasing official risk a court determination that he has failed to give preference to local products, or a contractor that he did not give preference to Iowa labor?

Florida, which disclaims restrictive foreign purchasing practices, was reported to have lost $200,000 on a $1.7 million bulkhead project for a seaport because the original specifications for the project prohibited the use of foreign steel. After considerable protest by the American Institute for Imported Steel, the project was readvertised, but excluded Bessemer-process steel and provided for "numerous inspection requirements" designed to hamper foreign bidders.[65]

Massachusetts has arrayed its preferential purchasing program in order, requiring first preference to supplies and materials in areas of local unemployment in Massachusetts, second to those manufactured and sold within the commonwealth, and finally to goods manufactured and sold within the United States.[66] No provision is made for purchases outside the United States.

In 1963 the Texas Association of Steel Importers successfully invalidated an order of the Texas Highway Commission, apparently in force since 1961, prohibiting the use of imported steel.[67] The association argued that the order denied equal protection of the laws; interfered with the federal regulation of foreign commerce; violated the General Agreement on Tariffs and Trade; contravened specific bilateral treaty commitments of the United States; and violated a Texas statute requiring competitive bidding. The court confined its rationale to the last-named ground.

California requires that "the governing body of any political subdivision, municipal corporation, or district, and any public officer or person charged with the letting of contracts for (1) the construction, alteration, or repair of public works or (2) for the purchasing of materials for public use, shall let such contracts only to persons who agree to use or supply only such manufactured materials as have been produced in the United States, substantially all from materials produced in the United States."[68]

65. *Wall Street Journal,* Oct. 2, 1962, p. 20.

66. Mass. Ann. Laws chap. 7, secs. 22, 17 (1958).

67. See *Texas Ass'n. of Steel Importers, Inc. v. Texas Highway Comm'r.,* 364 S.W. 2d 749 (Tex. Ct. App. 1963).

68. 32 West's California Codes (Government) Ann. sec. 4303 (1966); see generally secs. 4300–05.

Its code lists specific exclusions from the act's coverage, requires inclusion of buy-American language in every contract, and provides for posting the names of noncomplying persons. Its laws regarding award of contracts to the lowest responsible bidder are subordinated specifically to the state buy-American and California preference provisions. The state procurement preference calls first for goods grown, manufactured, or produced in California, and second for goods partly attributable to California, "price, fitness and quality being equal."[69]

State buy-American acts such as California's raise two types of constitutional issues. Are such acts consistent with international agreements of the United States, and, if not, are they to be deemed to be invalid under the supremacy clause of the U.S. Constitution, pursuant to which self-executing treaties and agreements of the United States override inconsistent enactments? Do such state laws regulate interstate and foreign commerce in such a way as to trench on Congress's power so to regulate, and are they in consequence precluded by the exclusive power granted by the Constitution to a branch or branches of the federal government in this regulatory area?

The first question reached the California courts in 1962. The city and county of San Francisco had issued an invitation for bids to furnish turbines and related equipment for a generating station that contained a place of manufacture specification essentially incorporating the provisions of the California buy-American act. Allis-Chalmers Manufacturing Company had submitted a single bid of $1,308,550 in accordance with the place of manufacture specification. Baldwin-Lima-Hamilton Corporation had submitted a bid of $1,337,036 on the same basis, and an additional bid of $1,237,036 that called for certain parts from foreign sources. The lower Baldwin bid was accepted and a contract awarded.

Allis, complaining that the Baldwin bid did not comply with the buy-American provision, sought an injunction requiring that the award be made to it. The Superior Court of San Francisco set aside the award to Baldwin but refused to order that the award be made to Allis. Baldwin then appealed, and California's Appellate Court ruled that "the California Buy-American statute and the above 'place of manufacture' clause in the bid call of November 20, 1961, are unenforceable in the situation now

69. Ibid., sec. 4331.

before us since they conflict with certain treaties and agreements and thus with the 'supreme law of the land.' "[70]

The court thus lent judicial approval to the holding of the California attorney general that the General Agreement on Tariffs and Trade, which he considered to be a self-executing treaty within the meaning of the supremacy clause, required nondiscriminatory treatment of foreign goods of signatories of GATT *unless* such goods are solely for governmental use.[71] Since the Baldwin contract was for equipment the state intended to use to generate electric power for *commercial resale,* it was not within the governmental use exception of the General Agreement on Tariffs and Trade.

Governmental Use Exception of GATT

A number of GATT articles are relevant to state buy-American acts. Article III provides:

4. The products of the territory of any contracting party imported into the territory of any other contracting party shall be accorded treatment no less favourable than that accorded to like products of national origin in respect of all laws, regulations and requirements affecting their internal sale, offering for sale, purchase, transportation, distribution or use. . . .

5. No contracting party shall establish or maintain any internal quantitative regulation relating to the mixture, processing or use of products in specified amounts or proportions which requires directly or indirectly, that any specified amount or proportions of any product, which is the subject of regulation must be supplied from domestic sources. . . .

6. The provisions of paragraph 5 shall not apply to any internal quantitative regulations in force in the territory of any contracting party on July 1, 1939, April 10, 1947, or March 24, 1968, at the option of the contracting party. . . .

8. (a) The provisions of this Article shall not apply to laws, regulations or requirements governing the procurement by governmental agencies of products purchased for governmental purposes and not with a view to commercial resale or with a view to use in the production of goods for commercial sale.

Article XXIV provides:

12. Each contracting party shall take such reasonable measures as may be available to it to ensure observance of the provisions of this Agreement by the regional and local governments and authorities within its territory.

70. *Baldwin-Lima-Hamilton Corp. v. Superior Court,* 208, Cal. App. 2d 819, 25 Cal. Rptr. 798, 808.
71. 34 Op. Cal. Att'y Gen. 302 (1959); 36 Op. Cal. Att'y Gen. 147 (1962).

The GATT Protocol of Provisional Application provides that on and after January 1, 1948, the signatories will apply Parts I and III of the agreement, and Part II (which includes Article III) to the fullest extent not inconsistent with existing legislation.

Thus, products of another signatory country are to be treated no less favorably by an importing country than its own products. When products are acquired for purely governmental purposes, however, Article III(4) gives way to III(8a)—if acts by state and local governments are "governmental" within the meaning of the latter paragraph.

It clearly appears that they are. Article XXIV(12) specifically recognizes that there are "regional and local governments and authorities" that have taken and can take measures affecting international trade. Thus provisions of state buy-American acts that cover purchases by a state or local government for government use are not inconsistent with the GATT, and hence do not raise any question under Article VI of the U.S. Constitution of conflict with GATT treaty obligations as the "supreme law of the land."

Under these circumstances, where purchases are limited to governmental use, the only constitutional basis for questioning the provisions of state acts is that of preclusion because they encroach on the exclusive congressional power to regulate interstate and foreign commerce. Both the preclusion and the supremacy clauses, however, may apply to goods purchased for resale.

Resale Provisions

State buy-American provisions that cover resales are clearly in conflict with Article III of GATT. The question, for supremacy clause purposes, is whether Article III's substantive provisions are intended to be self-executing and therefore to override inconsistent state legislation. Whether or not the state legislation antedated 1948, it appears to be incorrect to consider the GATT provisions self-executing.

First, Article XXIV(12), calling on a federal government to "take such reasonable measures as may be available to it to ensure observance of the provisions [of GATT] by the regional and local governments and authorities within its territory," is quite antithetical to self-execution. Far from bespeaking an intention to have the agreement operate as domestic law, the language of the drafters implies futurity, which U.S. Supreme

Court decisions have clearly interpreted as non-self-executing.[72] The negotiating and legislative history of Article XXIV(12) supports this view: Australia and Canada, two federal states, secured inclusion of the article because they had no power to compel governmental subdivisions such as Victoria, New South Wales, or Ontario to change local laws to conform with GATT obligations, or did not wish to exercise such power.[73]

Secondly, the Protocol of Provisional Application, which permits the continued application of pre-1948 legislation that is inconsistent with Part III (including Article III), is persuasive that state legislation was not intended to be treated differently from federal legislation. The California court's Baldwin decision, accordingly, cannot be considered sound.

Is there no way, then, to challenge successfully on constitutional grounds state buy-American legislation? One such ground—preclusion—has considerable promise. A long line of U.S. court cases, including two Supreme Court cases, establishes the proposition that certain areas in which the federal government is given the power by the Constitution to regulate or tax are precluded from regulation or taxation by the states and their subdivisions. The Supreme Court decided in 1827 that a state law requiring an importer of foreign goods to obtain a state license for a fee was invalid.[74] In recent years the preemption doctrine has been applied to invalidate an Oregon meat labeling law based on country of origin, not quality; a similar Tennessee meat labeling statute; and a New Jersey statute requiring that every advertisement for maritime passage indicate the flag of registry of the vessel.[75] The Supreme Court used the doctrine in 1964 to invalidate a state tax that discriminated against imports.[76]

Only one very recent state court case has applied the doctrine in the

72. *Foster v. Neilsen,* 27 U.S. (2 Pet.) 253, 314 (1829); *United States v. Percheman,* 32 U.S. (7 Pet.) 51 (1833). See also *Robertson v. General Electric Co.,* 32 F. 2d 495, 500 (4th Cir. 1929); *Fujii v. State,* 38 Cal. 2d 718, 721–22 (1952).

73. See John Howard Jackson, *World Trade and the Law of GATT* (Bobbs-Merrill, 1969), sec. 4.11, pp. 110–17. Jackson takes the contrary view, however.

74. *Brown v. Maryland,* 25 U.S. (12 Wheat.) 419 (1827). Some recent cases involving local regulation of imports have been decided on grounds other than preemption; see, for example, *Territory v. Ho,* 41 Hawaii 565 (1957); *Texas Ass'n. of Steel Importers, Inc. v. Texas Highway Comm'r.,* 364 S.W. 2d 749 (Tex. Ct. App. 1963).

75. *Ness Produce Co. v. Short,* 263 F. Supp. 586 (D. Ore. 1966), *aff'd* 385 U.S. 537 (1967); *Tuppman Thurlow Co., Inc. v. Moss,* 252 F. Supp. 641 (M.D. Tenn. 1966); and *Cunard S.S. Co. v. Lucci,* 94 N.J. Super. 440 (Super. Ct. 1966).

76. *Dept. of Revenue v. James B. Beam Distilling Co.,* 377 U.S. 341 (1964).

buy-American area. The plaintiffs, Bethlehem Steel Corporation, had unsuccessfully sought to prohibit the award of certain contracts to the low bidders who proposed to use Japanese steel. One contract was for steel beams to enlarge an aqueduct, which could involve governmental use only. The other was for steel to be used in electrical transmission towers, which could possibly supply power to private distributing companies. The appellate court ruled:

The crucial and determinative issue presented by these appeals is whether this act, as applied to certain purchases of steel products manufactured abroad, violates the United States Constitution. We have concluded that the California Buy American Act is an unconstitutional encroachment upon the federal government's exclusive power over foreign affairs, and constitutes an undue interference with the United States' conduct of foreign relations.[77]

The court regarded the enormous federal presence as a preemptive occupation of the area of foreign trade and therefore found that the alleged absence of conflicting federal legislation was immaterial:

The California Buy American Act, in effectively placing an embargo on foreign products, amounts to a usurpation by this state of the power of the federal government to conduct foreign trade policy. That there are countervailing state policies which are served by the retention of such an Act is "wholly irrelevant to judicial inquiry" (*United States v. Pink,* 315 U.S. 203, 233, 62 S.Ct. 552, 86 L.Ed. 796) since "(i)t is inconceivable that any of them can be interposed as an obstacle to the effective operation of a federal constitutional power." (*United States v. Belmont, supra,* 301 U.S. 324, 332, 57 S.Ct. 758, 81 L.Ed. 1134.) Only the federal government can fix the rules of fair competition when such competition is on an international basis. Foreign trade is properly a subject of national concern, not state regulation. State regulation can only impede, not foster, national trade policies. The problems of trade expansion or nonexpansion are national in scope, and properly should be national in scope in their resolution. . . . Certainly, such problems are beyond the purview of the State of California. As stated in *United States v. Pink, supra,* 315 U.S. 203, 232, 62 S.Ct. 552, 566, 86 L.Ed. 796: "These are delicate matters. If state action could defeat or alter our foreign policy, serious consequences might ensue. The nation as a whole would be held to answer if a State created difficulties with a foreign power."[78]

The court went on to state that it did not base its opinion on GATT and the supremacy clause:

It is vigorously asserted by defendants and denied by plaintiff that the Buy

77. *Bethlehem Steel Corp. v. Board of Commissioners of Department of W and P,* 80 Cal. Rptr. 800, n. 24 at 802 (1969).
78. Ibid., p. 803 (treaty citations omitted).

American Act is violative of the General Agreement on Tariffs and Trade (GATT, 6; Stat. Pts. 5 and 6, as amended), of which this nation is a signatory. In *Baldwin-Lima-Hamilton Corp. v. Superior Court,* 208 Cal. App. 2d 803, 819–820, 25 Cal. Rptr. 798, as one column of a twin pedestal upon which its decision was based, the court held that the California Buy-American Act had been superseded by GATT. In *Territory v. Ho,* 41 Hawaii 565, similar legislation was invalidated on the premise that it was in conflict with GATT. *Since we have concluded that the federal power, whether or not exercised, is exclusive in this field, we find it unnecessary to delve into an extensive analysis of the effect of GATT.*[79]

Despite this broad language, indeed perhaps because no distinction is made between "governmental use" and "resale" or with respect to actual preemption in the buy-American area (federal preference legislation not by its terms or rationale being preclusive of parallel state legislation), dramatic changes in state attitudes favoring buy-American policies are not likely to occur. A ruling by the U.S. Supreme Court, or clear legislative action by the Congress, or the negotiation of an international agreement that is clearly self-executing as to the states and that puts severe limitations on the present governmental use exception in GATT might cause a change. The latter possibility might be accomplished by excluding areas of state activity other than the construction of state office buildings and similar traditional activities. Less dramatic changes could be encouraged through strong action by the federal executive in its state-aid programs and in challenges to state policies by the Justice Department on grounds similar to those stated in the Bethlehem case. Whatever method is used to attack the problem, difficult questions of federal–state relations are raised because of the overlapping of jurisdiction and the tension between the federal power to regulate foreign commerce and foreign affairs and the states' powers to determine for themselves matters relating to their own health, safety, welfare, and internal governmental operations.

Effective Negotiations on Buy-American Policies

With the existing pattern of buy-American laws and policies, is it likely that the United States can negotiate an effective international agreement on this nontariff barrier, and if so, under what limitations?

The United States' capacity to negotiate effectively is limited by the

79. Ibid., pp. 804–06. Italics added.

absence of specific legislative authority to conclude agreements in this area without congressional approval or acceptance, statutory limitations imposed by the current act, and the relatively unsettled question of federal authority to control effectively state regulation. Moreover, it would appear that any agreement in this area would have to include an escape mechanism that would permit imposition of buy-American standards in such important policy areas as national security.

Absence of Authority to Negotiate

At present the President has no specific legislative authority to negotiate an agreement with respect to discriminatory governmental purchasing policies. That has not, of course, prevented his utilizing his constitutional power over foreign affairs as the basis for negotiating international agreements, where he felt the need existed—for instance, in the recent Antidumping Code (discussed in Chapter 4). He runs a risk when he does so, however, particularly if the terms of the agreement he negotiates are arguably inconsistent with an existing statute. Then, congressional hostility is likely to develop, as the current congressional emasculation of the Antidumping Code graphically proves.

Fortunately, however, the federal Buy American Act contains great flexibility in the manner and degree of preference it legislates, and the President has exercised this flexibility within the range of 6 percent to 50 percent. Hence, an international agreement within that range could certainly not be criticized as unprecedented.

Consistency with Current Laws

Because there is existing legislation in the area, the international agreement must be consistent if it is to be effective. Otherwise it runs the risk of being invalidated either by the courts as an ineffective attempt by the executive to derogate from Congress's constitutionally exercised powers over foreign commerce, or by congressional action designed to reassert the statutory balance of interests that Congress believed to be correct.

In short, any agreement negotiated on the President's authority acting on his own should stay within the limits contemplated by the federal buy-American statute. Since the act contains no minimum percentage of preference, and specifically refers to "unreasonable" prices which it acknowledges harm the U.S. Treasury, the range of discretion is very wide indeed. For example, if the President were to agree internationally not to apply the statute unless the foreign bid undercuts the domestic bid by less than 6 percent including duty (or 10 percent without duty), he would be doing nothing more drastic than he had done before. In all likelihood the domestic repercussion would be no greater than any that had occurred earlier—no argument of illegality based on inconsistency with prior administrative determinations could remotely hold water, thus distinguishing the case from that of the Antidumping Code. An international agreement negotiated within the substantial leeway open to the President would tend to satisfy a very basic objection to the Buy American Act, by sharply reducing the margin of preference to a level that would not be a significant deterrent to international trade.

It would be most important in this connection, however, to eliminate the possibility of invocation of a balance of payments or gold flow exception to raise the margin of preference. Otherwise, foreign trading partners of the United States, remembering those instruments for raising the 6 percent preference to 50 percent five years later, would remain unimpressed by the seeming change of policy. In short, no balance of payments exception should be incorporated in the agreement.

A complete elimination of this barrier could be achieved, of course, if Congress were to repeal the act, either prior to negotiations or upon reciprocal action from other countries as a result of negotiations. But the formidable difficulties in the path of this solution seem to render it ill-advised. For it invites a confrontation between free traders and protectionists that can be resolved favorably for free traders only with a major political commitment by the administration in power, which is unlikely in the absence of a major international political event such as the birth of the Common Market. In the context of more normal bargaining, such as nontariff barrier negotiations, it is not prudent to expect unusual congressional tolerance.

Ability to Regulate State Policies

One of the objects of foreign nations' negotiations with the United States would be to obtain an agreement that would not only effectively curtail federal but also eliminate state and local discriminatory purchasing policies. If revenue sharing should become substantial, this objective would obviously be even more important. Despite the preclusion holding in the

Bethlehem case, the question is still open whether the Supreme Court will adopt and apply it across the board to state buy-American laws. An international agreement, however, could be framed in clearly self-executing terms and be made applicable to state and local governments. Either the general authority to conclude trade agreements, granted by the trade agreements legislation, or the presidential authority could be used to execute an agreement. While the latter method is more vulnerable to political attack, an agreement within the leeway of federal legislation is unlikely to be open to legislative repudiation.

Escape Mechanisms

Perhaps the greatest difficulty in negotiating an international agreement with respect to federal and state buy-American policies is determining the special situations that would permit discriminatory purchasing. In part the problem is a substantive one of each nation deciding which of its national policies, such as alleviation of unemployment in impacted areas, it would be most tempted to withhold and yet be willing to bargain for without destroying the agreement itself. But it is equally as much a drafting problem, of framing exceptions and escape mechanisms in such a manner that they will not be easily employed. For example, the national security exception under Executive Order 10582 has been employed at times against goods whose purchase could only remotely, by the greatest stretch of the imagination, affect U.S. "national security" as that term is reasonably understood. Since good faith is the ultimate binding force in most international agreements in any event, and since nothing conduces to it more than a requirement to explain to a skeptical audience in advance the reasons and motives for a nation's actions, a provision requiring consultation with affected parties *prior* to a deviation from the agreement would encourage strict compliance.

Past practice in the United States indicates that the more probable areas where exceptions or escapes would be sought are those affecting the national security and labor-surplus areas.

Reciprocity

An important, if not crucial, part of any international agreement on buy-national laws and policies is reciprocity. Enactment of the Buy American Act in 1933 was greatly facilitated by the British preference then in existence, duly noted by congressional advocates of the American counter-part. Today there is little question that every important trading country employs domestic preferences in government purchasing in kind and degree at least as restrictive as those of the United States. The major difference is that U.S. provisions are set out in laws and regulations, while foreign preferences are largely expressed in the form of internal, unpublished, instructions. No international agreement is possible in this area without reciprocal undertakings, with reciprocity reflected in governmental purchases made without regard to the foreign origin of the product except in specified situations.

Institutional Arrangements

Because escapes are highly likely to be required, and reciprocity is in fact necessary to an agreement on buy-national laws and policies, there must be some forum for consultation. This consultative organ could well be a committee of the GATT or perhaps the Organization for Economic Cooperation and Development. In all events, a small staff will be necessary to assist in the advance consultation required for escapes and in handling the inevitable complaints of failure to afford equality of opportunity brought by parties to the agreement. There is no reason why such an organ could not assist in administering other nontariff barrier agreements that might be negotiated from time to time.

Conclusion

Under existing law a relatively effective agreement, consistent with existing federal legislation, could be negotiated to lower very significantly the restrictions imposed by federal buy-American legislation. To be effective in controlling state policies it should be self-executing, thereby invoking *Missouri v. Holland*'s holding of the supremacy of international agreements over state law. It should also narrowly and carefully define escapes and exceptions from the general rules concerning discrimination, requiring advance consultation before any may be invoked. The agreement should be reciprocal, applying to other major participants in world trade that act similarly, and a consultative organ should be employed to assist in its administration.

A more successful relaxation could only come about with the cooperation of Congress, through the amendment or repeal of the present federal
act, perhaps coupled with a prohibitive directive to the states. Such a result
is unlikely in the immediate future. But its absence need not stultify the
effort to curtail drastically a most important nontariff barrier to international trade. Substantial immediate progress is feasible through the use
of the presidential agreement within the leeway of existing federal legislation.

CHAPTER FOUR

Antidumping and Countervailing Duties

MANY COUNTRIES, including the United States, impose duties to offset the advantage to imports secured through lower prices than the goods command elsewhere (antidumping duties), or through subsidization by the exporting country (countervailing duties). The practices of a number of countries imposing these duties are considered by many to create unjustified barriers to trade.

ANTIDUMPING DUTIES

IN ITS PRECISE ECONOMIC SENSE, dumping means price discrimination between national markets. It is usually employed, however, to denote sales for export at prices lower than those charged domestically.[1] Thus a Japanese manufacturer of, say, "tuners (of the type used in consumer electronic products)" who sells his product in the United States at a lower price than in Japan is said to be dumping the tuners in this country.

Dumping is only a special case of price discrimination between buyers. Theoretically, no difference exists between the Japanese firm and a Maryland manufacturer who sells a product at a lower price in New York City than in Baltimore. Like the Japanese concern, the Maryland firm may be

1. Jacob Viner, *Dumping: A Problem in International Trade* (Augustus Kelley, 1966), pp. 4–6. The discussion of various kinds of dumping in this chapter relies on this work.

selling at a lower price because the buyer is in a stronger bargaining position than others, or because the firm wishes to break into a new market, maintain long-run connections in a currently unprofitable market, eliminate competition and then subsequently raise prices, supplement relatively inelastic demand in the local market, or profitably utilize its production capacity by selling outside the local market.

In the United States, federal law prohibits price discrimination between national markets and in interstate commerce. The Robinson-Patman Act makes it unlawful for sellers "to discriminate in price between different purchasers of commodities of like grade and quality . . . where the effect of such discrimination may be substantially to lessen competition or tend to create a monopoly . . . or to injure, destroy, or prevent competition with" the discriminating seller.[2] The Antidumping Act of 1921 imposes a dumping duty on the importer of foreign merchandise that is sold for less in the United States than in the country of exportation if an industry in the United States is thereby being injured.[3] In both cases Congress intended to eliminate the use of price-cutting tactics that impair the competitive position of domestic sellers. The Antidumping Act applies, however, without regard for the competitive structure of the industry being affected by price discrimination.

Neither law takes into account the consumer interest in lower prices brought about by price discrimination between markets. Both are aimed at keeping manufacturers in business, even though they may be quite inefficient or refuse to engage in price competition.[4] Price discrimination, however, is only economically harmful to society at large if it leads to higher prices after destroying, or preventing the emergence of, competitive industry. The Antidumping Act, however, has been administered without regard to the anticompetitive impact of duties imposed on lower priced imports at the behest of domestic monopolists, oligopolists, or cartels.

Dumping as an Economic Phenomenon

Price discrimination between national markets includes not only export sales at lower prices than domestic sales but sales at different prices in

2. 49 Stat. 1526, 15 U.S.C. sec. 13(a) (1964).
3. 42 Stat. 11, 19 U.S.C. secs. 160–73 (1964).
4. See Paul A. Samuelson, *Economics,* 6th ed. (McGraw-Hill, 1964), p. 504; discussion of the economics of dumping in this chapter relies on this work.

different export markets or at higher prices abroad than at home. For example, china produced in Britain for export to North America may be sold in the United States at one price and in Canada at a different price. Dumping is taking place even though there are no sales whatever in the home market. Or a Japanese manufacturer of Christmas tree ornaments may charge higher prices in foreign markets than in his relatively unimportant domestic market. This kind of discrimination is known as "reverse dumping."

Sales at identical prices in two markets may conceal markedly different terms. In these concealed dumping cases, provisions for technical assistance and servicing, advertising and selling costs, commissions, credit terms, warranties, research and development costs, costs of containers and other expenses incurred in readying goods for shipment, and shipping costs may differ substantially in foreign and domestic sales. Thus identical prices may in actuality mean a lower price for the foreign purchaser if he is getting more for his price.[5] By the same token, of course, the lower price may benefit the home buyer.

All instances of price discrimination between national markets can be characterized as either sporadic dumping, short-run or intermittent dumping, or long-run or continuous dumping. Scattered, isolated instances of dumping are considered unimportant; permanent dumping is beneficial to the country dumped in (if not to certain of its producers) because consumers are provided with a less expensive source of merchandise, but short-run dumping may on balance be harmful.

Sporadic dumping includes sale of an (unintentional) overstock in a foreign market at a lower price in preference to holding the surplus for sale at a later date or lower price in the home market. It also includes unintentional dumping of goods that could not be sold at the anticipated profitable price in the foreign market.

Short-run dumping is, by definition, always carried on intentionally. It may be designed to maintain market position or trade connections in a foreign market when competitors' prices are temporarily lower than those in the home market. It may be a means of breaking into a new market. Introduction of a new product or of a new supplier of a familiar product

5. Exchange dumping is another variety of selling for less abroad than at home. When a currency is depreciating, its internal purchasing power is higher than its external purchasing power and export prices are thus lower in terms of foreign currency.

through a loss-leader is a time-honored method of developing a market. Attempts to eliminate or suppress competitors in a market, or bring them to price terms—the infamous predatory dumping—are "the most objectionable form of dumping from the point of view of the country dumped on."[6] Retaliatory dumping seems to fall in the predatory category; the foreign manufacturer, faced with an influx of dumped goods in his home market, retaliates by dumping in the dumper's home market.

Long-run dumping practiced by manufacturers whose home market demand is inelastic (for reasons of market or product or both) is designed to raise profits through export of excess production. Among others, the American chemical industry has engaged in this activity.[7] Inelastic demand means that a lower selling price in the home market will not stimulate sales but simply lower the manufacturer's total revenue. On the other hand, for the individual manufacturer, world demand is so elastic that any price for his product in excess of his marginal cost of production will add to his profit.

The manufacturer must, however, be able to control substantially home market prices. If competition forces prices down, they may equal or fall lower than the foreign market price. In order to control home market prices, the dumper must be a monopolist or oligopolist or participate in a price-fixing cartel, and he must be protected by tariff or nontariff barriers from foreign competition in the home market.[8] Conceivably, domestic prices could be kept higher than foreign through external measures alone —tariffs, unstable foreign exchange rates, buy-national policies, and so forth.

Is Dumping Harmful?

The basic assumption that dumping is, on balance, harmful to the economy or other national interests of the country being dumped in is highly

6. Viner, *Dumping,* p. 26.

7. See ibid., pp. 28–29. Socialist and communist countries, selling through state-controlled trading agencies, may engage in long-run dumping on mercantilist grounds. Such dumping in the United States seems unlikely at this time because of the high U.S. tariff barriers applicable to communist-controlled countries.

8. See Horace J. DePowdin and Barbara Epstein, *The British Power Transformer Industry and Its Excursions into the United States Market: A Case Study in International Price Discrimination* (New York University, Graduate School of Business Administration, 1969).

doubtful. Consumers probably can purchase goods of the kind being dumped at a lower price than they would otherwise pay. Even when a dumper's prices are not lower than domestic prices, his presence stimulates competition. But when dumped goods cost less than domestic goods, the consumer will benefit by the difference. If the domestic industry responds to the competition, the benefit to consumers may be even greater, as the price of all goods of the class or kind dumped falls.

The resources thus saved by consumers increase the total resources available to them. If the dumped goods are used as raw materials or components of other products, prices of those products should also fall. And if dumped goods are finished products, their ultimate consumers will have available additional resources for other purchases. In general, the country dumped in benefits as a whole from the lower prices resulting from dumping; its production-possibility curve is shifted outward and real per capita income is higher.

Dumping also creates competition for industries that are monopolistic or oligopolistic in structure or that otherwise restrict free competition. Despite U.S. antitrust laws, legal action has been taken to improve industry structure in only a few of the most flagrant instances.[9] Typically, oligopolists and monopolists attempt to administer their prices in such a way as to earn excess profits. This not only produces an undesirable distribution of resources but a deadweight loss to the economy through lower production at higher prices than would prevail under competitive conditions. The pressure of low priced imports forces domestic industries to lower prices or face the loss of a substantial part of their sales. Dumping can therefore have the salutary effect of introducing competition where it has been nonexistent.

The negative aspect of dumping to the country dumped in is, of course, the harm done to domestic producers of the goods dumped. However, unless the attendant price discrimination can be shown to be an unfair method of competition, domestic producers harmed by the dumping are in exactly the same position as those harmed by cheap imports that are not being dumped. Thus the same arguments for free trade, or for protectionism, should obtain in both cases.

Only predatory dumping can reasonably be considered unfair compe-

9. See, for example, *United States v. United Shoe Machinery Corp.*, 110 F. Supp. 295 (D. Mass. 1953), *aff'd per curiam*, 347 U.S. 521 (1954).

tition to the country being dumped in. By definition, it is intended to destroy, injure, or suppress competition. Usually intent on preventing local industry from becoming established, or on squeezing it out if it has started operating, the predatory dumper hopes to be able to charge monopolistic prices for his products or to discourage competitors from price competition. When it is retaliatory—directed at suppressing the competition of a foreign manufacturer in the dumper's home market—predatory dumping is frequently characterized by sales at less than the marginal cost of production.

The argument that other forms of dumping are unfair is based primarily on the notion that the low prices are founded on discrimination between buyers, not on superior efficiency or production. This totally misstates the concept of price competition. The most efficient producer does not necessarily charge the lowest prices for his goods even in a highly competitive market. A producer who is less efficient because he is smaller may engage in vigorous price competition, making no profit or losing money in the short run, in order to increase sales, enlarge plant capacity, and thus become more efficient by taking advantage of the economies of scale. If domestic manufacturers are in fact more efficient than dumpers, they should have no hesitancy in meeting price competition by lowering prices.[10]

A corollary argument, that dumping is unfair because it is subsidized by the high prices the dumper receives in his protected home market, has major flaws. It assumes that overhead (fixed) costs are completely recovered in the home market and that the manufacturer greatly increases his profit by selling in foreign markets at a price above marginal cost of production. While inelastic demand precludes increased sales in the home market, the market price for those goods is usually fixed. That kind of restrictive business practice is widespread. Dumping is therefore a symptom of a worldwide misallocation of resources. Antidumping duties levied on a few articles imported at low prices are obviously an impossible means

10. Viner takes the position that short-run dumping is on balance more harmful than not: "Short-run dumping, whatever its objective, may result in serious injury to or even the total elimination of the domestic industry. The gain to the consumer from a short period of abnormally low prices may not be nearly great enough to offset the damage to the domestic industry." *Dumping,* p. 140. Strangely, this argument seems to assume that the industries affected are infant ones, unable to defend themselves against price competition.

of controlling the price fixing. The country receiving the dumped goods can be legitimately concerned if they are seriously injurious. It is hardly in a position to object to price fixing in other countries in the name of "misallocation of world resources" while it tolerates such practices in its home market.

Price discrimination between national markets is not predicated on overhead costs being recovered in the high price market, but on economies of scale. By increasing output without expanding facilities, a manufacturer can usually lower his average cost. Each additional unit produced decreases the percentage of overhead cost allocable to all units. The efficiencies of larger scale operation may also decrease the marginal cost of production. The effect of a sharp drop in average cost can vary, as Table 1 illustrates.

It is the drop in average cost inherent in full utilization of production facilities, in combination with inelasticity of demand in the high price market, that makes long-run discrimination between national markets a rational business decision. Short-run dumping may also be based on those factors, or on the equally fair business considerations involved in developing a new market and maintaining trade connections in a temporarily unfavorable market. Only predatory dumping—price discrimination between national markets coupled with an intention to achieve a monopoly and then charge monopoly prices or to injure competitors until they reach a tacit or express price level agreement—can reasonably be considered unfair competition as far as the country dumped in is concerned.

Table 1. *Profit from Domestic and Export Sales in a Fixed-Price Market*

Total output, units	Per unit cost of production, dollars			Price per unit, dollars		Sales, units		Total profit, dollars
	Indirect	Direct	Total	Domestic	Export	Domestic	Export	
100,000	1.00	3.50	4.50	4.75	4.75	100,000	0	25,000
200,000	0.80	2.80	3.60	4.75	3.50	100,000	100,000	105,000
200,000	0.80	2.80	3.60	3.70	3.70	200,000	0	20,000

Source: Jacob Viner, *Dumping: A Problem in International Trade* (Augustus Kelley, 1966), p. 125.

The Antidumping Act of 1921

Although most predatory dumping has been unlawful since the passage of the Sherman Antitrust Act in 1890,[11] the Antidumping Act has since 1921 prohibited almost all other forms of dumping. For the purposes of the act, dumping consists of all price discrimination (sales at less than fair value) between national markets by which "industry in the United States is being or is likely to be injured, or is prevented from being established, by reason of the importation of such merchandise into the United States."[12] Neither the consumer's interest in obtaining low priced goods nor the nation's interest in promoting competition is reflected in the act.

The Antidumping Act is substantially identical to a portion of the Underwood tariff bill, introduced in 1913, that appeared again, after World War I, in the Sixty-Sixth Congress.[13] These provisions are, in turn, almost verbatim copies of a Canadian statute enacted in 1904 and redrafted three years later.[14] Ironically, the Canadian law was directed at American dumping and was developed in large part as the result of predatory dumping by the United States Steel Corporation in Canada.[15]

The key provision of the Antidumping Act is as follows:

Whenever the Secretary of The Treasury . . . determines that a class or kind of foreign merchandise is being, or is likely to be, sold in the United States or elsewhere at less than its fair value, he shall so advise the United States Tariff Commission, and the said Commission shall determine within three months thereafter whether an industry in the United States is being or is likely to be injured, or is prevented from being established, by reason of the importation of such merchandise into the United States. The said Commission, after such investigation as it deems necessary, shall notify the Secretary of its determination, and, if that determination is in the affirmative, the Secretary shall make public a notice . . . of his determination and the determination of the said Commission . . . [which] shall be deemed to have made an affirmative determination if the commissioners of the said Commission voting are evenly divided as to whether its determination should be in the affirmative or in the negative. The Secretary's finding shall include a description of the class or kind of mer-

11. 15 U.S.C. secs. 1–7.
12. 19 U.S.C. sec. 160.
13. See H.R. 2, 63 Cong. 1 sess. (1913), p. 455; and H.R. 9983 and H.R. 10071, 66 Cong. 1 sess. (1919).
14. 6–7 Edward VIII, Vol. I–II, p. 134 (Can.).
15. Viner, *Dumping,* pp. 85–86.

chandise to which it applies in such detail as he shall deem necessary for the guidance of customs officers.[16]

The act goes on to provide that when the secretary of the treasury has reason to believe or suspect that there have been sales at less than fair value, he shall publish a notice of such belief or suspicion in the Federal Register and shall authorize withholding of appraisement on the merchandise for from up to 120 days prior to the date that the dumping question was raised until such time as a final determination of dumping or no dumping has been made. The secretary must publish dumping determinations and the Tariff Commission must publish its injury determinations in the Federal Register along with the grounds for such determinations. The amount of the dumping duty is established as the difference between the "purchase price" or "exporter's sale price" and the "foreign market value" (or the "constructed value").

The Customs Simplification Act of 1954 amended the Antidumping Act by transferring the injury determination authority from the secretary of the treasury to the Tariff Commission, and provided that such determination be made within three months from the determination of the question of "fair value" by the secretary. It also provided that the secretary's authority to withhold appraisement be limited to merchandise entered or withdrawn from warehouse, for consumption, not more than 120 days before the question of dumping was first raised.[17]

The only other change in the 1921 act provides that where the commissioners are evenly divided it shall be deemed that the commission made an affirmative determination of injury.[18]

Objective of the Act

An antidumping policy and implementing legislation presuppose a definition of dumping—the unfair trade practice that is their target. The statute did not incorporate the imprecise, colloquial use of the term that manufacturers faced with competition from abroad apply to every form of price differential caused by imports, whether resulting from prices below those of comparable domestic goods or below those prevailing in the producing country. The legislative history of the act forcefully demon-

16. 19 U.S.C. sec. 160(a).
17. *Customs Simplification Act of 1954,* 68 Stat. 1138.
18. *Trade Agreements Extension Act of 1958,* 72 Stat. 583, 585.

strates that Congress did not intend to prohibit as "dumping" every instance of price discrimination, but was concerned only with those it deemed to constitute unfair trade practices.

In 1916 it was made a crime to dump goods into the United States "with the intent of destroying or injuring an industry in the United States, . . . or of restraining or monopolizing any part of trade or commerce in such articles in the United States."[19] It is clear that Congress was concerned with eradicating the kind of predatory price-cutting practices of foreign producers that the Sherman Act deals with. In the debate over the bill Senator Boies Penrose (Republican of Pennsylvania) called attention to predatory dumping by German cartels.[20]

Although the 1921 statute attacks the problem in broader language, there can be little doubt that the congressional conception of the evils of dumping had not changed. The sanctions of the antitrust laws were dropped because of their unworkability, not because of a divorcement of dumping and unfair monopoly practices in the congressional mind.

Thus, a 1919 Tariff Commission report to the Congress reiterated concern over the predatory tactics of the German dye industry and found it injurious because domestic businesses are forced "to sell their entire output at a small margin of profit, or even at a loss."[21] And the House report stated the antidumping bill was designed to protect industry and labor against "now common species of commercial warfare of dumping goods at less than cost or home value if necessary until our industries are destroyed, whereupon the dumping ceases and prices are raised at or above normal levels to recoup dumping losses."[22] The bill's principal proponent in the Senate declared that it was aimed at a "condition in which some foreign business concern desiring to enter the American market may be willing to slaughter its profits for a given length of time for the purpose of destroying the American industry."[23]

Even clearer evidence of the limited definition of dumping appeared during Senate debate on the bill. Senator Stanley (Democrat of Kentucky) divided dumping into three categories. Dismissing sporadic and surplus-

19. 39 Stat. 798, 15 U.S.C. sec. 72.
20. *Congressional Record,* Vol. 53, 64 Cong. 1 sess. (1916), pp. 14147–48.
21. U.S. Tariff Commission, *Dumping and Unfair Competition* (1919), p. 20.
22. *Emergency Tariff Bill,* H. Rept. 1, 67 Cong. 1 sess. (1921), p. 23.
23. Remarks of Congressman Fordney (Republican of Michigan), in *Congressional Record,* Vol. 61, 67 Cong. 1 sess. (1921), pp. 1011, 1021; see also pp. 254, 262.

production dumping as not being within the ambit of the bill, Senator Stanley declared, "This act is ostensibly designed to meet the condition described . . . as unfair price cutting, the object of which is to injure, destroy or prevent the establishment of an American industry."[24]

Unfortunately, this legislative history has been largely lost sight of in the expanded application of the act's terminology in recent years.

Operation of the Act

The act has been applied somewhat differently than its framers intended.[25] The act comes into operation when a foreign producer sells to U.S. importers at a lower price than he charges in his own country, with resultant injury to U.S. industry. The dumping duty assessed on the imports is determined by the difference between the two prices.

To justify such action, both price discrimination and injury must be found. Though price discrimination typically involves a lower price to the United States than the price charged in the producer's home market, some exporters have few or no home market sales to use as a measure. In those cases the price to the United States is measured against the price to a third country—that is, another purchaser of the producer's exports— or against the foreign producer's cost of production if he sells only to the United States.

For example, price discrimination might be found in the sale of bicycles for a producer's home market at $15 and for export to the United States at $12. Or if the producer sells no bicycles in his home market but exports to third countries at $15 and to the United States at $12, this would be price discrimination. If he exports only to the United States and his cost (including overhead and profit) is $15, while his sale price is $12, this also would be price discrimination.

Discrimination must be accompanied by injury, which within the meaning of the Antidumping Act is found if an industry in the United States is being or is likely to be injured or is prevented from being established by the imports. The statute does not define *injury*.

The usual dumping case begins with a claim by a U.S. producer,

24. Ibid., p. 1194.
25. See James P. Hendrick, "The United States Antidumping Act," *American Journal of International Law,* Vol. 58 (1964), p. 914.

directed to the commissioner of customs, that a particular product is being dumped with resultant injury to him. If the commissioner is satisfied that there is reason to believe there may be price discrimination, he will initiate an investigation. Representatives of both the foreign producers and the domestic industry are given opportunity informally to present their views and arguments. If, on the basis of the commissioner of customs' report, the secretary of the treasury decides that there is price discrimination, jurisdiction over the case is transferred from the Treasury Department to the U.S. Tariff Commission. The commission investigates whether the imports are causing or threatening injury to an industry in the United States. It holds a hearing at which opposing interests may present evidence and argument. If its injury determination is positive, a dumping finding is signed by the secretary or assistant secretary of the treasury and duties are assessed on all imports on which there is price discrimination. If the injury determination is negative, the case is closed.

While any case is pending under the Antidumping Act, appraisement may be withheld on any such imports that the secretary of the treasury has "reason to believe or suspect" are being sold at less than home price (or third country price, or cost). The result is to postpone the fixing of any duties until the dumping determination is made. The withholding does not deny entry to merchandise. It does, however, allow retroactive assessment of dumping duties on imports that entered up to 120 days before the dumping complaint was filed and that have not cleared customs (that is, are held in bonded warehouses). Imports that enter at a price equal to or higher than home price are not affected by a withholding order.

Administration

Except in the determination of injury, responsibility for the administration of the act is vested in the secretary of the treasury. He is empowered to promulgate regulations necessary for enforcement of the act.[26] The secretary may initiate an antidumping proceeding on his own motion when information provided him or a subordinate supports the suspicion that the purchase price of imports or the exporter's sales price is less than

26. See Alexis Coudert, "The Application of the United States Antidumping Law in Light of a Liberal Trade Policy," *Columbia Law Review,* Vol. 65 (1965), p. 189.

the foreign market value (or the constructed value) of the goods.[27] Proceedings are most apt to be instigated by customs appraisers or other principal officers of the Customs Service. (A customs appraiser or his superior must inform the commissioner of customs if either has grounds to suspect an instance of sales at less than fair value.) Also, "any person outside the Customs Service" (a domestic producer, for example) having information as to sales at less than fair value may communicate it, together with supporting reasons, to the commissioner of customs.[28] By far the overwhelming number of proceedings is triggered by domestic producers' complaints.

The commissioner, on receiving a complaint, may conduct a brief preliminary investigation to determine whether reasonable grounds exist to "believe or suspect" that sales are being, or are likely to be, made at less than foreign market value. If the answer to that inquiry is affirmative, he conducts a more thorough, though confidential and informal, investigation to provide the secretary with the additional information necessary to make his determination as to fair value.[29] Questionnaires are submitted to the foreign producers, who are permitted to supply the commissioner with information tending to establish that their products have not been sold in the United States at less than fair value. This information is compared with that of domestic producers and with information already available to customs officers or obtained, when circumstances warrant it, at the foreign producer's plant.

If the commissioner decides, after either preliminary or full-scale investigation, that there are reasonable grounds to suspect a case of sales at less than fair value, he publishes a "withholding of appraisement notice" in the Federal Register and notifies the secretary.[30] He also advises the customs appraisers, who then withhold appraisement of merchandise that has been entered and stored in bonded warehouses or that was withdrawn from warehouses not more than 120 days before the question of dumping was raised (goods already appraised would of course not be

27. *Customs Simplification Act of 1954,* sec. 301, 68 Stat. 1138, as amended, 19 U.S.C. sec. 160 (1959).

28. 19 C.F.R. sec. 14.6(b) (1964), as amended, 29 Fed. Reg. 16320 (1964).

29. 19 C.F.R. sec. 14.6(d)(2) (1964). If the answer is negative, the commissioner may either initiate a full-scale investigation or recommend to the secretary that such investigation is not warranted by the facts and that the case be closed by a finding of "no sales at less than fair value." 19 C.F.R. sec. 14.6(d)(3).

30. 19 C.F.R. secs. 14.6(e), 14.9, 29 Fed. Reg. 16320, 16322 (1964).

affected retroactively). Although withholding of appraisement does not directly deny entry to the imported merchandise, it does postpone the fixing of ordinary duties; any dumping duty later assessed will be added to such ordinary duties.

In practice, before 1968 the period from the date of notice to the date of the secretary's finding of dumping (after the Tariff Commission's injury determination) was a year or more. The burden on foreign producers could be increased by as much as 120 days when appraisement was withheld retroactively. In contrast, most foreign dumping laws and regulations authorize neither retroactive withholding of appraisement nor assessment of dumping duties prior to the promulgation of the dumping finding.[31] The ordinary effect of the U.S. procedure was severe; because it was impossible for the importer to determine his final sales price during the withholding period, the importation of the merchandise ceased during this time. For this reason, foreign governments severely criticized the appraisement withholding procedures.

After completing the investigative inquiry, the secretary of the treasury must make a prompt, tentative determination whether or not there are sales at less than fair value; he then publishes in the Federal Register a "notice of tentative determination" which includes a statement of the grounds on which the determination is based. Interested persons then may present additional written submissions or argument. The secretary may, in his discretion, afford an opportunity for argument and confrontation among all interested persons. As soon as possible thereafter, he will make a final determination, except that he may defer making an affirmative determination during the pendency of any other antidumping proceedings that relate to the same kind of merchandise imported from another foreign country. No determination that sales are not below fair value will be deferred. If the secretary determines that sales are being made at less than fair value, he will so advise the Tariff Commission.

Until 1970, Treasury had a practice of stopping a dumping proceeding when it determined that although price discrimination may have been present it had been discontinued and was not likely to be reinitiated—in other words, when the alleged dumper agreed to revise his prices upward to avoid the dumping finding. The practice was justified on grounds that the cost of making a final determination was not justified

31. See testimony of Assistant Secretary of the Treasury Kendall in *Amendments to Antidumping Act of 1921,* Hearings, pp. 55, 88–90.

by the possibility of only slight, if any, monetary or other benefit that might be derived from a dumping finding.[32]

THE FAIR VALUE FORMULA

In determining whether foreign merchandise is being sold or is likely to be sold within the United States at a price below its fair value, the Treasury Department compares the purchase price or exporter's sale price with the foreign market value or constructed value.[33] The purchase price is the f.o.b. factory or point of export price charged the American importer plus, if not already including, cost of packing and expenses incident to conditioning the merchandise for shipment, and export taxes and internal taxes imposed by the country of export that have been rebated or waived because of export.[34] If the sale price includes costs incident to transporting the merchandise from the shipping point in the exporting country to the place of delivery in the United States, or United States import duties, or duties imposed for violation of the U.S. Antidumping Act, these are deducted in calculating the purchase price.[35]

The exporter's sale price is applicable where foreign merchandise is sold to American purchasers after export either on consignment or by an agent in the United States.[36] It is the purchase price before or after

32. See Hendrick, "United States Antidumping Act," pp. 918–19. 19 C.F.R. sec. 14.7(b)(8) provided that no determination would be made if the quantity involved in sales, or the differential between the price compared, was "not more than insignificant."

33. See Lowell E. Baier, "Substantive Interpretations Under the Antidumping Act and the Foreign Trade Policy of the United States," *Stanford Law Review,* Vol. 17 (1965), pp. 409, 414–16.

34. 19 U.S.C. sec. 162. See *Amendments to Antidumping Act of 1921,* Hearings, pp. 12–13; and *Rayon Staple Fiber from West Germany,* 26 Fed. Reg. 3387 (1961).

35. See *Rayon Staple Fiber from Cuba,* 26 Fed. Reg. 3387 (1961); *Portland Cement from Holland,* 26 Fed. Reg. 1971 (1961); and 19 C.F.R. sec. 14.9(f) (1964). "A warranty of nonapplicability of dumping duties granted to an importer with respect to merchandise which is (1) purchased, or agreed to be purchased, before publication of a 'Withholding of Appraisement Notice' with respect to such merchandise, and (2) exported before a determination of sales below fair value is made, will not be regarded as affecting purchase price or exporter's sales price." 29 Fed. Reg. 16320 (1964).

36. "The price to the United States is called 'purchase price' if the foreign producer and the United States importer are dealing at arm's length. It is called 'exporter's sales price' if the foreign producer and the importer are related." Baier, "Substantive Interpretations," p. 415, quoting James P. Hendrick, deputy assistant secretary to the assistant secretary of the treasury.

import plus, to the extent not included in the agreed sale price, cost of packing and conditioning the merchandise for shipment, and import duties and internal taxes imposed by the exporting country that have been rebated or waived because the goods are exported. Conversely, export taxes imposed by the country of export, cost of transporting the merchandise from the point of shipment to the place of delivery in the United States, U.S. import duties, and commissions and expenses incurred by the exporter related to selling the merchandise are deducted from the agreed sale price if they have been included.[37] Any dumping duties refunded to the importer are also deducted.

Foreign market value is the price at which merchandise is sold or offered for sale in usual wholesale quantities in the ordinary course of trade in the principal markets of the exporting country at the time of export. If, however, the merchandise is not sold or offered for sale in the exporting country, or the quantity sold is too small to form an adequate basis for comparison with sales to the United States, then the export price to other countries is the basis for determining the foreign market value.[38] The cost of packing and conditioning the merchandise for shipment must be included in determining the foreign market value. Allowances for differences in quantities sold are carefully defined:

Consideration will be given . . . to the practice of the industry in the country of exportation with respect to affording in the home market (or third country markets, where sales to third countries are the basis for comparison) discounts for quantity sizes which are freely available to those who purchase in the ordinary course of trade. Allowances for price discounts based on sales at large quantities ordinarily will not be made unless (i) the exporter during the six months prior to the date when the question of dumping was raised or presented had been granting quantity discounts of at least the same magnitude with respect to 20 percent or more of such or similar merchandise which is sold in the home market (or in third country markets when sales to third countries are the basis for comparison) and that such discounts had been freely available to all purchasers, or (ii) the exporter can demonstrate that the discounts are warranted on the basis of savings specifically attributable to the quantity involved.[39]

37. 19 U.S.C. sec. 163.
38. 19 U.S.C. sec. 164; 19 C.F.R. secs. 14.7(a)(1) and (2) (1964). See *Welded Standard Steel Pipe from Luxembourg,* 29 Fed. Reg. 2951 (1964); 19 C.F.R. sec. 14.7(a), n. 15, example 2 (1964); *Amendments to Antidumping Act of 1921,* Hearings, p. 12.
39. 19 C.F.R. sec. 14.7(b)(1) (1964), as amended, 29 Fed. Reg. 16321 (1964). See, for example, *Portland Cement from Belgium,* 26 Fed. Reg. 1971 (1961).

Allowances are also made for differing circumstances of sale where the differences bear a reasonable, direct relationship to the sales under consideration. Differences in credit terms, guarantees, warranties, technical assistance, servicing, commissions, and the assumption by a seller of a purchaser's advertising or other selling costs are generally recognized as warranting reasonable allowance.[40] Allowances are not made, however, for differences in costs of research and development, production, and advertising, or other selling costs unless attributable to a later sale by a purchaser, and they must bear a reasonably direct relationship to the sale under consideration. If, during the Treasury Department's inquiry, the home market price fluctuates, an average or weighted average of the changing prices is calculated to determine the foreign market value.

A constructed value, based on the foreign cost of production, is calculated if there is insufficient information to ascertain the market value of the merchandise in the country of exportation. Constructed value is an aggregate of the cost of materials, fabrication, and processing; general expenses equaling not less than 10 percent of the cost of materials, fabrication, and processing; and profit equaling not less than 8 percent of all packing and other expenses incident to conditioning the merchandise for shipment.[41]

DETERMINATION OF INJURY

Prior to 1954 the secretary of the treasury not only determined when sales were being made for less than fair value, but whether by reason of such sales "an industry in the United States is being or is likely to be injured, or is prevented from being established."[42] The latter function was transferred to the Tariff Commission in 1954.[43] As in the case of fair value, there is no definition of what constitutes an injury in the act itself. Nor does the legislative history give dispositive guidance, though key

40. See, for example, *Radio Tubes from Japan,* 26 Fed. Reg. 6276 (1961); *Portland Cement from Belgium,* 26 Fed. Reg. 1971 (1961); and *Portable Typewriters from West Germany,* 26 Fed. Reg. 1413 (1961).

41. 19 U.S.C. sec. 165(a).

42. 19 U.S.C. sec. 160. For standards of injury required by other countries, see General Agreement on Tariffs and Trade (GATT), *Antidumping and Countervailing Duties* (1958), pp. 16–17.

43. The transfer was made by the *Customs Simplification Act of 1954,* sec. 301, 68 Stat. 1138, 19 U.S.C. sec. 160(a) (1958), because of the commission's experience in making injury determinations under escape clause actions.

senators made it plain that the degree of injury would need to be quite serious.

The Tariff Commission has thus had to deal with the causation and injury issues in its written opinions with less than clear direction. Its investigations have centered on the disposition of substantive questions related to the meaning of "an industry," the standards for determining whether there is "injury," the degree of probability required in order to have a "likelihood of injury," and the required causal connection between the dumping and the injury.[44] In none of these areas is there a fixed or even a stable commission position that can be compared to an authoritative line of cases decided by a court. The commission's membership changes every year (each year the term of one of the six commissioners expires), thus guaranteeing a continual flux of deciding personnel. Most commissioners come to the job with little background in trade, or in administrative agencies, and it is doubtful that they reach their decisions in any systematic way. Their decisions thus avoid general principles, each case not only concentrating on its own facts, but being based solely on those facts. As has been noted by several commentators, in each area of issues there is no clear line of principles—the decisions are "all over the lot."[45] Certain lines of reasoning seem, however, to have been dominant prior to the 1968 advent of the Antidumping Code.

Defining an industry. One of the threshhold questions is whether injury to less than all members of a national industry can constitute injury to an industry. The Tariff Commission has held that it can, but usually only in cases of heavy, low-value products for which the high cost of transportation restricts the geographical area of effective competition. For instance, the commission has held that the domestic suppliers of cement in a limited "competitive area" qualified as "an industry" that has suffered injury from dumped imports,[46] and in several cases involving heavy steel products and chromic acid a majority of the commission held that

44. See James C. Conner and Gerold Buschlinger, "The United States Antidumping Act: A Timely Survey," *Virginia Journal of International Law,* Vol. 7 (1966), pp. 117, 133. See also Baier, "Substantive Interpretations"; and "Note," *Yale Law Journal,* Vol. 74 (1965), p. 707.

45. *International Antidumping Code,* Hearings before the Senate Committee on Finance, 90 Cong. 2 sess. (1968), p. 17 (testimony of Special Representative for Trade Negotiations William H. Roth), and pp. 369–80 (statement of Tariff Commission Chairman Metzger and Commissioner Thunberg).

46. *Portland Cement from the Dominican Republic,* 28 Fed. Reg. 4047 (1963).

although the industry involved was the entire national industry, injury suffered by members who sold within a definable competitive market area was injury to "the industry."[47] While the commission has refused to segment the industry on other grounds, it has recently seemed inclined to do so.[48]

In a 1961 report prepared for the contracting parties to the General Agreement on Tariffs and Trade (GATT), a group of experts, concerned about this kind of decision, stated that "as a general guiding principle judgment of material injury should be related to a total national output of the like commodity concerned or a significant part thereof."[49] On the other hand, an earlier GATT report had observed that it would be hard to imagine a case of danger to a whole national industry, and that most countries seem to take into account only effects on the "relevant" branch.[50]

The greatest harm in a finding of injury to a geographical segment of an industry is that duties on the imported product increase nationwide. Thus, uninjured segments of the industry receive added protection they may not require. Nor does the fact that existence of injury to producers in one segment of the national industry may, under some circumstances, create a "likelihood of injury" to the rest of the industry[51] offset this bonanza to the uninjured segment, for in every case that segment benefits while only some cases would fall in the "national likelihood" category.

The Tariff Commission has at times defined the relevant industry as including only producers or their subdivisions making goods in competition with the dumped import. This approach accords in general with principles applied under the U.S. antitrust laws, although two members of the commission dissenting in a pair of cases called the majority's definition of the industry too narrow.[52]

47. *Chromic Acid from Australia,* 29 Fed. Reg. 2919 (1964); *Carbon Steel Bars and Shapes from Canada,* 29 Fed. Reg. 12599 (1964). See also *Ellis K. Orlowitz Co. v. United States,* 50 C.C.P.A. (Customs) 36 (1963); *White Portland Cement from Japan,* T.C. Pub. No. 129 [AA 1921–38] (1964) (dissent).

48. In *Steel Bars, Reinforcing Bars, and Shapes from Australia,* T.C. Pub. No. 314 (February 1970).

49. GATT, *Antidumping and Countervailing Duties: Report of Group of Experts* (1961), p. 10.

50. GATT, *Antidumping and Countervailing Duties* (1958), p. 17.

51. See *Ellis K. Orlowitz Co. v. United States,* 50 C.C.P.A. (Customs) 36, 41–42 (1963).

52. *Carbon Steel Bars and Shapes from Canada,* T.C. Pub. No. 135 [AA 1921–

Defining injury. The GATT and the laws of most countries require that injury be material in order to be actionable. Although the U.S. law merely speaks of "injury," the Treasury Department interpreted this as meaning "material injury" when it had the job of investigating injury. Some members of the Tariff Commission apparently agree, since they have used the term "material injury" in their opinions.[53] However, in 1964 two commissioners asserted that "an injury need not be fatal, permanently crippling or universal to be material,"[54] and in some recent decisions, by divided votes, the commission has held that anything greater than a de minimis (too trifling to waste time over) amount of injury falls within the meaning of the statute.

Where prices of imports have been higher than or equal to domestic prices, the Tariff Commission has found no injury. Where foreign merchandise has been priced below domestic prices, the commission has found injury if the lower import prices were accompanied by a domestic price break or if they prevented domestic manufacturers from participating in a price rise that was otherwise called for.[55] On the other hand, the commission has held on occasion that there was no injury when the effect on domestic prices was "insignificant" or the domestic producers' price cut was due to "competitive aggressiveness" vis-à-vis all competitors, not just foreign goods.[56] If domestic prices have risen despite the influx of imports, an injury ruling is likely only if there is some other strong evidence of injury.

Capture of a substantial share of the market by dumped imports— varying from 47 percent to 10 percent—has frequently been regarded as strong evidence of injury[57] or of likelihood of injury.[58] On the other

39] (1964); *Steel Reinforcing Bars from Canada,* T.C. Pub. No. 122 [AA 1921–33] (1964).

53. See *White Portland Cement from Japan,* 29 Fed. Reg. 9636 (1964).

54. *White Portland Cement from Japan,* T.C. Pub. No. 129 [AA 1921–38] (1964) (dissent of Commissioners Culliton and Sutton).

55. For example, *Azobisformamide from Japan,* 30 Fed. Reg. 6130 (1965); *Chromic Acid from Australia,* 29 Fed. Reg. 2919 (1964); and *Carbon Steel Bars and Shapes from Canada,* 29 Fed. Reg. 12599 (1964).

56. *Titanium Dioxide from Japan,* 29 Fed. Reg. 5522 (1964); *White Portland Cement from Japan,* 29 Fed. Reg. 9636 (1964).

57. *Bicycles from Czechoslovakia,* 25 Fed. Reg. 9782 (1960); *Chromic Acid from Australia,* 29 Fed. Reg. 2919 (1964); *Carbon Steel Bars and Shapes from Canada,* 29 Fed. Reg. 12599 (1964). See Baier, "Substantive Interpretations," pp. 420–22.

58. *Steel Reinforcing Bars from Canada,* 29 Fed. Reg. 3840 (1964).

hand, when imports had a 7 percent share of the market, the commission found there was no injury or likelihood of injury.[59]

The Antidumping Act does not require a finding of predatory intent—that is, intent to weaken or injure competition or to obtain a monopoly in the United States.[60] Nevertheless, the absence of intent to penetrate the U.S. market by dumping—sometimes inaccurately called "predatory intent"—has occasionally been part of the basis for a finding of no injury,[61] and the presence of such intent has sometimes been a factor in favor of a finding of injury[62] or of likelihood of injury.[63] This latter is curious, since intent to penetrate a foreign market is not evidence of existing injury, although it may be some evidence of a likelihood of future injury.

Other factors that the commission has deemed important from time to time are the amount of the dumping margin, loss of customers due to dumped imports, the trend of domestic production and sales, the volume and the trend in volume of imports sold at less than fair value, and the idling of domestic production facilities.

Likelihood of injury. Like GATT Article VI, the U.S. law authorizes dumping duties where there is only a likelihood of injury. On several occasions a majority of the Tariff Commission has found there was a likelihood of injury where the foreign producer had the capacity, incentive, and intent to continue dumping.[64]

Causation. The Tariff Commission seems, from time to time, to have required a showing that the dumped imports were the "significant factor" in the causation of any injury suffered. In one group of cases it ruled that dumped products that merely met the price of fairly priced imports did not cause whatever injury had been suffered by the domestic industry.[65]

59. *Plastic Baby Carriers from Japan,* 29 Fed. Reg. 13990 (1964).

60. But compare Baier, "Substantive Interpretations," pp. 428–44; "Note," *Yale Law Journal,* Vol. 74 (1965), p. 707.

61. For example, *Peat Moss from Canada,* 29 Fed. Reg. 4843 (1964). See Baier, "Substantive Interpretations," pp. 417–19, 430–32.

62. *Portland Gray Cement from Portugal,* 26 Fed. Reg. 10010 (1961).

63. *Portland Cement from the Dominican Republic,* 28 Fed. Reg. 4047 (1963). Intent to penetrate the market by dumping has sometimes been inferred from a foreign producer's past pricing policies, its excess productive capacity, and a market incentive to continue exporting on an incremental cost basis. Ibid. But see *Cast Iron Soil Pipe from Australia,* 29 Fed. Reg. 5253 (1964).

64. See, for example, *Steel Reinforcing Bars from Canada,* 29 Fed. Reg. 3840 (1964); *Portland Cement from the Dominican Republic,* 28 Fed. Reg. 4047 (1963).

65. See *Hot-Rolled Carbon Steel Wire Rods from France,* 28 Fed. Reg. 7368

The commission has also found that dumped imports did not cause the injury where the significant causes were the domestic industry's marketing practices (product development, sales, engineering, pricing)[66] or the imports were the result of a very strong demand for imported products without regard to the price.[67]

On the other hand, cases during the 1969–71 period suggest the commission's test is only that dumping be a contributing factor rather than the principal factor in causing injury. This is ironic, in light of the stringent causal requirements of the International Antidumping Code to which the United States is signatory.

APPLICATIONS OF THE LAW

In a case involving no price discrimination, a U.S. producer of macaroni products complained that a Canadian competitor was dumping. The Canadian producer had a substantial market for his product in Canada, and the price he charged the American importer was in fact higher than the price he charged in Canada. Price discrimination is within the purview of the Antidumping Act only if the price of the import is the lower of the two prices compared. In this case, therefore, the complaint was dismissed. The Canadian home price in this case constituted the fair value of the goods, and the imported macaroni had not been sold at "less than its fair value."[68]

In a case involving price discrimination but no injury, rayon staple fiber from France was sold to U.S. importers at a price below the French home price. This constituted sales at "less than fair value." But further inquiry showed that, during the period under consideration, U.S. producers of rayon staple fiber, "as a result of aggressive pricing practices of that industry, had lowered their prices to such levels that the importer did not generally meet the lower average domestic prices and, as a consequence thereof, his sales in the United States of the imported fiber declined

---

(1963); *Hot-Rolled Carbon Steel Wire Rods from West Germany,* 28 Fed. Reg. 6606 (1963); *Hot-Rolled Carbon Steel Wire Rods from Luxembourg,* 28 Fed. Reg. 6476 (1963); *Hot-Rolled Carbon Steel Wire Rods from Belgium,* 28 Fed. Reg. 6474 (1963).

66. *Titanium Dioxide from France,* 28 Fed. Reg. 10467 (1963); *Titanium Dioxide from Japan,* 29 Fed. Reg. 5522 (1964).

67. *Vital Wheat Gluten from Canada,* 29 Fed. Reg. 5921 (1964).

68. 27 Fed. Reg. 7367 (1962).

sharply compared to sales of the like domestic fiber. The importer gained no customers during this period and there is no evidence that he sold at a price lower than that charged by the domestic producers for the same fiber." It was determined that there was no injury; the fact that there had been price discrimination was therefore irrelevant.[69]

In a case involving both price discrimination and injury, bicycles were imported from Czechoslovakia. It was established that there was price discrimination and consideration was accordingly given to the question whether the lower priced sales to the United States resulted in injury. A finding was made that due to the pricing of the Czechoslovakian imports, "the importer has sold, and continues to sell, bicycles in the United States at prices below the prices at which domestic producers are able to produce comparable models." It was also found that "the sales of the Czechoslovakian bicycles have been, and are likely to continue to be, in sufficient volume to displace a significant part of the United States market for low-price bicycles." Finally, it was found that "the importation of Czechoslovakian bicycles purchased at prices below fair value is continuing and there is indication of an intent on the part of the exporting organization to continue its practice of selling the bicycles at less than fair value." The conclusion was therefore reached that there was injury to United States industry and a dumping finding was published.[70]

In a price revision case, cement was imported from Yugoslavia at a price, it became evident, that involved discrimination. However, no imports were being made at the time the complaint was filed and those that had already entered had been appraised (thus no dumping duties could be collected on them). Furthermore, evidence was submitted showing that the foreign producer had no intention of selling to the United States in the future at less than fair value. Technically, the case could have gone on to a consideration of injury. But, practically, what would have been the use? No duties could be collected on the past imports and there apparently would be no future imports. From the standpoint of the foreign producer, a dumping finding would be ineffective. From the standpoint of the U.S. industry, further inquiry might take away its protection if there were a determination of no injury and the dumper decided to resume sales involving discriminatory pricing. From the standpoint of the taxpayer, additional

69. 26 Fed. Reg. 1671 and 4428 (1961).
70. 25 Fed. Reg. 6657, 9782, and 9945 (1960).

processing of an essentially meaningless case would involve useless expenditures. Under these circumstances, no further action was taken.[71]

The International Antidumping Code of 1968

One of the successes of the Kennedy Round of trade negotiations held
under the auspices of the General Agreement on Tariffs and Trade was the
negotiation of an International Antidumping Code. Its purposes were to
make injury prerequisite to assessment of dumping duties; to "define and
flesh out some of the key concepts" used in antidumping actions; and to
reach agreement on a set of open and fair procedures to protect those
against whom a complaint of dumping is brought.[72]

Foreign objections to certain procedures under the U.S. Antidumping
Act were the primary stimulus to negotiation of the code. Inevitably, therefore, certain code provisions differ in language and somewhat in substance
from certain American procedures. The code's drafters, recognizing that
this would be the case, required that each party to the agreement "take
all necessary steps of a general or particular character, to ensure, not later
than the date of the entry into force of the Agreement for it, the conformity of its laws, regulations, and administrative procedures with the provisions of the Antidumping Code."[73]

From the outset, many segments of U.S. industry viewed negotiation of
the code not only as an unwanted liberalization (that is, a tightening of
the law in the interest of freer "liberal" trade policies) of a rarely enforced
antidumping law, but also as an encroachment by the executive on an
area traditionally reserved to Congress. Notwithstanding vocal support of
this view in the Senate, a U.S. official signed the code on June 30, 1967, to
be binding one year later, the special representative for trade negotiations
announcing that, in view of the code's consistency with the Antidumping
Act of 1921, only limited changes in existing regulations and interpretations of the Treasury and the Tariff Commission would be required.[74]

71. 28 Fed. Reg. 41 (1963).
72. *International Antidumping Code,* Hearings, p. 13 (testimony of Roth).
73. "Agreement on Implementation of Article VI of the General Agreement on
Tariffs and Trade, June 30, 1967 (effective July 1, 1968), The Contracting Parties,"
International Legal Materials, Vol. 6 (1967), pp. 920, 930.
74. Press release 90, Office of the Special Representative for Trade Negotiations,
"Kennedy Round Concluded," June 29, 1967, p. 1.

This announcement prompted further dispute. Members of domestic industry, members of Congress, and three of the five-member Tariff Commission (there was one vacancy at the time) argued that the code should not govern American antidumping proceedings unless Congress enacted it into law. The key issues in the debate were the President's authority to negotiate the code and the code's consistency with the U.S. Antidumping Act.

Executive Authority to Negotiate

Authority for the negotiation of the code could have been derived from the President's general constitutional powers over foreign affairs, or from the Trade Expansion Act of 1962. The act, the only possible legislative source of authority, allows the President to enter agreements to modify existing "import restrictions."[75] The legislative history of the Antidumping Act of 1921 suggested that it was not considered to be an import restriction in the trade-barrier sense, but a measure to prevent injurious international price discrimination. The legislative history of the Trade Expansion Act did not indicate that Congress intended it to encompass American antidumping or countervailing duty law or practice.

The President's constitutional authority was relied on in agreeing to the code.[76] If, however, there was inconsistency between the code and the U.S. Antidumping Act, a question of priority in domestic law between a self-executing presidential agreement and a prior inconsistent federal statute was presented. The Supreme Court has never decided that question. Indeed, it went out of its way in 1955 to make clear that it was not taking the position of a lower court that had held that federal statute had priority and executive agreement was in consequence void.[77] The basic position expressed by the lower court, however, has received strong support, which the executive branch undoubtedly recognized.[78] The belief that there was no inconsistency between the code and the act led the executive to bottom its case on the premise that there was no question about priorities.

---

75. *Trade Expansion Act,* sec. 201.
76. *International Antidumping Code,* Hearings, p. 12 (testimony of Roth).
77. *United States v. Guy W. Capps, Inc.,* 348 U.S. 296 (1955).
78. Influential support is expressed in American Law Institute, *Restatement (Second) of the Foreign Relations Laws of the United States* (1965), sec. 144(1)(b).

LEGISLATIVE HISTORY OF THE TRADE EXPANSION ACT

Even if the Antidumping Act of 1921 was not originally intended to serve as an import restriction, Congress may have since concluded that it had outgrown its intended purpose and become a nontariff trade barrier. And Congress may have meant to include it in the "import restrictions" it gave the President authority to modify in the Trade Expansion Act.

During consideration of the trade expansion measure, members of Congress referred only generally to the scope of the delegated authority. The Senate Finance Committee, elaborating on the Trade Expansion Act's relation to other laws, stated: "Section 257 (h) provides that Section 22 of the Agricultural Adjustment Act and import restrictions imposed thereunder shall be unaffected by the bill. *Other laws not to be affected include the Antidumping Act and Section 303 of the Tariff Act of 1930, which relates to countervailing duties.*"[79]

The administration's views at the hearings on the act were similar. Secretary of the Treasury Dillon stated that he did not think the bill affected American antidumping legislation at all. Secretary of Commerce Hodges pledged that the government would take no action in tariff policy that would undermine existing protections against unfair competition.[80]

Moreover, the Antidumping Act was never included in discussions of import restrictions. The House report on the bill mentioned only quotas;[81] Senator Curtis listed embargoes, quotas, import licenses, currency manipulations, and quarantines;[82] and Secretary Hodges alluded to "quota restrictions, prohibitions, discriminatory tax measures, surcharges, burdensome customs procedures, unwarranted sanitary, food and drug regulations."[83]

After enactment of the Trade Expansion Act, it became apparent that U.S. representatives in Geneva were planning to negotiate an international

79. *Trade Expansion Act of 1962,* S. Rept. 2059, 87 Cong. 2 sess. (1962), p. 19. Italics added.

80. *Trade Expansion Act of 1962,* Hearings before the House Committee on Ways and Means, 87 Cong. 2 sess. (1962), Pt. 2, pp. 897–98, and Pt. 1, p. 81.

81. *Trade Expansion Act of 1962,* H. Rept. 1818, 87 Cong. 2 sess. (1962), pp. 2, 14.

82. *Congressional Record,* Vol. 108, 87 Cong. 2 sess. (1962), p. 19764.

83. *Trade Expansion Act of 1962, H.R. 11970,* Hearings before the Senate Committee on Finance, 87 Cong. 2 sess. (1962), Pt. 1, p. 54.

antidumping code. The initial reaction from Congress seemed to indicate that modification of the Antidumping Act was not within the intended sphere of executive authority. Senator Abraham Ribicoff and a number of others introduced a resolution providing:

It is the sense of the Congress that, in the conduct of or in connection with negotiations to carry out the Trade Expansion Act of 1962, no agreement or other arrangement which would necessitate the *modification of any duty or other import restriction* applicable under the laws of the United States should be entered into except in accordance with legislative authority delegated by the Congress prior to the entering into of such agreement or arrangement.[84]

The Senate Finance Committee, advocating passage of the resolution, expressed its disturbance over "reports that the current Kennedy round of tariff negotiations may be broadened to include U.S. offers of concessions with respect to matters for which there is no existing delegated authority." It remarked that one reported area "concerns the American selling price method of valuation."

Another area may involve the treatment of "dumped" goods by the country in which the dumping occurs. This problem concerns unfair trade practices in a domestic economy and it is difficult for us to understand why Congress should be bypassed at the crucial policymaking stages, and permitted to participate only after policy has been frozen in an international trade agreement.[85]

Following floor remarks that reiterated this objective, the Senate passed the resolution by a nearly unanimous vote.

Although the resolution was introduced and supported to stress the absence of executive authority under the Trade Expansion Act to modify the Antidumping Act, its language seemed to describe the Antidumping Act as an "import restriction." Since the President had clearly been authorized to modify "import restrictions" in the Trade Expansion Act, the resolution might well have strengthened the case for presidential negotiation of the code. But the House failed to consider the resolution. At all events, the sentiment within the Senate was unmistakable, and it ensured that the President would not base key actions in negotiating the code on the Trade Expansion Act, but would rely on his constitutional powers.

---

84. *Sense of Congress Regarding Certain Trade Agreements,* S. Rept. 1341, 89 Cong. 2 sess. (1966), p. 3. Italics added.

85. *Congressional Record,* Vol. 112, 89 Cong. 2 sess. (1966), p. 14704. Only Senator Jacob Javits (Republican of New York) voted against the resolution. Ibid., p. 14709.

Consistency of the Code with the Act

Both during and after the negotiation of the code, administration representatives insisted that the code provisions were entirely consistent with American domestic law as provided for in the Antidumping Act and would necessitate only procedural changes in Treasury regulations. Shortly after the code was signed the Treasury Department, which had been involved in the negotiations and concurred in the administration's view, amended its regulations.

Congressional dissent was immediately expressed in the introduction of a resolution that would have declared it the sense of Congress that the code was inconsistent with, and in conflict with, the Antidumping Act; that the President should submit the code to the Senate for its advice and consent; and that the code should become effective in the United States only at a time specified in legislation enacted by Congress to implement the code.[86] The issues were debated on the Senate floor as well as in extensive trade policy hearings held by the House Committee on Ways and Means.[87] The Tariff Commission reported to the Senate Finance Committee that a 3–2 majority of the commission believed certain provisions of the code conflicted with the act.[88] Their position was not surprising, for commission appointments are confirmed by the Senate Finance Committee, and members are often sensitive to the views of powerful committee members.

Thus, the two groups charged with administering the act, and various people within Congress, took opposite positions on the question of whether the code and the act were consistent. If the administration was correct, then no harm, other than a possible wounding of congressional pride, had occurred to domestic interests as a result of the negotiation of the code, regardless of the basis of authority under which the President negotiated the code. On the other hand, if the code and the act were not consistent, troublesome questions concerning the propriety of negotiating such a code, and the duties of domestic agencies in respect of taking it into account in their administration of domestic law, would certainly arise.

86. S. Con. Res. 38, *Congressional Record,* daily ed., Aug. 2, 1967, p. S10572.

87. See remarks of Senator Hartke (Democrat of Indiana), ibid., p. S10571; Senators Javits and Hartke, ibid., Aug. 23, 1967, p. S12106, and Aug. 27, 1967, p. S13792; Senator Hartke, ibid., April 4, 1968, S3867, and April 25, 1968, p. S4459.

88. U.S. Tariff Commission, "Report of the U.S. Tariff Commission on S. Con. Res. 38, Regarding the International Antidumping Code," in *International Antidumping Code,* Hearings, p. 321.

SIMULTANEOUS INVESTIGATION OF DUMPING AND INJURY

Among the Treasury regulations revised to conform to the code was that dealing with investigations. The code requires that: "Upon initiation of an investigation and thereafter, the evidence of both dumping and injury should be considered simultaneously. In any event the evidence of both dumping and injury shall be considered simultaneously in the decision whether or not to initiate an investigation."[89]

The Antidumping Act, however, is silent both on how an investigation must be initiated and the kind of information it must be based on. Immediately prior to the new regulations, the Treasury had required only information concerning sales at less than fair value and the total value and volume of the domestic production of the merchandise in question.[90] The amended regulations required, in addition, that communications pertaining to suspected dumping contain "information indicating that an industry in the United States is being injured . . . or prevented from being established."[91] The commissioner of customs, in a summary investigation, could close the case if he believed any of the information to be patently in error, or the merchandise to be imported in insignificant quantities and not likely to be imported in significant quantities, or for other reasons.[92] Otherwise, he was required to publish an "antidumping proceeding notice" which specified "that there is some evidence on record concerning injury to or likelihood of injury to or prevention of establishment of an industry in the United States."[93]

Treasury's position, during congressional consideration of the code, was that it would now scan dumping complaints to assure there was a bare allegation suggesting that the dumped merchandise was causing injury; responsibility for actual investigation and determination of injury would remain with the Tariff Commission. Two members of that commission, including the chairman, saw no inconsistency between the new regulation and the act; so read, the regulation complies literally with the code's requirement that "evidence . . . of injury shall be considered."[94]

89. "Antidumping Code," pt. 1, art. 5(a), *International Legal Materials,* Vol. 6, pp. 920, 924.
90. Treas. Reg. secs. 14.6(b)(2), (3), 19 C.F.R. sec. 14.6(b)(2)–(3) (1968).
91. Treas. Reg. sec. 53.27(e), 33 Fed. Reg. 8244, 8247 (1968).
92. Treas. Reg. sec. 53.29, 33 Fed. Reg. 8244, 8247 (1968).
93. Treas. Reg. sec. 53.30, 33 Fed. Reg. 8244, 8247 (1968).
94. See Tariff Commission, "Report on S. Con. Res. 38" (remarks of Chairman Metzger).

Nonetheless, it is a constricted reading of the code's obligations that could have (though it has not) raised questions from other signatories whether the regulation complies with the code's spirit as well its letter. Of course, those who see an inconsistency between regulation and act could scarcely have cared less about such complaints; they were interested solely in retaining in the Tariff Commission the untrammeled power to determine injury questions, because a protectionist statutory majority of the commission had been finding injury on the slimmest kind of evidence.[95]

WITHHOLDING OF APPRAISEMENT

The code permits application of provisional measures only when there has been a preliminary decision as to dumping and there is sufficient evidence of injury. In addition, it requires that, except under special circumstances, provisional measures may not be imposed for a period of longer than three months.

The only provisional measure specifically authorized by the Antidumping Act is withholding of appraisement:

Whenever . . . the Secretary has reason to believe or suspect . . . that the purchase price is less, or that the exporter's sales price is less or likely to be less, . . . than the foreign market value . . . he shall . . . publish notice of fact in the Federal Register and shall authorize under such regulations as he may prescribe, the withholding of appraisement reports as to such merchandise entered.[96]

Thus, while the act does not require a finding of sufficient evidence of injury as a condition to withholding of appraisement, and does not set a limit on the period during which appraisement may be withheld, nothing precludes the Treasury Department from so providing in its regulations.

MEANING OF INJURY

The Antidumping Act gives the Tariff Commission responsibility to determine "whether an industry in the United States is being or is likely to be injured, or is prevented from being established by reason of the importation of merchandise at less than fair value."[97] Among the issues that this directive raises is the meaning of injury.

95. Under the statute, if the commission is evenly split on a decision as to injury, this constitutes a majority in favor of a positive injury determination.
96. 19 U.S.C. sec. 160(b).
97. 19 U.S.C. sec. 160(a).

In conformance with the language of the GATT, Article 3(a) of the code provides that a determination of injury shall be made only when there is material injury to a domestic industry.[98] The Antidumping Act merely requires the Tariff Commission to determine whether an industry in the United States "is being or is likely to be injured" by reason of sales at less than fair value. Both the Treasury Department and the Tariff Commission had officially termed *injury* and *material injury* synonymous, though no further definition was made. Arguments to the Congress that the code and the act were in conflict because of the act's use of the bare word *injury* were quite unconvincing. The act's legislative history discloses that a high degree of injury is required—higher than is normally connoted by the inexact adjective *material*—and in recent years the commission has utilized that adjective in a similar vein. Protectionist groups—led by the cement and steel industries and their lawyer-lobbyists—nonetheless seized upon the alleged discrepancy.

CAUSATION

The code permits relief only when "dumped imports are demonstrably the principal cause of material injury." It further requires that the authorities in making their decision "weigh, on the one hand, the effect of the dumping, and, on the other hand, all other factors taken together which may be adversely affecting the industry."[99]

The Antidumping Act requires the Tariff Commission to determine if an industry has been injured "by reason of" the importation of dumped merchandise into the United States.[100] This clearly requires a causal connection between the dumped merchandise and injury, but it provides no clear guideline for the balancing and treatment of other factors that might be affecting the industry, nor does it indicate to what degree the injury must be caused by the dumped imports. The legislative history of the act also fails to establish a guideline. The Tariff Commission has at times used a "significant factor" test and at others "the principal factor" test.

Those who saw conflict argued that the act permitted an interpretation that the statutory requirement of causation was met if there were some connection between imports at less than fair value and injury, while the

98. "Antidumping Code," art. 3(a), *International Legal Materials,* Vol. 6, pp. 920, 922.
99. Ibid.
100. 19 U.S.C. sec. 160(a).

code required that the imports be the major cause of the injury. Such a loose construction of the act was attacked as unnecessary and erroneous. To read "by reason of" to mean "contribute to" is a strained and unreasonable construction of the act.

DEFINITION OF INDUSTRY

As a general rule a domestic industry, according to the code, must be defined in terms of either all domestic producers of like products, or the domestic producers whose collective output constitutes a major proportion of the domestic production of like products. Producers within a competitive market may be regarded as an industry separate from the rest of the domestic industry, however, if there is injury to all or almost all of the total production of the product in a segment of the industry, and either transportation costs cause the regional producers not to sell beyond that market and outside producers not to compete in the market, or special regional conditions such as traditional patterns of distribution or consumer tastes isolate the producers in the same fashion.[101]

Unlike the code, the act provides no criteria for determining what constitutes "an industry in the United States" that is being or is likely to be injured, and thereby allows discretion to the administering agency in interpreting the term. In most instances the Tariff Commission has employed the term with reference to all producers of the relevant product in the United States; in a few cases it has recognized a particular geographical region. Its decisions were not attempts to establish general restrictions or any doctrinal definitions of segmentation; each case was decided on its merits. While opponents of the code argued that the commission "could not have found" segmentation in these cases had the code been binding, their argument was based on selected facts and the most strained interpretations of the terms of the code. Their case was less than convincing, though not so far fetched as to be able to be laughed out of court. In short, it was arguable, and thus useful to those who wished to kill the code.

Fate of the Code

In the fall of 1968, opponents of the code almost succeeded in preventing it from affecting administration of the U.S. Antidumping Act in any

---

101. Article 4(a) of the code.

way. Following a one-day hearing, a receptive Senate Finance Committee attached an amendment to the House-passed Renegotiation Amendments Act of 1968, which would have suspended the code until approved by Congress, preserved those Treasury regulations in force prior to the effective date of the code, and prohibited the Treasury from dismissing dumping complaints upon assurances by a foreign producer that he would no longer sell at less than fair value.[102] The Senate passed the amendment, but opposition from House members of the conference committee resulted in an act that provides:

Nothing contained in the International Antidumping Code, signed at Geneva on June 30, 1967, shall be construed to restrict the discretion of the United States Tariff Commission in performing its duties and functions under the Antidumping Act, 1921, and in performing their duties and functions under such Act the Secretary of the Treasury and the Tariff Commission shall—

(1) resolve any conflict between the International Antidumping Code and the Antidumping Act, 1921, in favor of the Act as applied by the agency administering the Act, and

(2) take into account the provisions of the International Antidumping Code only insofar as they are consistent with the Antidumping Act, 1921, as applied by the agency administering the Act.[103]

The President was required to report to Congress on the administration of the U.S. act and on antidumping actions by foreign countries during the period July 1, 1968 to June 30, 1969. Thus the act requires that any clear conflicts between the code and the act be resolved in favor of the act. The Tariff Commission could continue to make injury determinations untrammeled by any sense of obligation to apply the code.

TREASURY DEPARTMENT RESPONSE

When the new law was enacted, the Treasury Department did not revise the regulations it had drawn up after U.S. signature of the Antidumping Code. It apparently interpreted the new act as prohibiting only such regulations as were clearly inconsistent with the Antidumping Act, which it believed was not the case in respect of the new regulations. The most favorable changes in the new regulations from the viewpoint of liberal trade principles were in withholding of appraisement; whereas prior to negotiation of the code, no maximum limit was placed on the time, after

102. Remarks of Senator Hartke in *Congressional Record,* daily ed., Sept. 9, 1968, p. S10477.

103. *Administration of the Antidumping Act,* Pub. L. No. 90, sec. 201(a).

filing of initial notice, that appraisement could be withheld, under the new regulations forward appraisement could only be withheld for a maximum of three months.[104] Furthermore, both forward and retroactive appraisement periods were to be measured from the date on which a *determination* of sales at less than fair value was made, rather than at the initiation of *investigations*.

In one area, however, the Treasury Department has fallen short in complying with the code's letter and spirit. On May 27, 1970 the Customs Bureau changed its price revision procedure. The old regulation provided that upon price revision, the secretary would publish a notice stating the facts that led him to believe that there "are not and are not likely to be sales at less than fair value," and that "unless persuasive evidence or argument to the contrary is presented within 30 days the Secretary will determine that there are not and are not likely to be sales at less than fair value."[105] Under the new regulations, the only notice and determination made are whether "the investigation has been (or will be) discontinued."[106] Price assurances by a potential dumper are not accepted until "a final decision of the Treasury Department is published in the Federal Register" to that effect.[107] Apparently the changes are intended to restrict price revision assurances (as a basis for termination of antidumping cases) to those situations where "the home market price, third country price, or constructed value of the merchandise under consideration exceeds the purchase price or exporter's sales price by an amount that is considered minimal in relation to the total volume of sales."[108] The new regulations have resulted in an increase in the number of cases in which positive determinations of sales at less than fair value are made. Although the Antidumping Code does not deal with price revision procedures, the new Treasury regulations are clearly contrary to its spirit.

TARIFF COMMISSION RESPONSE

Unlike the Treasury Department, the Tariff Commission in its decisions since September 1967 has shown a marked tendency not only to avoid compliance with the code but to ignore its existence, as well as the

104. 19 C.F.R. sec. 53.34(a) (1970). With the exporter's consent the maximum could be increased to six months. 19 C.F.R. sec. 53.34(b).
105. 19 U.S.C. sec. 53.15 (1970).
106. 35 Fed. Reg. 8275 (1970).
107. Ibid.
108. Ibid.

legislative history of the Antidumping Act itself and the weight of prior injury determinations. This attitude has no doubt been bolstered by the commission's assumption that the Congress in its 1968 action intended the commission to be free to construe the act as it wished. From 1969 to 1972 a protectionist majority prevailed in injury determinations. With the exception of two members, the commission appeared to be guided by the conviction that little more than de minimus injury need be shown, and that the sales at less than fair value need only be a *contributing* cause of that injury.

De minimis injury. The legislative history of the Antidumping Act, past determinations, and the Antidumping Code support the proposition that injury findings should be based on material injury. While *material injury* has never been defined precisely, the code, and indeed the history of the 1921 act, indicates that it connotes the kind of harm to a domestic industry that would result in substantial losses in profits, employment, sales, and other indicators of economic health.

In recent years, however, particularly in a series of cases since September 1967, the Tariff Commission has ignored these considerations. For example, an increase in penetration of Dutch eggs in the U.S. market from 1 percent to 7 percent over a four-year period was sufficient to justify a positive injury determination by two commissioners, without regard to whether the domestic industry was doing nicely or badly.[109] The two constituted a statutory majority in the case.

Since 1967 the protectionist majority has held that "an affirmative determination will ensue if the degree of injury is greater than *de minimis,* that is, more than trifling injury."[110] In deciding whether more than a trifling injury has occurred, these commissioners have looked at one or two measures of industry health—particularly sales volume, market penetration, and price trends—ignoring all the other factors that should be considered in assessing whether an industry is suffering overall bad economic health, that is, injury.

A contributing cause of injury. After injury has been found, the Tariff Commission still must determine that such injury was caused by the sales at less than fair value in order to make a positive injury finding. In a sub-

109. *Whole Dried Eggs from Holland,* T.C. Pub. No. 332 (July 1970).
110. *Potassium Chloride from Canada, France, and West Germany,* T.C. Pub. No. 303 (November 1969), p. 5; see also *Whole Dried Eggs from Holland,* T.C. Pub. No. 332 (July 1970), p. 3.

stantial number of cases prior to 1968, such sales were shown to be the most important single factor in causing injury, and in virtually all cases at least a significant factor. The code also requires that less than fair value sales be "the principal cause" of injury—another way of saying "the most important single factor."

Recently the Tariff Commission has applied the proposition that if the sales in any way contribute to the injury, such contribution—however small—is adequate causation under the act. In 1971 three commissioners voted an affirmative determination for an industry suffering depressed prices and sales, holding "the major causal factor" to be "a diminished market" rather than sales at less than fair value. Their causation standard was that only "if injury is attributable solely to factors other than sales at LTFV [less than fair value]" should a negative determination be made.[111] This test has been applied in other cases as well. One commissioner wrote strong dissenting opinions in these cases, finding insufficient causation.[112]

In another drastic departure the commission went so far as to add less than fair value sales from Japan to those from France in order to compensate for the very small amount of offending French sales; in so doing, the commission departed from the practice of the Treasury Department up to 1954 and its own practice since that time.[113]

There has also been a marked tendency deliberately to segment a national industry in order to find injury. The majority of commissioners in one case determined injury on the basis of the Pacific Northwest market, even though the dumping duties would apply to the imports wherever sold, and even though the competitive market for which the same price prevailed for these commodities was the entire nation, after taking account of transportation costs. As the dissenting commissioners pointed out, less than fair value imports amounted to only 0.5 percent of the national market and only 5.5 percent of consumption in Oregon and Washington; in addition, proof of injury was unconvincing.[114]

111. *Ferrite Cores from Japan*, T.C. Pub. No. 360 (January 1971), pp. 4–5.

112. See Will E. Leonard, in *Ceramic Wall Tile from the United Kingdom* and *Clear Plate, Float, and Sheet Glass from Japan*, T.C. Pub. Nos. 381 and 382 (April 1971). See also *Ice Cream Sandwich Wafers from Canada*, T.C. Pub. No. 460 (February 1972) for a case where Leonard and Young dissented from an injury finding.

113. *Aminoacetic Acid from France*, T.C. Pub. No. 313 (February 1970) (Commissioner Leonard dissenting).

114. *Steel Bars, Reinforcing Bars, and Shapes from Australia*, T.C. Pub. No. 314 (February 1970).

The disposition of cases brought since passage of the Antidumping Act is shown in Table 2. During the period from 1955 to September 30, 1967, the Tariff Commission made affirmative injury determinations in only 8 percent of the cases where the Treasury had made positive determinations of sales at less than fair value; from 1967 through 1971, roughly 80 percent of the commission determinations were affirmative. In only three of the fifteen cases in the latest group did the commission find no injury—twice unanimously, and once by a 5–1 vote. Their affirmative determinations were on two unanimous votes, two 4–1 votes, two 4–2 votes, one 3–2 vote, and four 2–2 votes. Recently, from 1972 through the first quarter of 1973, the commission more frequently found no injury, the record being 11 no injury determinations and 12 affirmative injury findings, though there was no indication that the commission had allowed itself to embrace code principles.

The plain fact of the matter is that since the code went into force the commission has contained a statutory majority of protectionist commissioners who have consciously avoided compliance with the code and have departed drastically from past interpretations of the act by the Tariff Commission.

PROPOSALS TO AMEND THE ANTIDUMPING ACT

In 1970 the Congress considered major new trade legislation, including amendments to the Antidumping Act. The legislation, which reflected the strength of protectionism in Congress, was not enacted. Its passage by

Table 2. *Injury Determinations under the Antidumping Act, 1921–71*

Determination	1921– Jan. 1, 1955	Jan. 1, 1955– Sept. 30, 1967	Sept. 30, 1967– April 1971
Negative			
No sales at less than fair value	80	228	n.a.
No injury	115	40	3
Price revision	0	87	0
Reason unavailable	123	0	0
Affirmative	65	11	12
Total cases	383	366	15

Sources: *Compendium of Papers on Legislative Oversight,* prepared for the Senate Finance Committee, 90 Cong. 2 sess (1968); and "Note," *New York University Journal of International Law and Politics,* Vol. 4 (1971), pp. 212–13.
n.a. = not available.

the House of Representatives indicates, however, that for the present, at least, negotiators must move cautiously against certain nontariff trade barriers.

Among other things, the legislation would have abbreviated complaint procedures under the Antidumping Act. There is no time limit within which the secretary of the treasury must act following a complaint that imported articles are being sold in the United States at less than their fair value; indeed, there never has been a limit. The necessities of proper investigation have dictated against a time limit.

The major tasks for the Treasury Department in determining whether there has been a sale at less than fair value are to determine the base price —whether home market or third country—and whether that price reflects the same circumstances of sales as those involved in sales in the United States. The U.S. sales price may include discounts for large quantities, or it may reflect differences in credit terms, guarantees, warranties, technical assistance, servicing, and assumption by a seller of a purchaser's advertising or other selling costs. It may also legitimately reflect differences in the seller's research and development, production, and advertising and other selling costs. Practically all of these data must be assembled by the foreign seller. They are evaluated by Treasury, which often asks for additional information. Attorneys for the foreign supplier in the United States are very often involved. They must confer with Treasury in order to be better able to elicit from their overseas clients the proper information in correct form. Communication is often difficult because of language problems, as well as the intrinsic complexity of accounting practices and of the nature of the question at issue.

This complex process was deliberately foreshortened in the 1970 trade bill to four months after the secretary concludes that "there is reason to believe or suspect" sales at less than fair value. The beginning of the period is triggered by the customs collector's decision to open a formal investigation, a decision that must be made within thirty days after a complaint is filed. The Ways and Means Committee reported these abbreviated procedures were adopted to "protect effectively American industry," acknowledging that deadlines for furnishing information and rebutting information "will in many instances create hardships."[115] As for results, the committee dryly observed that "additional work [for the Tariff Commission] is ex-

115. *The Trade Act of 1970,* H. Rept. 1435, 91 Cong. 2 sess. (1970), p. 45.

pected from the tightening up of Treasury's procedures under the Anti-dumping Act, 1921."[116]

There can be no doubt that the committee's prediction was wholly safe. As the committee itself stated, Treasury would be "compelled to act on the basis of the best information available to it," even though it were inadequate.[117] Since the initial prices in a dumping case ordinarily do differ (that is, 90 cents U.S. sales price, $1.00 home market price), the important factor in the investigation is differing circumstances of sale, and the time for explaining and calculating them would be short-circuited. Inevitably, there would be more determinations of "reason to believe or suspect" dumping at the end of a mere four-month period; the accompanying withholdings of appraisement would act as a Damocletian sword over all subsequent imports, threatening an unknown additional dumping duty before they could clear customs.

The probabilities are that a great many more dumping and withholding of appraisement determinations would have been made. Tariff Commission determinations that less than fair value sales caused injury are highly likely. The likelihood that complaints could withstand four months of investigation becomes greater as many complaints tax a relatively small Treasury staff. Those industries intent on curtailing imports would doubtless make substantial use of the new procedures, even if a campaign to that end were not organized, aided, or abetted by protectionist groups.

During the past several years, protectionist pressures have made the Antidumping Act an increasingly important nontariff distortion of trade, much more important than it was during the Kennedy Round negotiations, when European countries were concerned about its inhibiting effect on trade. The inclination in both the executive and congressional branches of government in the United States to bow to these pressures makes any abatement of abuses under the act highly unlikely at this time. Moreover, the backlash against the Antidumping Code in 1967–68 forewarns that further attempts to improve the antidumping picture through international negotiations would be at least equally difficult at this time and for the near future. Indeed, the recent history of antidumping argues that the forces arrayed on one side and the other domestically on this issue must reach some area of accommodation through the legislative process before inter-

116. Ibid., p. 50.
117. Ibid., p. 45.

national negotiations will ever be really feasible. This means that codes of conduct falling short of agreements are interdicted as much as international agreements themselves. After all, a fairly good code was negotiated in 1967, and it has been ignored.

COUNTERVAILING DUTIES

A COUNTERVAILING DUTY is a charge, added to normal customs duties, imposed on imports whose exportation has been facilitated through a "bounty or grant" in the exporting country. The additional duty is intended to neutralize the foreign subsidy, and thereby to prevent injury to the producers of comparable products in the importing country who operate without the benefit of the subsidy.

The Tariff Act of 1930 demands the imposition of countervailing duties whenever it is found that a country or political subdivision thereof, or any "person, partnership, association, cartel, or corporation," pays or bestows a bounty or grant, directly or indirectly, on the "manufacture, production or export" of merchandise produced in that country. The duty is applicable only to merchandise that is otherwise dutiable and applies whether or not the merchandise is imported in a different condition, through remanufacture or otherwise, than it was when exported, and whether or not it was imported directly from the country of production. The secretary of the treasury is required to "ascertain and determine, or estimate" the net amount of the bounty or grant, to declare his findings, and to assess a duty equal to the net amount.[118]

The practice of encouraging commercial exports through governmental subsidy has long been recognized as a threat to the natural and most efficient allocation of resources in international trade. Adam Smith condemned the artificial stimulation of exports as early as 1776: "The effect of bounties, like that of all the other expedients of the mercantile system,

118. *Tariff Act of 1930,* sec. 303, 19 U.S.C. sec. 1303 (1964). For a good discussion of countervailing duties, see Peter Buck Feller, "Mutiny Against the Bounty: An Examination of Subsidies, Border Tax Adjustments, and the Resurgence of the Countervailing Duty Law," *Law and Policy in International Business,* Vol. 1 (1969), p. 17; and E. Bruce Butler, "Countervailing Duties and Export Subsidization: A Reemerging Issue in International Law," *Virginia Journal of International Law,* Vol. 9 (1968), p. 120, which have been relied on for some portions of this chapter.

can only be to force the trade of a country into a channel much less advantageous than that in which it would naturally run of its own accord."[119]

Since then, trading nations have entered a variety of bilateral and multilateral agreements to combat the trade-diverting effects of direct or indirect export subsidies. The Brussels Sugar Convention of 1902, for example, attempted to end a ruinous trade war among beet-sugar-producing countries that were caught in a spiral of rising subsidy costs. The signatories agreed to cease subsidizing the production or exportation of sugar and to impose special duties on sugar imports from countries giving bounties. More recently, the Treaty of Rome has outlawed the use of export aids within the European Economic Community if such aid "distorts or threatens to distort competition by favouring certain enterprises or certain productions."[120] Likewise, Article XVI of the GATT directs contracting parties to terminate those export subsidies (except on primary products) that enable products to be sold at lower prices abroad than in the home market.[121]

In the United States, attitudes toward export subsidies and the role of countervailing duties have altered somewhat since Alexander Hamilton, in 1791, proposed a special duty on certain subsidized commodity imports to fund a subsidy program for the domestic production (including production for export) of such commodities.[122] Hamilton believed that the greatest obstacle to the growth of fledgling industries in the United States was the system of export bounties maintained by foreign countries "to enable their own workmen to undersell and supplant all competitors in countries to which these commodities are sent."[123] The special duty was accordingly to be levied not only to protect specific infant industries from foreign economic marauders, but to nurture their growth.

No legislation approximating Hamilton's proposal was adopted until 1890, when Congress enacted the world's first countervailing duty law. It was limited to protecting American sugar producers from their highly sub-

119. Adam Smith, *An Inquiry Into the Nature and Causes of the Wealth of Nations,* ed. J. Rogers (Oxford: Clarendon Press, 1869), p. 80.

120. *Treaty Establishing the European Economic Community, March 25, 1957,* art. 92, 298 U.N.T.S. 1451.

121. GATT, *Basic Instruments and Selected Documents (BISD),* p. 30.

122. Alexander Hamilton, *Report on Manufactures,* in F. W. Taussig (ed.), *State Papers and Speeches on the Tariff,* Vol. 1 (Harvard University Press, 1893), p. 66.

123. Ibid., p. 31.

sidized European competitors. It subjected refined sugar imports to a sur-tax, and provided a bounty for all domestically produced sugar.[124] The bounty system was discontinued in the Tariff Act of 1894, but the surtax provision was expanded to cover raw as well as refined sugar.[125]

The first general countervailing duty measure in American law, applicable to all bounty-fed imports that were otherwise dutiable, was contained in the Tariff Act of 1897.[126] Congress delegated the authority to determine the amount of the subsidy to the secretary of the treasury and directed him to assess a duty equal to that amount.

Because the high tariff levels at that time reflected a dominant protectionist trade policy, foreign export subsidies on American imports were viewed chiefly as a means of negating the effect of the U.S. tariff wall.[127] The countervailing duty law, therefore, was intended to function as a repair mechanism to insure the integrity of that wall in the face of threatened breaches. This largely explains the absence of a provision requiring proof of injury to a domestic industry, such as that found in the Antidumping Act, and the fact that the act applied only to dutiable articles. Since the tariff itself was designed as a protection for domestic industries, a specific injury provision would have been inapposite or superfluous. By the same logic, duty-free merchandise was considered noncompetitive and foreign subsidies of such goods consequently no cause for concern. Subsidies were thus not considered inherently "evil" in the antitrust sense. A provision for determining price competitiveness was apparently thought unnecessary, since bounties were assumed to enable foreign producers to undersell domestic producers; in fact, foreign bounties are frequently given to bring the price of exports down to a competitive level in foreign markets, rather than below that level. In brief, the thrust of the countervailing duty law at the outset was to protect domestic interests, rather than to protect competition as such.

The 1897 provision was reenacted without alteration in the Tariff Acts of 1909 and 1913. To prevent its circumvention, the law was extended in 1922 to cover bounties or grants bestowed on the manufacture or production of commodities, and not only on their exportation.[128] It was also

124. *Tariff Act of 1890,* chap. 1244, sec. 231, 26 Stat. 583.
125. *Tariff Act of 1894,* chap. 349, 28 Stat. 521.
126. *Tariff Act of 1897,* chap. 11, 30 Stat. 205.
127. Percy Wells Bidwell, *The Invisible Tariff* (New York: Council on Foreign Relations, 1939), p. 87.
128. *Tariff Act of 1922,* chap. 356, 42 Stat. 838.

extended to include bounties derived from private sources. The present law, found in the Tariff Act of 1930, amended the 1922 provision to permit the secretary of the treasury to estimate the amount of foreign subsidy.[129] Basically, however, the countervailing duty statute has remained virtually unchanged since 1897.

Scope of the Law

The terms *bounty* and *grant* are not defined in either the U.S. countervailing duty statute or the administrative regulations issued under it. Moreover, it is often impossible to establish from the official records of a countervailing duty proceeding which practice in the foreign country has led the Treasury Department to impose a duty.

Subsidies may be direct or indirect, but most of those countervailed have been indirect. They may be granted on export, manufacture, or production, though almost all have been export subsidies. In addition, they may be imposed even on products that have been shipped to a third country for processing or incorporation into other products.

The act does not permit the secretary of the treasury to take into account the lack of potential injury to a domestic industry from the imported goods, or to consider the fact that the subsidy may have been granted in order to bring the price down to the generally competitive level in the American market. While the secretary may decide that a given practice does not amount to a bounty or grant, and refuse to countervail, if he once finds that there is such a subsidy, he has no option to refuse to act on any ground whatever.

The countervailing duty law is fully as capable of being used as a trade weapon as of serving as a protective device against artificial export stimulants. Indeed, a literal application of all its terms could produce harsh and economically unjustified results. For example, the law takes no account of the purpose for which a particular subsidy was established or of its trade effect. Thus, foreign government assistance to entrepreneurs for the purpose of promoting regional development, reducing unemployment, encouraging plant and equipment modernization, or fostering national self-sufficiency in particular industries—all recognized as legitimate gov-

129. *Tariff Act of 1930,* sec. 303, 19 U.S.C. sec. 1303 (1964).

ernmental functions—could technically come within the ambit of the law without regard to the actual effect on exports from that country to the United States. With a few exceptions, however, countervailing duties have not been levied against foreign practices that were not plainly export subsidies, or that were not intended to increase exports, or that did not result in an increase in exports.

There is no evidence that subsidies provided by private, as distinct from governmental, sources have ever been countervailed. But the entrepreneur who establishes his son in business by means of a gift of money oɪ no-interest loan puts the exports of that business in jeopardy under the countervailing duty law, even though the business may be primarily oriented toward the domestic market.

Administrative Procedure

One of the most striking aspects of countervailing duty administration in the United States is the almost total lack of procedural safeguards in official proceedings. Neither statute nor regulations make any provision for hearings and the usual ancillary procedures according substantial elements of procedural due process to parties or countries affected by a countervailing duty imposition. The lack of procedural safeguards is peculiarly disturbing in view of the very great discretion delegated to the secretary of the treasury and, through him, to the Bureau of Customs.

The customs regulations provide for the initiation of countervailing duty investigations upon information furnished by interested persons or developed within the Customs Service. As a general rule, however, investigations are only undertaken in response to complaints filed by domestic producers. A "notice of countervailing duty proceeding" is published in the Federal Register at some stage in the inquiry to advise the public that the matter is under consideration and to elicit comments within a specified time (usually 30 days).[130]

A decision is reached after consideration of the commentary. If the decision is affirmative (that the imports in question are subsidized), a countervailing duty order will be published in the Customs Bulletin and the Federal Register. No provision is made for the publication of negative determinations.

130. 32 Fed. Reg. 13276 (1967).

The effective date of countervailing duty orders is uniformly delayed at least 30 days.[131] Goods entering the United States between the date of publication and the effective date of the order will not incur countervailing duties. There is no provision for withholding of appraisement, as in the Antidumping Act.

Cases involving the assessment of countervailing duties are heard in Customs Court. In 1953 an importer challenging a countervailing duty order charged that the secretary of the treasury's action was in the nature of rule-making, and that he had not followed certain requirements of the Administrative Procedure Act. The government, on the other hand, contended the ruling was an adjudication because "the Secretary has no discretion as to whether or not to assess countervailing duties once it has been ascertained that a bounty or grant exists. Congress has taken this function out of the Secretary's hands and left him nothing to 'legislate'."[132]

The Customs Court ruled in the government's favor but left undecided the question whether the administrative determination constituted rule-making or adjudication. The Court of Customs and Patent Appeals also overlooked the question when it reversed the lower court on other grounds.[133] No judicial resolution of the problem has been reached.

From 1897 through 1969, approximately 65 countervailing duty orders were issued.[134] Thirty-two of those, issued since May 1, 1934, when record-keeping methods were improved, resulted from at least 193 cases processed by the Bureau of Customs. There was a long relatively quiet period from 1958 to 1966. After a 1969 change in customs regulations requiring publication of investigations initiated,[135] a stricter enforcement policy was generally expected. Thus far, a relatively small number of complaints has been received each year, and the portion resulting in countervailing duty orders has remained small, though recent cases portend greater utilization of the statute in the future.

131. This is apparently required by the Tariff Act of 1930, sec. 315, 19 U.S.C. sec. 1315(d) (1964).

132. *Energetic Worsted Corp. v. United States,* 53 C.C.P.A. 36, 51, 54 (1966).

133. Ibid., 36.

134. *Selected Provisions of the Tariff and Trade Laws of the United States and Related Materials,* prepared by the staff of the House Committee on Ways and Means, 90 Cong. 2 sess. (1968), p. 139.

135. See 19 C.F.R. sec. 16.24 (1972).

Judicial Review

An importer of merchandise covered by a countervailing duty order may challenge the administrative determination that a bounty or grant exists; he must file a written protest within sixty days of the duty order, for action by the district director of customs. Rejected claims can be taken to the Customs Court for determination. American manufacturers, producers, or wholesalers may not normally challenge a negative determination as to the existence of a bounty or grant. The Court of Customs and Patent Appeals in a recent decision held that the Tariff Act of 1930 did not confer such jurisdiction on the Customs Court (though it left open the possibility that in rare instances the regular federal courts—not the Customs Court—might have jurisdiction). The court held that a countervailing duty determination could not be characterized as a "classification" or a "rate of duty"—which a domestic producer may have reviewed —but was an "exaction."[136]

Though the Tariff Act specifies that "all decisions" of the customs authorities "as to the rate and amount of duties chargeable" are subject to protest by the importer,[137] the Court of Customs and Patent Appeals has ruled that the secretary of the treasury's findings as to the *amount* of countervailing bounties or grants are "final so far as any revision or examination by the courts is concerned."[138] The same court has, however, reviewed and struck down Treasury decisions on amount as not supported by substantial evidence.[139]

Relationship to Antidumping Act

The Antidumping Act and the countervailing duty statute clearly have an interlocking conceptual basis. Indeed, the practice of subsidizing exports has often been described as "bounty dumping" in trade writings. Moreover, foreign antidumping and countervailing duty measures are typically combined into one law and are frequently indistinguishable. In the United States, however, the Antidumping Act has traditionally been

136. *U.S. v. Hammond Lead Products,* 440 F. 2d 1024 (C.C.P.A. 1971).
137. 19 U.S.C. sec. 1514 (1964).
138. *Franklin Sugar Ref. Co. v. United States,* 178 F. 743 (C.C.P.A. 1910).
139. *Energetic Worsted Corp. v. United States,* 53 C.C.P.A. 37 (1966).

restricted to dealing with the unfair trade practices of private interests, whereas the countervailing duty law—despite its express inclusion of privately distributed bounties—has in practice only been applied as a remedy against official bounties. Yet, there is a significant overlap in these two provisions.

Administration of the Law

The phrase *bounty or grant* is not defined in statute or in regulation, and the legislative history of the act offers little guidance to its intended scope or meaning. The definitional problem is compounded by the fact that the Treasury Department has not issued negative determinations.[140] Thus, neither the practices considered legitimate under the countervailing duty law, nor the rationale for decisions thereunder, can be known. For some seventy years no public notice was given when countervailing matters were under investigation.[141] In consequence, published countervailing duty orders are the primary source of evidence of administrative interpretations of the phrase, and many of them contain only sketchy information about the foreign practices deemed to be subsidies.

Along with the duty orders, court cases, testimony presented to congressional committees, public statements of officials, GATT reports, and other sources yield a structure of practices that have incurred countervailing duties, or that are generally regarded as subsidies for purposes of the statute.[142] They appear to fall into roughly eight categories, some with

140. But see T.D. 67-142, 1 Cust. Bull. 292 (1967), where the Treasury Department found that no bounty or grant was bestowed by the Mexican government on litharge imported into the United States and accordingly that the rate of duty thereon had been validly assessed. This ruling was reversed in *Hammond Lead Prods. Inc. v. United States,* 289 F. Supp. 533 (Cust. Ct. 1968), which in turn was reversed in *U.S. v. Hammond Lead Products,* 440 F. 2d 1024 (C.C.P.A. 1971).

141. An exception was made in a case involving motor vehicle parts from Canada. 29 Fed. Reg. 7249 (1964).

142. *Subsidy,* as used here, is not necessarily identical to the term as used by economists. The following definition is applicable: "A subsidy is an act by a governmental unit involving either (1) a payment, (2) a remission of charges, or (3) supplying commodities or services at less than cost or market price, with the intent of achieving a particular economic objective, most usually the supplying to a general market a product or service which would be supplied in as great quantity only at a higher price in the absence of the payment or remission of charges. Government loans made at lower than market rates of interest or at rates below the cost of funds

overlapping characteristics. The terms *bounty or grant* and *subsidy* do not necessarily have identical meanings.

Direct Subsidy Payments

The classical method of subsidizing exports involves the giving of outright premiums, bonuses, or cash payments to producers on their export sales. For example, it was found in 1959 that the Spanish government paid eight pesetas per kilo to exporters of almonds. An equivalent countervailing duty was levied until the offending practice was abandoned.[143] More recently, a countervailing duty was assessed against merchandise from France to offset "temporary measures" adopted by the French government in the wake of the student-worker disturbances of May 1968.[144] The "temporary measures" included payments to exporters equal to 6 percent of the labor costs of all exported products. Exports of tomato products from France and Italy that involved outright cash payments by the respective governments were also recently countervailed.[145]

The Supreme Court early in the century upheld a countervailing duty against importations of certain British spirits. Under British law, spirits were entitled to drawback of import duties, as well as to forgiveness of "all inland revenue tax" upon their exportation. In addition, an "allowance" was paid out of the public treasury to the exporter for each gallon exported. The lower court specifically excluded from its consideration the question of the drawback and remission of internal charges, upon which no countervailing duty had been assessed. Although the importer attempted to characterize the allowance as mere compensation for the added administrative expenses needed to comply with rigid British regulations governing distillers, the lower court held it to be a bounty or grant. The Supreme Court affirmed, confining its judgment to the issue of the allow-

---

to the government and government insurance provided at lower than private insurance premium rates may also appropriately be considered as subsidies." *Subsidy and Subsidy-effect Programs of the U.S. Government,* prepared by the staff of the Joint Economic Committee, 89 Cong. 1 sess. (1965), p. 39.

143. T.D. 54792, 94 Treas. Dec. 94 (1959), revoked in T.D. 55184, 95 Treas. Dec. 355 (1960).

144. T.D. 68-192, 2 Cust. Bull. 11 (1968).

145. T.D. 68-111, 2 Cust. Bull. 23 (Weekly No. 18, May 1, 1968); T.D. 68-112, 2 Cust. Bull. 25 (Weekly No. 18, May 1, 1968).

ance which, in effect, was an outright bonus payment to the exporter from the British treasury.[146]

Excessive Tax Rebates

Tax rebates and customs duty drawbacks exceeding tax or duty liability have frequently been used as a subsidy device. In a sense such overcompensation is nothing more than a direct subsidy payment in the guise of an otherwise legitimate tax adjustment; typically, however, the subsidy elements are hidden behind complex and circuitous regulatory arrangements.

The Supreme Court, in another early case, upheld the imposition of a countervailing duty against Russian sugar exports.[147] All Russian production was subject to a normal excise tax, and that in excess of a quota fixed at the level of domestic consumption to an additional tax. Exporters were entitled to remission of both taxes, even though the additional tax would probably not have been applicable if the sugar were sold in the domestic market. The total remission thus tended to exceed the amount of tax owing or paid.

In a case involving sugar imports from Holland, countervailing duty action was also upheld.[148] Under Dutch law, an excise tax account was maintained for each manufacturer of sugar. Credits were permitted for all sugar processed, with a higher rate of credit for more highly refined sugar. The excise tax credit, as a practical matter, never exceeded the tax for a nonexporting manufacturer. Because exported sugar was exempt from excise taxes, an exporting manufacturer virtually always had an excess of credits over debits, for which the government paid him.

In 1963, Canada adopted a complex plan designed to increase exports of motor vehicles and parts. The plan ostensibly provided for the remission or drawback of customs duties paid on imports of automobile equipment by Canadian motor vehicle manufacturers equal to the excess of the "Canadian value content" of their exports over that value during a designated base period. While the total drawback could not be greater than the duty on imports for the appropriate period, the only correlation required between the imported and exported articles was that both be

---

146. *Nicholas & Co. v. United States,* 249 U.S. 34 (1919). See Feller, "Mutiny Against the Bounty," p. 41.

147. *Downs v. United States,* 187 U.S. 496 (1903).

148. *United States v. Hill Bros. Co.,* 107 F. 107 (2d Cir. 1901).

broadly described as automotive equipment. Thus a manufacturer who imported valves to be used in the manufacture of carburetors would be entitled to a duty remission on his exports of finished carburetors equivalent to the duty paid on the valves, even if all of the imported valves were not exported as components of carburetors. In other words, he would receive drawback of duties on valves for his exports of the other carburetor components, which were produced in Canada.[149]

Drawback of customs duties on imported merchandise is a generally accepted international trade practice for merchandise that is subsequently exported either in an unchanged condition or in a commercially advanced form. Drawback is also allowed on a more or less identical article produced by the exporting manufacturer. A manufacturer of radios, for example, who produces some dials and imports others need not show that those he exports as part of complete radio sets are the dials he actually imported in order to receive drawback of customs duties. He may instead export only those he produced himself or a mixture of both and still receive a drawback equal to the duties paid on the imported dials. This substitution principle is limited to imported and exported articles that are substantially alike.

The Canadian plan further provided that motor vehicle manufacturers were permitted to include, as part of the value content on which drawback was earned, the automotive parts exported by an entirely independent Canadian parts manufacturer (who did not himself qualify as a motor vehicle manufacturer), so long as those exports were to be used in the manufacture, repair, or maintenance of motor vehicles produced by a foreign affiliate of the Canadian motor vehicle manufacturer.

In June 1964 the Treasury Department, pursuant to a complaint filed by an American manufacturer of automobile radiators, issued a Federal Register notice that it was investigating the Canadian plan and invited comments by interested parties. While the case was pending, the United States–Canadian Automotive Agreement was negotiated, establishing a limited "free trade area" between the two countries by providing for the elimination of duties on a wide range of original motor vehicle equipment.[150] The Canadians abandoned their controversial remission plan and

149. Feller, "Mutiny Against the Bounty," p. 43.
150. *Agreement Concerning Automotive Products with Canada, Jan. 15, 1965*, 1 U.S.T. 1372, T.I.A.S. No. 6093. Implemented by the *Automotive Products Trade Act of 1965*, 19 U.S.C. secs. 2001–33 (Supp. III, 1965–67).

the question of a countervailing duty, which can be applied only to dutiable merchandise, was rendered moot.

Preferred Income Tax Treatment

Another form of subsidy includes credits, preferential tax rates for export income, tax-free export reserves, and accelerated write-offs for export-related investments. Although countervailing action has not been taken against this type of subsidy, the possibility has been raised in the case of an alleged accelerated depreciation allowance relating to French export sales.[151]

A good illustration in U.S. law of this kind of subsidy is the Western Hemisphere Trade Corporation Act. A reduced income tax rate is available for any domestic corporation that conducts all of its business in the Western Hemisphere and derives 95 percent of its income from sources outside the United States.[152] Although originally intended to apply to operations based in Latin America, the law has been increasingly used to gain favorable tax treatment for export sales from the United States.[153] Since 1962 the Internal Revenue Code has also afforded favorable income tax treatment for export trade corporations. The most recent boost—in the 1971 Revenue Act which is a response to the President's call for new U.S. trade expansion initiatives—allows export companies to qualify as domestic international sales corporations, which, like foreign-based corporations, would incur no federal income tax liability. In turn, one-half of shareholders' current earnings, whether distributed or not, may be deferred for tax purposes, so long as it is reinvested in the qualifying corporation or in Export-Import Bank obligations.[154]

Government Price Support Systems

Usually associated with agricultural commodities, governmental intrusion into the marketplace to maintain relatively high domestic prices, and to facilitate the export of surplus production at lower world prices, is

151. See *Journal of Commerce* (New York), Oct. 11, 1968, p. 11.

152. *Internal Revenue Code of 1954*, secs. 921–22.

153. Stanley S. Surrey, "Current Issues in the Taxation of Corporate Foreign Investment," *Columbia Law Review*, Vol. 56 (1956), pp. 815, 830.

154. Title V, Pub. L. No. 92-178, 85 Stat. 536; see U.S. Department of Commerce, Domestic International Sales Corporation, *A Handbook for Exporters* (1972).

widely practiced by trading nations.[155] The methods used include government purchase plans designed to soak up oversupply with subsequent resale to exporters at the lower, going world price, and guaranteed price programs to insure that the net return to exporters is equal to the domestic price for like commodities.

In such a case, Treasury imposed countervailing duties in 1937 on exports of Lithuanian butter that benefited from a government guarantee of export sales at no less than the domestic price.[156] In 1939, imports of Dutch pork products were countervailed upon a finding that a government monopoly purchased pork from exporters at the domestic price and promptly sold it back at the lower world price.[157] In view of the widespread American practices of agricultural price supports and similar export subsidies, it is not surprising that there have been no recent countervailing duty actions against the frequent European use of these techniques under the Community's common agricultural policy.

Export Loss Indemnification

Governmental assumption of losses suffered in export transactions, including credit-risk guarantees, is an obvious incentive for producers to engage in the export trade. It differs from the guaranteed price technique because, among other things, it bears no direct relation to domestic prices.

In 1935, the Treasury Department issued a countervailing duty order against imports of Danish butter pursuant to a finding that butter exporters received "compensation trade premiums" amounting to approximately 10 percent of their selling prices.[158] Under the Danish plan, exporters would file a formal application for reimbursement of losses, stating the cost of materials, labor, and overhead applicable to their exports, as well as their selling prices and losses sustained. The granting of import licenses to Danish importers of American goods was conditioned on the payment of the Danish exporters' losses then outstanding.[159] In effect, the Danish system established a variable import license fee that rose or fell in relation to export losses, and that was designed to offset those losses.

---

155. See Oscar Zaglits, "Agricultural Trade and Trade Policy," in D. Gale Johnson and others, *Foreign Trade and Agricultural Policy* (GPO, 1967), pp. 125–269; Kenneth Dam, "The European Economic Community and Agriculture," *Columbia Law Review*, Vol. 67 (1967), pp. 209, 264–65.
156. T.D. 49122, 72 Treas. Dec. 241 (1937).
157. T.D. 49809, 74 Treas. Dec. 366 (1939).
158. T.D. 47896, 68 Treas. Dec. 305 (1935).
159. Feller, "Mutiny Against the Bounty," p. 46.

Subsidies for Specific Costs

Over the years governments have sought to lower the production and distribution costs of their exporting businesses by directing their subsidy activities to specific cost factors. Such government-sponsored devices include favorable insurance and inland freight rates, preferred borrowing rates and terms for financing of export-related investments, government financing or "overexpensing" of export promotion costs, and the sale of government-owned raw materials to export producers at favorable prices. It does not appear that subsidies of this kind have been countervailed under United States law, although complaints against special rail rates from factory to port in Italy and against subsidies for participation in international trade fairs have been filed with the Customs Bureau.[160]

Currency Manipulation Plans

Although the Articles of Agreement of the International Monetary Fund seek to achieve a unitary system that fixes the value of national currencies in terms of gold, the practice of encouraging export trading by means of official manipulation of currency exchange rates to accord favorable treatment to exporters persists. It presents a most difficult countervailing duty problem.

In part, the difficulty grows out of the variety of purposes for which flexible or multiple exchange-rate systems are used. Multiple rates are primarily attractive to less developed countries because they represent an administratively simple means of raising revenues and because they can be used to help in economic stabilization and to solve balance of payments problems. Countervailing duty findings in this area seem to have been influenced by an assessment of the purpose and trade effects of multiple exchange practices—when they appear to be directed at stimulating certain exports, countervailing duties have been held to be appropriate. A general devaluation of currency is apparently not considered a bounty or grant, even though one of its major purposes is to increase exports by cheapening their price.

In the 1930s the German government instituted a system of controlled currency accounts in which large sums of marks were held. These controlled marks could not be freely circulated in Germany. American im-

160. *New York Times,* Oct. 30, 1968, p. 63; Oct. 10, 1968, p. 1.

porters could purchase the marks at a substantial discount, so that, although the nominal prices of German imports remained the same, the actual cost was reduced. Exporters also benefited because they could receive payments in controlled marks, which improved their competitive positions in foreign markets, and they were entitled to redeem them for an equal number of the higher value free marks used in the German economy. On the basis that the German system constituted a partial depreciation or devaluation of currency to encourage exports, Treasury imposed countervailing duties equivalent to the difference between the normal exchange rate for free marks and that for controlled marks.[161]

In another important case dealing with the problem of multiple exchange rates, Treasury, after an extended public controversy, issued a countervailing duty order in May 1953 against imports of wool tops from Uruguay. Under the Uruguayan system, exporters were required to surrender to the central bank the foreign exchange proceeds of all export sales in return for which they received pesos at varying official rates of exchange, depending on the particular commodity sold. In order to determine whether the exchange rate for wool tops gave rise to a bounty or grant, Treasury computed a benchmark rate based on an average of all the rates used, for both import and export transactions, in a given year. The benchmark figure proved to be 18 percent lower than the Uruguayan wool top export rate at the time the countervailing duty action was taken.[162]

In recent world monetary crises, border fiscal devices have been used as an ad hoc mechanism to adjust for disequilibrium in currency exchange rates. Their use has been condoned particularly among "key currency" countries, whose monetary stability is truly a matter for international concern; moreover, a consensus is emerging that surplus countries should share the burdens of correcting payments disequilibriums.

Cooperative action among industrial nations in the last decade has served to avert a collapse in the system. When Great Britain introduced

161. T.D. 49821, 74 Treas. Dec. 389 (1939); and T.D. 48360, 69 Treas. Dec. 1008 (1936).
162. T.D. 53257, 88 Treas. Dec. 105 (1953). The importer in the case filed a protest in Customs Court and was overruled, in *Energetic Worsted Corp. v. United States,* 224 F. Supp. 606 (Cust. Ct. 1963). In an appeal to the Court of Customs and Patent Appeals, the decision was reversed on grounds that the benchmark rate was based on 1951 rates whereas the shipments occurred in 1953. *Energetic Worsted Corp. v. United States,* 53 C.C.P.A. 36 (1966).

an import surcharge between 1964 and 1966, in an effort to halt its deteriorating balance of trade position, its trading partners refrained from taking retaliatory action permitted under the GATT. In the converse situation West Germany in 1968 took steps to reduce its trade surplus by lowering its export rebates and its import charges during the crisis over the French franc. At the same time France raised its value added tax rate and repealed its payroll tax to strengthen its international trade account.

Unjustified Tax Remissions

Whether tax remissions are justified or not depends on their economic impact on export sales. The remission of "direct taxes or social charges on industrial or commercial enterprises" is considered unjustified in the GATT concept of nondiscriminatory world trade.[163] Essentially, those tax remissions that have the same economic effect as direct subsidy payments are not considered justified; however, remission of indirect taxes, such as consumption and excise taxes, is not considered an export subsidy.

Prior to 1967, the only countervailing duty actions involving tax remissions and duty drawbacks were those in which overcompensation for indirect taxes was given by the governments concerned.[164] Mere remission of domestic excise taxes borne by the exported goods was not viewed as a bounty or grant. Beginning with a countervailing duty order against imports of Italian steel transmission towers in 1967, however, the nature of the indirect taxes and the effect of remissions on the export price of commodities have played a prominent role in countervailing duty cases. (A decision of the EEC Court of Justice that certain rebate practices of the Italian government on exports of steel products to other Common Market countries violated the Treaty of Rome may have contributed to this development.)

The rebates that were considered unjustified were against charges not directly related to the exported product or to raw materials or components

163. GATT, *BISD,* 9th Supp. (1961), p. 190.
164. See, for example, T.D. 19321, 1 Treas. Dec. 696 (1898), countervailing a drawback allowed by the French government on a shipment of chestnuts preserved in syrup. In 1958 the United States replied to a GATT questionnaire as follows: "Remission of internal taxes borne by a product is one method by which a bounty or grant can be bestowed indirectly. If the remission does not exceed the amount of taxes previously paid, however, then such remission is not considered a bounty or grant." GATT, *Antidumping and Countervailing Duties* (1958), p. 139.

incorporated in its manufacture. They included rebates of taxes or other charges related to the purchase of motor vehicles, advertising, licensing, and the transfer or registration of documents, all overhead expense items as distinguished from production costs.[165]

The GATT Approach to Subsidies

Since the countervailing duty is a device used to regulate the flow of international trade, it falls within the problems of governmental subsidies in the international community. The GATT defines a countervailing duty as a special duty levied for the purpose of offsetting any bounty or subsidy "bestowed, directly or indirectly, upon the manufacture, production or export of any merchandise."[166] The 1947 agreement declared that the remission of certain taxes upon export was not to be viewed as a subsidy.[167] In 1955, multiple currency practices were, in certain circumstances, recognized as a subsidy.[168] Otherwise, the GATT contains no definition of a subsidy or bounty.[169] A special panel on subsidies was unable in 1962 to agree on a definitive list of governmental acts that should be considered as subsidies.[170] The inability of the panel to define a subsidy is indicative of the reluctance of many nations to accept international regulation of the use of subsidies.

The use of countervailing duties by GATT member states is restricted. No duty may exceed the amount of the subsidy granted. Countervailing

165. *Foreign Trade and Tariff Proposals,* Hearings before the House Committee on Ways and Means, 90 Cong. 2 sess. (1968), Pt. 5, pp. 2214, 2219.

166. GATT, art. VI(3).

167. Ibid.

168. GATT, Interpretative Notes, art. VI, paras. 2 and 3, note 1.

169. The only international agreement containing a definitive list of subsidies is a decision of the Council of the Organization for European Economic Cooperation (OEEC), Decision of 14th January 1955 Concerning Measures Designed to Aid Exporters, reprinted in OEEC, *Code of Liberalization* (1959), pp. 174–81. The list was incorporated in the European Free Trade Association (EFTA) Convention, Annex C, 370 U.N.T.S. 3 (1960).

170. The panel in 1961 noted that the actions enumerated in the OEEC Council Decision (ibid.) were considered by some nations as forms of export subsidies but refrained from endorsing this conclusion. GATT, *BISD,* 9th Supp. (1961), pp. 185–201. In 1962 it noted that it was "neither necessary nor feasible to seek an agreed interpretation of what constitutes a subsidy." GATT, *BISD,* 10th Supp. (1962), p. 208.

duties and antidumping duties may not be invoked simultaneously. And countervailing duties may be levied only if the subsidization threatens "material injury to an established domestic industry, or is such as to retard materially the establishment of a domestic industry."[171]

The GATT rules govern all countervailing duty statutes enacted since the treaty came into force, which include those of most of the major trading nations; GATT thus provides a general standard which is applicable in international trade.[172] Since GATT does not require amendment of prior inconsistent legislation, however, its conflict with the mandatory U.S. countervailing duty statute, while resulting in considerable dissatisfaction on the part of the United States' trading partners, does not spell out a U.S. violation of an international agreement.

Rules Governing Subsidies

The original GATT provision dealing with subsidies merely required consultation between members or with the contracting parties of GATT when disputes arose over the use of subsidies. The 1955 amendment, however, added a number of provisions dealing affirmatively and substantively with export subsidies.

It acknowledged that an export subsidy "may have harmful effects for other contracting parties, both importing and exporting, may cause undue disturbance to their normal commercial interests, and may hinder the achievement of the objectives of the GATT."[173] While unable to agree to prohibit subsidies, the contracting parties did agree to abolish export sub-

171. GATT, art. VI(5); see also art. VI(2) and (4).

172. Both the EFTA Convention members and the Common Market have taken steps to regulate government subsidies in conformity with GATT rules. A study published in 1958 by GATT listed only eight countries that made use of their countervailing duty legislation at that time. Twelve other nations had general legislation that would permit countervailing duties, but none of them applied its law against governmental subsidies. Since that time, Germany, France, Italy, and the United Kingdom have all enacted countervailing duty legislation. See "Analysis of the Antidumping Laws of the Federal Republic of Germany, France, Italy and the United Kingdom," *American Bar Association Bulletin,* Section on International and Comparative Law, December 1965, p. 20; and Regulation 459/68, EEC Council, April 5, 1968, 1 CCH Comm. Mkt. Rep., par. 3883 (1968).

173. GATT, art. XVI, sec. B(2), in GATT, *BISD* (1958), Vol. 3, p. 30. See Michael Rom, "GATT: Export Subsidies and Developing Countries," *Journal of World Trade Law,* Vol. 2 (1968), p. 544, for a comprehensive discussion of the GATT rules.

sidies for nonprimary products and instituted rules regulating the use of subsidies for primary products.

NONPRIMARY PRODUCTS

The agreement on nonprimary products was not implemented until November 1962 and then only by the major trading countries in the GATT. Fourteen industrial nations of Europe and America have agreed to cease granting either direct or indirect export subsidies that reduce the price of the exported product below its price in the domestic market of the exporter.[174] Any subsidy that does not have this effect is still permissible.

Many of the other members of GATT signed a second declaration (a standstill provision in the 1955 agreement) against introducing new, or increasing existing, subsidies.[175] This declaration also provided that subsidies that were reduced or abolished could not be increased or reinstituted. The declaration was to remain in force for a year and to be automatically extended for two one-year periods unless notice of termination were given. By 1964, only Finland supported the standstill provision.

These declarations are only a small step toward an effective agreement on the abolition of governmental subsidies. Agreement on a definitive list of subsidies has not been possible. The declaration aimed at abolishing subsidies for nonprimary products is restricted by the requirement that the subsidy reduce the price of the exported item below the price of the domestic item. Not only is it clear that such subsidies still exist, but no nation has attempted to enforce the 1960 declaration by using the GATT machinery. In addition, the expiration of the standstill declaration leaves the basic regulation of governmental subsidies to the individual states importing the subsidized products.

PRIMARY PRODUCTS

The 1947 GATT agreement contained no specific provisions with respect to subsidies for primary products.[176] The unratified Havana Charter, establishing an International Trade Organization to succeed GATT, pro-

174. "Declaration of 19 November 1960, Giving Effect to the Provisions of of Article XVI(4)," in ibid., p. 34.
175. "Declaration of 19 November 1960, Extension of the Standstill Provisions of Article XVI(4)," in ibid., p. 34.
176. See John M. Leddy, "United States Commercial Policy and the Domestic Farm Program," in William B. Kelly (ed.), *Studies in United States Commercial Policy* (University of North Carolina Press, 1963), pp. 200–02.

vided relatively lenient treatment for subsidies of nonprimary products. It anticipated negotiation of intergovernmental commodity agreements, and thus provided generally that subsidies would not be applied to primary products that had the "effect of maintaining or acquiring for that Member more than an equitable share of world trade in that commodity."[177]

When the Havana Charter failed, the GATT provision for consultation among members was the only international agreement governing disputes over export subsidies. The 1955 amendment, under which the contracting parties agreed to seek to avoid the use of subsidies in the export of primary products, was a more specific, but rather unsuccessful, attempt to deal with the problem. It provides that a subsidy that increases exports of a primary product should not be applied in such manner as to give the subsidizing country more than an equitable share of the world export trade in that product, thus implicitly acknowledging that such subsidies will be a relatively permanent part of the international economic landscape.

In the only formal conciliation procedures so far invoked, Australia claimed that a French subsidy system for wheat or wheat flour was giving France more than an equitable share of world wheat exports. The conciliation panel heard statements by the parties and by Japan, which was also concerned about the French plan. After requesting further information and statistical data, the panel recommended specific measures that France could utilize to avoid the disruptive effects of her subsidy payments.[178]

The lack of agreement on the abolition of export subsidies for primary products is due basically to the fact that almost all countries, both industrial and developing, subsidize agricultural production, support domestic prices, and subsidize exports because they think it is in their interest and they wish to continue to be free to do so. While commodity agreements have provided some movement toward regulation and "stabilization" of trade in a few primary products, the prospects for future extended use of this device are dim. Especially in agricultural products, each trading nation continues to maintain its own protective structure, which includes domestic price supports and other forms of subsidization, import quotas,

177. Department of State, *Havana Charter for an International Trade Organization* (final draft, March 24, 1948), art. 28; see also arts. 28, 62–66. See generally John Howard Jackson, *World Trade and the Law of GATT* (Bobbs-Merrill, 1969), sec. 15.7, pp. 392–96.
178. GATT, *BISD*, 7th Supp. (1959), pp. 22, 46.

and other protective devices. Clearly, no progress toward eliminating these techniques of agricultural protectionism can be expected in the absence of systematic consultation concerning, and international regulation of, domestic agricultural policies.

Procedures for Resolving Disputes

Two procedural devices designed to clarify the proper use of subsidies were agreed to in the 1947 GATT. Neither has significantly aided international regulation of the use of governmental subsidies in international trade.

Any contracting party granting or maintaining a subsidy that directly or indirectly increases exports of any product from, or reduces imports of any product into, its territory is supposed to notify the contracting parties of the extent and nature of the subsidization, an estimate of its effect, and the circumstances making the subsidization necessary.[179] A provision requiring that a country give its trading partners information that could later be used against it would seem to offer few reasons for compliance, especially when there is no guarantee that the trading partners will be equally forthright. In 1961 fewer than half of the member states returned a subsidy questionnaire that had been sent to each state by the contracting parties. Those that were returned were obviously incomplete; for example, shipbuilding subsidies were referred to in only one instance, despite the fact that they are common.[180]

Self-reporting offers little chance of success toward reduction of subsidies. There are no effective means of forcing such reporting or of requiring changes of improper practices. A more realistic approach now being used provides for each nation to list those practices of every other nation that are deemed to impair the free flow of world trade. Reduction of these barriers through negotiation is then sought. Clearly, a more complete list will be compiled by those claiming injury than by the government accused of restricting international trade.

The special consultation procedures for countries granting subsidies that may be injurious to another are supplements to the general GATT

179. GATT, art. XVI, sec. A(1), in GATT, *BISD* (1958), Vol. 3, p. 30. See ibid., 11th Supp. (1963), pp. 58–59, for the procedures established for these notifications.

180. "Report Adopted 21 November 1961 Concerning Operation of Provisions of Article XVI," ibid., 10th Supp. (1962), p. 204.

consultation provisions. If the subsidies prove to be other than those permitted by GATT, the injured party may retaliate. The injured country may impose a countervailing duty, but as a unilateral measure it invites retaliatory strikes, and, like all unilateral punishment measures, affects adversely international amity, when its imposition is believed to be unjustified by a country whose interests are adversely affected.

The special consultation procedures in subsidy cases have been used infrequently. The contracting parties have received several formal complaints, but these have been settled in bilateral discussions between the governments concerned. Only the Australian-French dispute over French wheat exports has required formal conciliation.

The U.S. special representative for trade negotiations in 1969 recommended to the President that the United States seek international agreement on clear definitions of export subsidies for industrial products.[181] More than twenty-five years of being unable to agree on "clear definitions" reflects persistent divergence in views, however, as to what it is desirable or possible to proscribe as an undesirable export subsidy. No doubt this flows from national assessments of needs for particular devices.

For many devices a definition is not what is really needed. For example, there is little doubt that concessional credit terms for export financing—such as have been furnished, and consistently augmented, in recent years by the Export-Import Bank of the United States and comparable institutions in other countries—act as a subsidy to exports. The difference between the more favorable government terms and the available less favorable terms of private financial institutions constitutes the subsidy. The problem is not that of *defining* (or *identifying*) such conduct as subsidization; it is *convincing* countries to be prepared to forgo the exports that cessation of the subsidy would cause. And this is what nations are not prepared to do. Even a freeze on the levels of credit subsidization is extremely difficult to negotiate, to say nothing of elimination of this device for encouraging exports.

For many other devices the definitional problem is the familiar one of seeming to approve what is not defined as a subsidy. But how are future new devices that serve to subsidize to be treated? A catch-all—"and other devices which serve as subsidies"—brings the problem back to square one, where there is no definitive definition.

181. U.S. Special Representative for Trade Negotiations, *Report to the President: Future United States Foreign Trade Policy* (1969), p. 21.

Precisely the same considerations make the negotiation of a uniform code of countervailing duty practice equally difficult. Countries desiring to continue to subsidize exports in various ways will not agree to outlaw those methods. And they are unlikely to approve the methods used by others unless their own receive reciprocally beneficial treatment. It is highly likely that, in these circumstances, the unilateral reproach method —the use of the countervailing duty—remains the only instrumentality available for use, unhappy though that appears to be.

Consistency of the U.S. Statute with the GATT

The GATT and the U.S. act are not consistent in three particulars. The most glaring inconsistency stems from the failure of the U.S. statute to require a showing of injury to domestic competition. Article VI 6(a) of the GATT specifically provides: "No contracting party shall levy any . . . countervailing duty on the importation of any product of the territory of another contracting party unless it determines that the effect of the . . . subsidization . . . is such as to cause or threaten material injury to an established domestic industry, or is such as to retard materially the establishment of a domestic industry."

The U.S. legislation nonetheless does not violate the GATT because it falls within the "inconsistent legislation" exception, which applies if "the legislation on which it is based is by its terms or expressed intent of a mandatory character, that is, it imposes on the executive authority requirements which can not be modified by executive action."[182] The Treasury Department, taking the position that the U.S. statute is inconsistent with the provisions of Article VI, has never applied an injury test;[183] since the U.S. statute is mandatory in nature, the United States is not in violation of its international obligations under the GATT by virtue of the grandfather clause.

The United States did attempt to bring its law into conformity with the GATT in 1951, when the Treasury Department proposed an amendment to the countervailing duty statute that would have incorporated in it an

182. GATT, *BISD*, Vol. 2, p. 62.
183. See U.S. Department of State, "United States Laws Inconsistent with GATT Provisions," *Trade Agreements Extension Act of 1951*, Hearings before the Senate Committee on Finance, 82 Cong. 1 sess. (1951), Pt. 2, p. 1197.

injury provision similar to the one contained in the Antidumping Act. Although incorporation of an injury provision was favorably reported out by the House Ways and Means Committee, controversy over other provisions killed the legislation.[184]

Lack of an injury test is unfortunate since an injury requirement would benefit the American consumer and the lack of it hurts him. Under the present statute, once a grant or bounty has been found, the levy of the countervailing duty is mandatory. For consumers, the imposition of countervailing duties always means a higher price. Thus in situations where no unfair competition to American sellers is involved, the detrimental effect falls on the community as a whole, since the price of goods is not being raised to offset an injury caused by the subsidization. Restricting countervailing duty protection to dutiable goods is both an inflexible and a dubious method of dealing with the problem of injury. For while it might be argued that the domestic industry or firm benefiting from the duty usually believes it is suffering some injury in the market, there remains a long distance between belief and proof.

The basic objection of domestic competitors to the addition of an injury test is that injury is difficult to prove. That it is more difficult to prove than in antidumping cases, however, is unconvincing. The United States has had experience, albeit quite mixed, with injury provisions both under the Antidumping Act and under section 337 of the Tariff Act of 1930, which deals with imports involving unfair competition or unfair acts generally. The addition of an injury test to the countervailing duty statute would thus be consistent with U.S. policy relating to imports allegedly creating unfair competitive conditions. In addition, it would relieve the Customs Bureau of examining some foreign devices to stimulate exports that have very limited effects on American commerce and whose questioning damages American foreign relations, as is often the case where developing countries subsidize exports. An injury test would mean that minor forms of governmental assistance would escape the countervailing duty law because there would be no injury.

The special representative for trade negotiations has suggested also that the President be permitted to waive duties if he should determine that it is in the national interest to do so.[185] Such discretion would permit the

---

184. See *Simplifying Customs Administration and Procedures*, H. Rept. 1089, 82 Cong. 1 sess. (1951).

185. U.S. Special Representative, *Future U.S. Foreign Trade Policy*, p. 21.

executive branch to minimize serious disruption of the foreign relations of the United States through clearly defined statutory procedures, rather than by "avoidance" of the statute, which is the only way its rigors may now be moderated.

In the other two situations in which there is an inconsistency with the GATT, the U.S. statute has been administered in a manner consistent with the GATT obligations. The United States has never imposed countervailing and dumping duties for the same act, though it could do so. And long before the creation of the GATT, the Treasury had taken the position that only tax remissions in excess of that borne by the product would be countervailed. The amendments to the statute proposed in 1951 would have included a GATT-type statement with respect to tax remissions, thus formalizing long-standing practice.[186] Despite a favorable House report, the proposal died from the same cause as the proposed injury requirement —some opposition and neglect. Recently, a Customs Court decision held, contrary to this uniform practice and despite the Treasury Department's refusal to countervail, that mere remission of an excise tax was a bounty or grant within the meaning of the act. The U.S. government and the importer appealed to the Court of Customs and Patent Appeals, which reversed on jurisdictional grounds. In its opinion, however, the latter court recognized clearly the practical consequences—retaliation and foreign relations difficulties—that could ensue were its determination otherwise.[187]

U.S. ABILITY TO NEGOTIATE ANTIDUMPING AND COUNTERVAILING DUTY AGREEMENTS

THE CAPACITY of the United States to negotiate with respect to antidumping and countervailing duties is limited by the absence of clear authority for the President to conclude such agreements and translate them into domestic law without further reference to the Congress. The present

---

186. See *To Amend Certain Administrative Provisions of the Tariff Act of 1930 and Related Laws, and for Other Purposes,* Hearings before the House Committee on Ways and Means, 82 Cong. 1 sess. (1951), pp. 1–2. See generally "Statement of the United States Concerning Countervailing Duty," in GATT, *Antidumping and Countervailing Duties* (1958), Vol. 2, p. 139.

187. *United States v. Hammond Lead Products,* 440 F. 2d 1024 (C.C.P.A. 1971).

antidumping and countervailing duty statutes, and administrative interpretations of them, also impose severe limitations on negotiating leeway.

None of the methods of direct attack on the existing legislation seems feasible now. As in the case of buy-American practices, there is currently no clear legislative authority that would permit the President to negotiate a self-executing agreement with respect to antidumping and countervailing duties and proclaim it as domestic law. There are major difficulties to be overcome in order to secure such advance authority, given the entrenched position of the statutes, and the strength of protectionist forces to defend them. The chances of Congress in the near future granting to the President anything resembling a blank check on antidumping and countervailing duties, or, indeed, authority that could be taken to be a weakening of its resolve or that of protectionist groupings to strengthen these laws, cannot be rated high.

Nor does a general resolution indicating the sense of Congress that there should be negotiations, with the results brought back for approval by Congress, appear to be realistic. Those protectionist forces that are strong enough to prevent the authorization would likely be able also to defeat the approval; a prior resolution is not only unnecessary, since the President can always negotiate, but of doubtful weight politically.

Any self-executing agreement negotiated without advance congressional authorization or subsequent approval would have to be consistent with the antidumping and countervailing duty statutes to be effective. If past administrative interpretation of the language of those statutes is used as the yardstick, or is even taken seriously into account in measuring whether there is consistency, the limitations on negotiators' ability to conclude an effective agreement may be severe. For example, the misfortunes of the Antidumping Code arising from its asserted inconsistency with current practice under the Antidumping Act indicate that a new agreement cannot be negotiated while the existing statute remains unchanged. Likewise, any attempt to negotiate an agreement that would impose an injury requirement before countervailing duties were levied would run afoul of difficulties. Yet these kinds of provisions would be the very reason for negotiating international agreements in the area of nontariff barriers. If they cannot be implemented effectively, there is every reason for not negotiating them.

In short, it appears that under present law the United States cannot negotiate an effective self-executing agreement on antidumping and countervailing duties. One alternative, of course, is to negotiate a code that does not purport to be a binding international agreement. Like the Declaration of Human Rights, it could serve as a desirable international standard and, at the same time, put some pressure on those adhering to it to conform their domestic conduct to the standards recommended. But after GATT's lack of success despite a quarter of a century of experience with a countervailing duty principle (Article VI) and an Antidumping Code since 1967, a declaration seems less than appealing. Still another alternative is to seek legislation from Congress that would alter the present antidumping and countervailing statutes so as to permit the President more flexibility in negotiations, as well as to change substantively the objectionable portions of these statutes. When the time is ripe, no doubt this method will be the most efficacious.

In the meantime, however, much can be accomplished administratively to ameliorate the deleterious effects of the current Antidumping Act and the countervailing duty statute. Staunch secretaries of the treasury who will administer both statutes in as nonprotectionist a manner as possible, as has often been the case, and tariff commissioners selected for their knowledge and competence in the trade field and awareness of the important stake of America in an expanding world trade can do much to soften the impact of these laws, as well as carry out the letter and spirit of the Antidumping Code.

Indeed, administrative reforms of this nature would doubtless advance the day when statutory changes, and international negotiation, would be more feasible than they now appear to be. In terms of priorities for successful *negotiation* of reductions in nontariff barriers, antidumping and countervailing duty negotiation must of necessity be assigned a low priority.

CHAPTER FIVE

Quantitative Restrictions

THERE CAN BE little doubt that the quantitative restriction of imports—whether imposed by unilateral action of the importing country or by voluntary restraint over exports from the supplying country, induced by the country of destination—is one of the most potent instruments ever invented to restrain and reduce foreign trade. Though there are differences in effectiveness and in public control of the restraint—depending on whether it is enforced by the importing country or managed, formally or informally, by the exporting country—the adverse impact on trade is essentially the same. The import is quantitatively restricted regardless of its ability to compete successfully though paying high duties.

U.S. Quotas until 1947

As might be imagined, any patent on such a basic and potent device has long since expired. At least as far back as 1463, to speak only of the modern era, the English Parliament enacted a statute prohibiting imports of many manufactured articles—imposed a zero quota—because craftsmen could not "live by their skill because of foreign competition."[1] Over the years, quotas have been employed by all countries involved in international trade as a protectionist device to insulate domestic producers from competition with the lower priced import.

Historically the United States, particularly before World War I, made

1. John H. Clapham, *A Concise Economic History of Britain: From the Earliest Times to 1750* (London: Cambridge University Press, 1963), p. 178.

128

much less use of the quota to protect domestic industry than did other countries—high import duties constituted the principal U.S. import barrier. While certain nontariff restraints on U.S. imports were imposed by the War Trade Board during World War I, they were quickly abolished after the armistice, and in the 1920s the United States continued to rely predominantly on customs duties—those of the high-tariff Fordney-Mc-Cumber Tariff Act of 1922—for protection of domestic industry.[2] Indeed, the United States took the lead in the late 1920s and very early 1930s in seeking to outlaw quantitative restrictions, sponsoring a tightly drawn convention at the 1927 and 1928 international conferences on the abolition of import and export prohibitions and restrictions. The United States ratified the convention without conditions; only a few other countries were prepared, however, to accept it.

Again, in 1933 at the World Monetary and Economic Conference in London, the U.S. delegation strongly urged "that embargoes, import quotas, and various other arbitrary restrictions should be removed as quickly as possible." Later in that year at the Seventh International Conference of American States at Montevideo, a U.S. resolution, unanimously adopted, called for the removal of quantitative restrictions through trade agreements. No doubt the means referred to—agreements—induced the approval of many Latin American governments that doubted they would ever become parties to any.[3]

Since 1933, however, U.S. policy has been much more ambivalent. While continuing to campaign against quotas in general, and to resist them in particular, the United States has found increasingly that exigent economic and political pressures required its resort to them. This ambivalence began in the economic despond of the Great Depression. The failure of efforts to outlaw the quota, its increased use by other countries, and desperate economic conditions induced a broad variety of measures to raise prices, wages, and employment. Among them was the National Industrial Recovery Act of 1933, the first wholesale use of quotas by the United States. Under that act, codes of fair competition—then, as now, often a euphemism for industry cartel controls, governmentally blessed, whose

2. The historical material in this section is largely drawn from the able report of the U.S. Tariff Commission, *Quantitative Import Restrictions of the United States,* T.C. Pub. No. 243 (April 1968).

3. William B. Kelly (ed.), *Studies in United States Commercial Policy* (University of North Carolina Press, 1963), pp. 63–65.

purpose it is to limit production and raise prices—were established to aid the rehabilitation of sectors of the domestic economy.

Codes for the petroleum, lumber and timber, and alcoholic beverage industries provided for the imposition of import quotas, and such quotas were in fact imposed on crude oil and petroleum products (a premonition of the 1959 mandatory oil import quotas), Philippine mahogany, and alcoholic beverages.[4] Moreover, the President was authorized, after investigation by the Tariff Commission, to impose fees or quotas on other imports when necessary to prevent them from rendering the codes ineffective (a foreshadowing of the Agricultural Adjustment Act two years later). Of the fourteen cases referred to the Tariff Commission for formal investigation, seven were completed, four resulting in recommendations for restrictive action (quotas or import fees). In three of these cases the principal suppliers to the U.S. market agreed to restrict exports to specified quantities (foreshadowing the voluntary control over exports of the late 1930s as well as of the 1950s and 1960s). In the fourth case, import fees were recommended; later, a change in excise taxes drastically reduced the volume of imports and obviated the need for the fee.

These departures from the long-standing antagonism of the United States to quotas might appear to be aberrations, especially in light of the liberal tone of the Trade Agreements Act of 1934 and the twenty-nine bilateral agreements negotiated thereunder before 1947. Nonetheless, despite the demise of many import quotas after the Supreme Court declared key sections of the Recovery Act unconstitutional,[5] there appeared side by side with the new trade agreements legislation a number of acts authorizing—indeed, directing, under stated circumstances—quantitative restrictions of imports. Until the post-World War II period, however, these were limited to agricultural products. The 1934 Jones-Costigan Sugar Act, requiring quotas on foreign sugar in order to maintain the less efficient western and southwestern industry; the 1935 Philippine Cordage Act; and the 1935 Agricultural Adjustment Act, mandating import restrictions on agricultural products whose production or marketing was being restricted in the United States in the interest of lower production and higher prices, were not emulated in the industrial products areas during that period.

A large part of the agricultural sector was not covered by the relatively

4. See generally Robert L. Stern, "The Commerce Clause and the National Economy, 1933–1936," *Harvard Law Review*, Vol. 59 (1946), p. 645.

5. *Schechter Poultry Corp. v. United States,* 295 U.S. 495 (1935).

carefully drawn Agricultural Adjustment Act, though the groundwork was laid for the exclusion of the whole sector from the no-quota policy of the United States; the no-quota policy, however, continued to be pressed home for industrial products.

GATT Quota Provisions

The General Agreement on Tariffs and Trade (GATT) represented the high-water mark of all international efforts, led by the United States, to outlaw the quota. The twenty-three contracting parties in 1947, realizing that concerted action to reduce tariffs under the GATT framework could be rendered ineffective unless additional measures were taken to deal with other, easily substitutable, protective devices, decided to come to grips directly with the most important device—the quantitative restriction. The resultant Article XI was a marked advance over the standard U.S. bilateral friendship, commerce, and navigation treaty (which never sought to outlaw quotas),[6] as well as the bilateral trade agreements that preceded GATT, and all other prior multilateral agreements.

Article XI of the GATT provides: "No prohibitions or restrictions other than duties, taxes or other charges, whether made effective through quotas, import or export licenses or other measures, shall be instituted or maintained by any contracting party on the importation of any product of the territory of any other contracting party or on the exportation or sale for export of any product destined for the territory of any other contracting party."

Of course it was perfectly clear at the time that such a provision entailed complications. Not only would sound commercial policies have to bend to the necessities of war, pestilence, famine, short crop, or balance of payments difficulties, but existing, mandatory legislation in the contracting states was often inconsistent with the new prescription. Hence, a series of specific exceptions for the future was spelled out in the agreement:

1. Temporary export restrictions or prohibitions to prevent or relieve critical shortages of foodstuffs or other essential products (Art. XI[2][a]).

---

6. See, for example, *U.S.–Japan Treaty of Friendship, Commerce and Navigation of 1953*, T.I.A.S. 2863, art. 14.

2. Import and export prohibitions or restrictions necessary to the application of standards or regulations for the classification, grading, or marketing of commodities in international trade (Art. XI[2][b]).

3. Import restrictions on any agricultural or fisheries product, imported in any form, necessary to enforce governmental measures that operate to restrict the quantities of the like domestic product; or remove a temporary surplus of the like domestic product; or restrict quantities of animal products, the production of which is directly dependent on the imported commodity, if the domestic production of that commodity is relatively negligible (Art. XI[2][c]).

4. Restrictions on the quantity or value of merchandise permitted to be imported in order to safeguard a country's external financial position and its balance of payments (Art. XII).

5. Quantitative restrictions to foster the establishment of a particular industry for contracting parties with economies with low standards of living and in the early stages of development (Art. XVIII).

6. Escape measures for domestic industries threatened with or suffering serious injury as a result of increased imports generated by obligations incurred by a contracting party under the agreement (Art. XIX).

7. Restrictive measures taken to protect the wide range of activities encompassed by social welfare and health standards, that is, action to protect public morals, health regulations, patents and copyrights, and so forth (Art. XX).

8. Restrictive action necessitated by the security interests of the contracting party (Art. XXI).

A further, more general, exception is also important. It is notorious that, in legislating for economic control, a freeze is often practicable while a roll-back is rarely possible. The GATT was no exception. The Protocol of Provisional Application of GATT (still in effect after a quarter of a century) established a freeze by requiring the contracting parties to apply Part II (including Article XI) provisionally to the fullest extent not inconsistent with existing legislation (for the United States, legislation existing on October 30, 1947). By interpretation the contracting parties have indicated that "existing legislation" refers to mandatory, not merely authorizing, legislation. The United States, also by interpretation, has maintained that pre-1947 legislation that sounds mandatory—that is, the countervailing duty statute which applies to imports found to be bounty-fed—is saved by the protocol from being unlawfully inconsistent with substantive GATT commitments.

Neither the protocol nor the exceptions were sufficient, however, to save the United States from violation of Article XI when in 1951 it amended the Agricultural Adjustment Act to require quotas or fees on agricultural imports materially interfering, or practically certain to interfere, with any support program maintained by the U.S. Department of Agriculture.[7] This move to require import restrictions in aid of price support programs that did *not* involve marketing or production restrictions went beyond the scope of Article XI of GATT. Since a number of these pure price support programs were involved, the United States was forced to seek either a change in domestic law or a waiver of its GATT Article XI obligations in order to avoid a constantly running violation.

During the GATT revision negotiations in 1954–55 this issue was faced and decided. The U.S. negotiator, Winthrop Brown, felt he could negotiate a waiver for the illegal actions, but at a serious loss of leverage against similar restrictive actions in Europe and elsewhere adversely affecting U.S. exports, particularly agricultural exports. For the major European countries, like almost all countries possessing agricultural resources of consequence, possessed a network of protectionist measures rivaling, if not identical with, those in use in the United States. Mr. Brown was instructed to get the waiver—American agricultural interests were bent first on protecting their American market. It was to be almost another decade before the United States fully realized the consequences of its actions for American agricultural exports.

U.S. Quotas since 1947

The actual record of U.S. quantitative restrictions imposed since World War II indicates a constant use of unilateral import quotas on important agricultural products and an increasing use of voluntary agreements by foreign countries and industries to limit exports under threat of restraints

---

7. *Trade Agreements Extension Act of 1951,* sec. 22(f). See generally Stanley D. Metzger, *Law of International Trade: Documents and Readings* (Lerner Law Book, 1966), Vol. 1, pp. 688–730.

by the United States should they fail to cooperate. Both have been motivated by protectionist principles.

Agricultural Quotas

The principal quotas imposed under the Agricultural Adjustment Act at present apply to almost all of the dairy products; cotton, and cotton products; wheat and wheat flour; and peanuts. In addition, rye, barley, oats, shelled filberts, and tung nuts have been under quotas at one time or another during the past two decades.

For many years it has been the policy of the U.S. government to assist the agricultural sector of the economy by supporting prices for agricultural products. At various times, and under a variety of laws, programs of the Department of Agriculture have resulted in prices of some products being supported at levels higher than world prices.[8] Imports of such commodities, if unrestricted, would rapidly add to the supplies the Department of Agriculture would have to remove from the market. Hence, limitations on imports are a means of preventing material interference with the government programs. Provision for such restrictions of imports was initially made in 1935 by the addition of Section 22 to the Agricultural Adjustment Act of 1933.

PROCEDURE UNDER SECTION 22

Section 22, as amended, requires the secretary of agriculture to advise the President whenever he has reason to believe that any article or articles are being or are practically certain to be imported under such conditions and in such quantities as to render or tend to render ineffective or materially interfere with any price-support or other program related to agricultural commodities or any product associated with any such program. If the President agrees with this advice, he directs the Tariff Commission to conduct an investigation and submit a report to him of its findings and recommendations. The President, if he agrees with the report, is required to impose such fees or quotas on the importation of the articles involved as he determines necessary. The fees, imposed in addition to the basic import duty, may not exceed 50 percent of the price, and the quotas im-

8. See generally John M. Leddy, "United States Commercial Policy and the Domestic Farm Program," in Kelly, *Studies in U.S. Commercial Policy,* p. 174.

posed may not be less than 50 percent of the quantity imported during a previous representative period. In an emergency, the President may take action pending the report of the Tariff Commission.

In a similar manner, the secretary of agriculture may advise the President that conditions have changed in a sector of agriculture and that existing restrictions may, in his opinion, be relaxed. The President, following an investigation by the Tariff Commission, may liberalize or terminate the existing import controls.

The procedure has proved cumbersome. Despite appearances, it does not protect the public's interest in having as narrow an area of restraints over imports as possible, consistent with a sound overall agricultural policy. Dairy products afford a good example of quota restraints under Section 22. Between 1953 and 1968, new products were added to the quota list nine times as foreign exporters manufactured milk into various types of products. Practically all dairy products except high-quality table cheeses were under quota. In these cases, as in practically every Section 22 case, the Tariff Commission found as desired by the secretary of agriculture. Thus it found such exceptionally small percentages of import penetration as 1 percent or 2 percent of U.S. milk consumption to be materially interfering with price support schemes. Indeed, in some cases it recommended even more restrictive quotas than those desired by the guardian of the program, the secretary of agriculture.

There would appear to be no substantial reason for a Tariff Commission role in Section 22 proceedings, and many against. Were the secretary of agriculture, following a presidential determination to institute a formal proceeding looking to quota action, to establish an administrative proceeding before a departmental officer, with a record made that could be screened by the Office of the Special Representative for Trade Negotiations and members of his interagency committee, the decision to take restrictive action would be far better informed than at present. Possible retaliatory moves by the foreign countries who would be affected, including failure to take corrective action where they are already restraining American agricultural exports, could be weighed and assessed on a broader and more informed basis. The technical difficulties in administering particular types of quotas could be handled with the wisdom that comes of experience, and with responsibility; the spectacle of tariff commissioners recommending levels and types of quotas, when they have had neither experience in administering them nor responsibility for their outcome, could be avoided. Many years ago, Senators Wayne Morse and Allen Ellender urged elimination of the commission's role in Section 22 cases.[9] The State Department, then believing both that agriculture could be retained in the trade agreements program and that an independent investigation of the necessity for limitation by the Tariff Commission would assist in achieving that objective, opposed. The first belief was understandable, if somewhat naive; the second has proved to be mistaken. Better results would flow from a change in the structure of the Section 22 investigation.

THE EEC'S COMMON AGRICULTURAL POLICY

Though its derelictions in the agricultural products area may seem vast, the United States is by no means leader in agricultural protectionism. The common agricultural policy (CAP) of the European Economic Community (EEC) is more protectionist—a greater barrier to international trade in agricultural products. If the CAP continues to be applied extensively, Section 22 might have to be utilized for many years to come, and more extensively.

The workings of the common agricultural policy are graphically illustrated in the dairy products investigation of 1968.[10] Milk and other dairy products are among the key groups of agricultural products that the CAP was developed to provide a broad, Communitywide price-support program for. The CAP, while not a quota system, was designed to substitute a common policy for the multitude of price-support systems and protective controls existing in the member states prior to the EEC's establishment[11] and restrict the volume of imports in the interest of that policy.

The CAP price-support system for milk and other dairy products encompasses special prices, variable import levies, and export subsidies or refunds. The Community sets a target price for milk that is essentially a price goal; it is designed to assure an adequate standard of living and employment to domestic producers, to develop intra-Community trade, and to insure the sale of the domestic output of the product during the

9. Ibid., pp. 205–10.
10. See *Certain Daily Products*, T.C. Pub. No. 274 (December 1968), pp. 15, 23, 71.
11. See generally Eric Stein and Peter Hay (eds.), *Law and Institutions in the Atlantic Area: Readings, Cases, and Problems, with Volume of Documents* (Bobbs-Merrill, 1963), pp. 364–77.

marketing year. Intervention prices for butter, skim milk powder, and certain cheeses are actually support prices that member states stand ready to pay to assure that the domestic prices for these products do not fall below designated levels; they are the prices at which EEC governments are obliged to purchase all quantities of the domestic product offered on the market. The intervention prices are fixed at levels slightly below the corresponding target prices for the respective products. For twelve pilot products the CAP provides threshold prices, determined administratively as the minimum prices at which imports may be entered for sale in the domestic markets of member states; they are generally fixed on the basis of the internal market prices prevailing in each of the member states. The threshold prices are used as bases for determining the height of the Community's variable import levies, which are designed to isolate domestic products from foreign competition; they are employed to assure that imports do not enter the market at price levels that may interfere with the attainment of the target prices. Accordingly, they are fixed at levels that equate the cost of imports with the domestic prices of the respective products. The Community also encourages the member states to participate in world trade by authorizing refunds or subsidies to individual exporters. Their amounts are fixed at levels not to exceed the difference between exporters' f.o.b. prices and world prices. Thus, the Community's price-support system for milk and other dairy products is a closely knit, interdependent system in which pressure exerted on any one of its components will conceivably disturb the balance of the entire system.

The CAP regulations for milk and other dairy products, which went into full operation in 1964, were revised in 1968, purportedly to unify the Community dairy markets. The new regulations were approved by the EEC Council in the face of a milk market in serious disequilibrium, one in which the gap between production and consumption, including exports to non-EEC countries, grew wider and wider and led to a surplus of milk and the accumulation of large and increasing stocks of butter and other dairy products. In the period 1965–67, annual production of cow's milk in the EEC increased from 146 billion pounds to 162 billion pounds; output in 1968 was estimated to be about 167 billion pounds.[12]

The regulations issued in 1968 did not appreciably alter the broad

12. *Newsletter on the Common Agricultural Policy* (European Communities, Joint Information Service), No. 10, July 1968, p. 3.

framework of the price-support system for dairy products. In fact, the Council had left the structure unchanged because it had not "reached agreement as yet on the underlying economic and structural problems affecting milk policy, and in particular on the guidance to be given this policy, to produce a healthier situation in the dairying industry in the future."[13] The accumulation of surplus stocks most likely will continue unabated until the Council revises its policy regarding the production and marketing of milk.

As production of milk in the EEC in recent years increased, butter stocks rose 24 percent annually between 1965 and 1968.[14] Among the other outlets producers sought for the increased supply of milk was the U.S. market, where prices for dairy products were higher than world prices. Dairy processors in the EEC converted milk into canned milk and low-price cheeses, which were not subject to quantitative limitations in the United States. When U.S. imports of such products increased sharply, and every indication was that they would continue to do so, the President took emergency action to limit them.[15]

Because of its price-support policies, the EEC has had to rely on export subsidies to channel surplus dairy products into foreign trade. Table 3 shows, for various dairy products, the common export subsidy for shipments to the United States and the ratio of the subsidy to the export price. So long as the EEC encourages increased output and the resulting burdensome stocks, subsidies are likely to be available for dairy exports not subject to U.S. limitations. And so long as the EEC, in the interest of its CAP, closes its own market to third-country producers, such as those of Austria, dairy products of those countries will also seek outlets in the U.S. market.

THE FUTURE

We can see growing around the world the destructive pattern of high production stimulated by price supports leading to subsidies which in turn lead to trade distortions and new and increased import protection. This in turn gives

13. Ibid.

14. *Certain Dairy Products,* T.C. Pub. No. 274 (December 1968) (opinion of Chairman Metzger).

15. *Presidential Proclamation 3790,* 32 Fed. Reg. 9803 (1967). The proclamation limited imports, starting July 1, 1967, to three-fourths of the amount imported during previous years. See generally Carl H. Fulda and W. F. Schwartz, *Regulation of International Trade and Investment* (Foundation, 1970), pp. 281–89.

Table 3. *EEC Subsidies on Dairy Exports to the United States,*
by Amount and Rate, 1960s

Commodity and exporting country	EEC subsidy	
	Amount authorized, cents per pound	As a percent of export price
Evaporated milk, canned; Netherlands	13.61	111
Condensed milk, canned; Netherlands	4.99	37
Condensed or evaporated milk, in bulk; France	24.72	n.a.
Aged cheddar cheese; France	13.60	44
Processed Edam and Gouda cheese; West Germany	18.14	82
Italian-type cheese, not in original loaves; Italy	22.68	68
Other cheese; West Germany	15.22–20.87	61–84
Swiss cheese; West Germany	17.24	73
Gruyère-processed cheese; West Germany	17.24	68
Chocolate crumb; Netherlands	9.85	62
Butterfat-sugar mixtures; Belgium	32.37	158

Source: *Certain Dairy Products*, T.C. Pub. No. 274 (December 1968) (opinion of Chairman Metzger).
n.a. = not available.

still further impetus to the expansion of production in importing countries. Some way must soon be found to reverse the worsening trend. The problems are growing in number, scope and intensity. The European CAP, to cite but one example, has developed an extremely costly and highly protective system, the application of which has seriously exacerbated the problems of both importing and exporting countries.[16]

The U.S. delegate to GATT summarized the problem of a protective agricultural policy. As the EEC policy of protectionism grows, so inevitably will agricultural protectionism elsewhere.

Unfortunately, no one knows the precise nature and magnitude of the effects of worldwide agricultural protectionism, despite considerable concern that it is seriously detrimental to the efficient feeding of the world's population.[17] In 1968 the Tariff Commission instituted a study on the "effects on United States trade in agricultural products of national and regional agricultural measures affecting international trade in agricultural

16. Statement by Henry Brodie, U.S. delegate, at GATT, 25th session, Nov. 15, 1968.
17. See, for example, Fulda and Schwartz, *Regulation of International Trade,* pp. 298–99.

products."[18] The study, intended to provide agricultural policy makers a basis for gauging the effects of programs and policies, was completed in October 1973.

It outlines the wide scope and the substantial magnitude of distortions in trade of agricultural products that occur in consequence of the national programs of the main agricultural countries. It shows that a major economic task of future decades is to bring about a much greater degree of rationality in world agriculture policies than is now apparent.

MEAT CONTROLS

One unilateral control imposed by the United States—quotas on meat imports—is authorized by a separate act of Congress. In 1964, following a period of declining prices for many types and grades of live cattle, and concurrent large imports of beef, the Congress provided for the imposition of an absolute quota on fresh, chilled, or frozen beef, veal, mutton, and goat meat, if imports of these meats beyond specified quantities should be anticipated.[19] In the aggregate, these meats account for the bulk of U.S. meat imports.

The permissible level of aggregate imports of the meats was set at 725.4 million pounds annually. Each year, however, the amount is to be increased or decreased to assure that imports bear about the same ratio to domestic commercial production as they did, on the average, in the years 1959–63. Thus imports are limited to about 4.6 percent of domestic commercial production regardless of comparative advantage or other economic factors. The secretary of agriculture must estimate, prior to January 1, the expected domestic commercial production of these meats for the forthcoming year in order to compute the quota amount. He is also required to estimate the quantity of these meats that, but for the controls provided for in the law, would be imported. Should the estimate of imports exceed the quota amount by 10 percent or more, the President shall, by

18. *Notice of Study, Probable Effects of National and Regional Agricultural Programs on U.S. Foreign Trade in Agricultural Products,* 33 Fed. Reg. 17381 (1968). See Stanley D. Metzger, "New Roles for the U.S. Tariff Commission," *Law and Policy in International Business,* Vol. 1 (1969), pp. 1, 9–11; *Domestic and Foreign Government Programs and Policies Affecting U.S. Agricultural Trade,* T.C. Pub. No. 613 (October 1973).

19. Pub. L. 88-482, 19 U.S.C. sec. 1902 (1964).

proclamation, impose quotas. He may subsequently suspend or enlarge the quotas, as provided for in the law. The law does not specify precisely the manner in which quotas are to be administered, except that they are to be allocated on the basis of the shares that supplying countries exported to the U.S. market during a representative period.

In 1965, 1966, and 1967 the secretary of agriculture made estimates of domestic production and of imports of meats. The expected imports were significantly below the level that would have called for import quotas. In subsequent years, when it appeared that imports might reach levels calling for quotas, voluntary restraints were imposed by exporting countries in order to avoid the imposition of unilateral quotas by the United States. However, during 1970 there were substantial rejections of beef from nearly every country that is a normal exporter to the United States, and several rejections of veal and mutton.[20] In 1972 meat quotas were suspended in view of the limited supply, and excessive domestic prices, in the United States.

SECTION 204 REGULATIONS

The President has additional authority, under Section 204 of the Agricultural Act of 1956, as amended, whenever he deems it appropriate to negotiate with representatives of foreign governments in an effort to obtain agreements limiting the export from such countries and the importation into the United States of any agricultural commodity or product manufactured therefrom, or textile or textile product. He may regulate the entry or withdrawal from warehouse of any of those commodities to carry out such an agreement, and if a multilateral agreement exists among countries accounting for a significant part of world trade in the article concerned, his regulations may control trade in products of countries who are not parties to the agreement. The only agreement negotiated under this authority is the Long-term Arrangement Regarding International Trade in Cotton Textiles.[21] It is more properly classified, however, as a voluntary export control program by foreign countries acting under threat by the United States of imposition of unilateral legislative controls.

20. U.S. Department of Commerce, *Foreign Trade III* (December 1970).
21. Concluded in Geneva, Feb. 9, 1962; entered into force for the United States, Oct. 1, 1962, T.I.A.S. No. 5240.

Nonagricultural Quotas

While agricultural products have continued their aberrant way, outside the paths of the trade agreements program, the record of nonrecourse to quotas respecting industrial products is on the whole a creditable one. The number of disturbing occurrences has been growing in the past twenty years, however, and the end is far from sight.

The major sources of authority for the imposition of mandatory quotas by the United States on nonagricultural imports are the escape clause and the national security amendment of the trade agreements legislation.[22] Each has been used, albeit infrequently, to impose quotas—lead and zinc under the first, petroleum and petroleum products under the second.

QUOTAS UNDER THE ESCAPE CLAUSE

The escape clause provisions of the trade agreements legislation authorized quotas as well as upward revisions of rates of duty in order to remedy serious injury to domestic industry caused or threatened by concession-engendered increased imports.[23] The rationale for this seeming anomaly is that the escape is from all the international commitments contained in the GATT, including the commitment of Article XI not to impose quotas. No limits are placed on the means of remedying temporarily the injury found if quotas are employed.

This potent engine of trade restriction has several built-in safeguards, however. First, it is available only after what is, in essence, an adversary proceeding before the Tariff Commission, which must make a finding of injury due to a concession. Second, the President may accept or reject in whole or in part a commission finding of injury. Third, the recommendation of the commission is merely that, and the President may accept or reject it. Finally, the United States must compensate the exporting country through negotiation of a fresh concession on other products having equivalent trade effects, or through acquiescence in the exporting country's withdrawal of concessions to the United States having similar effects. This means that the President will do his utmost to avoid the quota technique—

22. *Trade Expansion Act of 1962,* sec. 301(b), 19 U.S.C. sec. 1901(b), and sec. 232, 19 U.S.C. sec. 1862.

23. This is true even if the concession was a mere duty reduction or binding and there had been no quantitative restriction against the imports of the same article prior to the trade agreement concession.

almost always the harshest in terms of trade restraint effectiveness—in the interest of successful foreign relations. Accordingly, the remedy has been infrequently recommended and seldom imposed—lead and zinc being the only major commodities involved.[24]

NATIONAL SECURITY AMENDMENT QUOTAS

The national security amendment of the trade agreements legislation, enacted in 1955, was expanded in 1958 and reenacted (in the 1958 form) in the 1962 Trade Expansion Act. While a number of domestic industries have sought to invoke this provision, only in the case of petroleum and petroleum products have quantitative restrictions been imposed on imports. The domestic oil industry for decades has sought to curtail imports of oil and oil products, since they undersell comparable American products by a wide amount. The industry, abetted by others such as the domestic fluorspar industry wanting similar quotas, succeeded in persuading the administration and Congress in 1955 to adopt the national security amendment, authorizing restraints, including quotas, on imports judged by the President to be impairing the national security. Originally, the objective was to provide a continuing mobilization base enabling the United States to fight a five-year war, if necessary; the base would fulfill essential wartime needs of industry and the public, assuming foreign sources were cut off. In 1958, however, this relatively conservative means of obtaining quota relief for obviously protectionist purposes was greatly changed by an amendment that was not fought by the administration, though it was heartily deplored. This expansion, far beyond the mobilization base concept, was accomplished through the addition of the famous "second sentence" which is now part of the 1962 act:

In the administration of this section, the Director [of the Office of Emergency Planning] and the President shall further recognize the close relation of the economic welfare of the Nation to our national security, and shall take into consideration the *impact of foreign competition on the economic welfare of individual domestic industries;* and any substantial unemployment, decrease in revenues of government, loss of skills or investment, or other serious effects resulting from the displacement of any domestic products by excessive imports

---

24. Reference has been made throughout to an absolute quota, not a tariff quota (such as a 10 percent ad valorem duty on the first 1 million pounds imported, 20 percent on all additional), which has been utilized fairly frequently. See Tariff Commission, *Quantitative Import Restrictions,* pp. 65–74.

shall be considered without excluding other factors, in determining whether such weakening of our internal economy may impair the national security.[25]

While the fear that this economic welfare conception would result in the section becoming a super escape clause has not yet been realized, there is little doubt that the national security amendment is a potent weapon available to any administration that is either determined to turn protectionist or is too irresolute to resist pressures in that direction.

OIL QUOTAS

The oil import restrictions, interestingly enough, did not commence life in consequence of the national security amendment. While the legislation was available, controls began in 1957 under a voluntary oil import program.[26] Importers were requested to cut imports of crude oil 10 percent below their average annual imports in 1954–56. The industry was soon dissatisfied with the result, especially since imports of finished petroleum products rose sharply.

Agitation for a system of mandatory restraints had begun long before 1957—at least as early as 1929, when a resolution of the Independent Oil Producers Association called for oil import restrictions. The relative ineffectiveness of the voluntary program merely bolstered these efforts. Thus, mandatory restrictions, following procedures instituted under the national security amendment, were first imposed on crude oil imports in March 1959 and a month later on oil products.[27] Until 1973, when the quota program terminated under pressure of the oil shortage, it was modified slightly from time to time but not in essentials. Under the mandatory program, imports were limited to 12.2 percent of domestic production of crude and unfinished oils.

While estimates of the cost of the program to the American consumer range from $4 billion to $6 billion annually,[28] there was little doubt that

25. *Trade Expansion Act of 1962*, sec. 232, 19 U.S.C. sec. 1862. Italics added. Though its motivating force was wholly from outside, Eisenhower administration officials were involved in drafting the legislation.

26. See generally Fulda and Schwartz, *Regulation of International Trade*, pp. 318–19.

27. *Proclamation 3279*, 24 Fed. Reg. 1781 (1959); *Proclamation 3290*, 24 Fed. Reg. 3527 (1959).

28. *Mandatory Oil Import Control Program, Its Impact on the Domestic Minerals Industry and National Security (Together with Dissenting and Separate Views)*,

the program was a bonanza to the domestic industry; the burden was borne by the consumer, in effect through a mechanism functioning like an excise tax, regressively employed.

The program itself was based on a rather broad interpretation of national security. In 1970, the President's Task Force on Oil Import Control drew from the empowering statute what it considered to be its two primary purposes. First, the program was to serve as protection against disruption of supplies needed to fill military and essential civilian demand for oil during periods when foreign supply might be cut off. Secondly, it was to insure that the domestic industry was not so weakened by imports as to weaken the national economy to a point detrimental to national security. The means adopted were limitation of imports, consequent higher prices, and, thereby, the provision of incentive to find new reserves in the United States to be utilized in a national security emergency.

The entire question of oil import quotas was examined by congressional committees and a White House interagency committee during 1969. Although changes designed to liberalize import restraints were recommended,[29] they were rejected by the President. It is noteworthy that wholly apart from the rationale for the program's restrictions, the drive of the oil industry for quotas on imports started long before sophisticated national security arguments were even considered.

Voluntary Quotas on Exports

The voluntary restraint of exports is a misnomer—it is an action of restraint taken by an exporting country threatened by unilateral quotas that might well be worse in trade effects. For every unilateral quota has within itself the seeds of its own continuity—the domestic industry groups that were strong enough to secure the quota will likely retain sufficient political power to assure its continuation far into the future. The mandatory controls on oil imports that followed quickly after the voluntary

Report of the House Committee on Interior and Insular Affairs, 90 Cong. 2 sess. (1968), minority views. See generally, *Mandatory Oil Import Control Program,* Hearings before the Subcommittee on Mines and Mining of the House Committee on Interior and Insular Affairs, 90 Cong. 2 sess. (1968).

29. Ibid., majority views.

restrictions, like Ol' Man River, just kept rolling along. The cotton and wheat quotas have had an even longer life, going back well over thirty years.

Voluntary quotas, on the other hand, being within the partial control of the exporting country, are bargainable in terms of duration as well as of severity of restraint. For example, when the Department of Agriculture in 1948 considered restricting potato imports, Canada indicated that it was prepared to control exports in order to avoid the quota.[30] The Department of Agriculture, for its part, was prepared to see the Canadian export control limited to a single crop year because the control could be implemented immediately rather than in the four months it took to process Section 22 quotas, and because the Canadian government had indicated that adverse political repercussions could be expected to attend U.S. application of unilateral quota controls. The Potato Agreement of 1948 was the result.[31]

The considerations that underlay that agreement have motivated most of the voluntary controls over exports negotiated since World War II. On the U.S. side, strong domestic interests desire to protect themselves against competitive imports. They either believe that they cannot qualify for escape clause relief (as in the cotton textile, manmade textile fiber, and shoe industries), or if they might qualify for national security amendment relief (the steel industry), they are at least aware that unilateral quotas could be taken to be unfriendly acts by America's trading partners, causing foreign relations problems. The cognizant congressional committees, as experienced in these problems as the executive, do not wish to force the administration's hand by legislating mandatory quotas; indeed, they may doubt that in the last analysis they could muster the

30. Canada was well aware of the longevity of Section 22 quotas once they had been introduced, having had its large wheat exports curtailed by the Section 22 wheat quotas.

31. T.I.A.S. No. 1896. Subsequently, this bypassing of Section 22 procedures was held by the Fourth Circuit Court to render void the agreement. The Supreme Court specifically disavowed that reason for denying relief to the government. *United States v. Guy W. Capps, Inc.*, 348 U.S. 296 (1955), affirming on different grounds 204 F. 2d 655 (4th Cir. 1953). During the 1952–54 period, however, the State Department avoided making agreements in areas covered by domestic remedial legislation because of the Fourth Circuit's opinion in Capps, and even thereafter preferred in negotiations not undertaken pursuant to congressional authorization to have unilateral voluntary controls notified to the United States, but not specifically agreed to by it.

strength to repass such a bill over a determined chief executive. Yet they, like the administration, are loath to treat all domestic industries—those with and those without major political strength—alike.

Those without domestic political strength must simply live with the foreign competition that cannot be stemmed under generally applicable domestic legal criteria. Those with such strength secure an extraordinary remedy—having the United States raise to the highest international nego-tiating levels the matter of securing curtailment of imports from friendly foreign countries, developing and developed alike, in the interest of relief to those who cannot show serious injury in consequence of increased imports, despite the substantial resultant losses to the country in higher consumer prices, retaliatory action by foreign countries, and so forth.

The Long-term Arrangement on Cotton Textiles of 1962, renewed in 1967 and 1970 for three-year periods, and the steel import limitation imposed by major foreign suppliers in 1969, and renewed in 1972, are good illustrations of this process.

Textiles before 1960

Control over textiles through the voluntary technique has an interna-tional history. Bilateral quotas, covering many textile items, were privately negotiated in the 1930s among France, Germany, Belgium, and Britain. Indeed, in 1931–32 approximately 150 industrial ententes were con-cluded under the auspices of the Franco-German Economic Committee, which had been established to foster them. These *contingents amiables, interlocutories, voluntaries,* or *contractuels* all functioned to limit im-portation into the protected country through a voluntary curtailment of exports by the exporting country.[32]

During the 1930s the United States negotiated voluntary arrangements with Japan restricting various cotton goods. Previously, imports of cotton textiles had come mainly from Europe; they were of high quality and not directly competitive with domestic production. Starting in 1933, however, imports of medium-quality cotton textiles competing directly with do-mestic production began to increase rapidly. Even though total imports of cotton manufactures remained below 5 percent of domestic sales and 3 percent of domestic production throughout the 1930s, while such im-

32. See Heinrich Heuser, *The Control of International Trade* (Blakiston, 1939), p. 119.

ports from Japan fluctuated around 1 percent of domestic sales, the domestic industry successfully argued that Japanese imports were rising rapidly, competing directly with domestic production, and, because concentrated in a few product lines, threatening the American industry.[33]

In two of the four voluntary agreements negotiated between Japan and the United States in the 1930s, the State Department conducted the negotiations; in the other two the negotiations were conducted by private industry groups in both countries. A two-year agreement limiting Japanese exports of cotton cloth was signed by the American Cotton Textile Mission and the representatives of the Japanese cotton textile industry in 1937 and renewed for two years. An agreement on cotton floor coverings, beginning for one year in 1934, and twice extended for a year, protected an industry in which imports exceeded American production, and most imports (99 percent in some years) originated from Japan. The National Association of Hosiery Manufacturers concluded a three-year agreement with the Japanese Knitted Goods Exporters Association in 1936 limiting cotton hosiery imports. Japan had replaced Germany as the main exporter of that product to the United States, and the Japanese association was collecting what amounted to a 5 percent ad valorem export duty on hosiery. Another agreement covered velveteens—an amount equal to 30–50 percent of domestic production was imported, more than 90 percent of it from Japan—and corduroys—the import portions were 3 percent and 90 percent, respectively. The 1937 agreement between the American Association of Velveteens and Corduroys and the Japan Cotton Yarn Piece Goods Exporters Association was for a period of two years.

As Jacques Henry states so well, the "entire story shows clearly that the United States–Japan voluntary export restraint agreements of the 1930s resulted mainly from American pressures and threats of unilateral, permanent, and possibly more restrictive action. . . . Nothing indicates that this pattern has been changed since."[34] The Japanese, for their part, accepted the agreements as the most practicable means of preserving a portion of their textile exports to the United States, and in the interest of

33. See Warren Seabury Hunsberger, *Japan and the United States in World Trade* (Harper & Row for Council on Foreign Relations, 1964), p. 353; Kenneth LeRoy Bauge, "Voluntary Export Restrictions as a Foreign Commercial Policy with Special Reference to Japanese Cotton Textiles" (Ph.D. thesis, Michigan State University, 1967); and Jacques Henry, "Voluntary Export Restraints" (Canadian Economic Policy Committee, November 1969), an excellent paper which much of the material in this section is taken from.

34. Henry, "Voluntary Export Restraints."

political harmony in this sphere of their relationships with the United States.

From 1945 until the mid-1950s the Japanese textile industry was recovering from the war and rebuilding and modernizing its plant. Exports then picked up very quickly. United States cotton-textile imports from Japan reached a peak in 1955 and 1956 and tended to decline toward the end of the decade. During the period from 1951 to 1962, total U.S. imports of cotton manufactures represented less than 2 percent of domestic production; of this, Japan's share represented less than 1 percent of domestic production.

In late 1955, in consequence of severe pressure from the domestic industry, the U.S. government advised the Japanese authorities that "they should exercise restraint in their exports and not attempt to capture so much of the American market that an American industry will be injured."[35] In May 1956, following government-to-government discussions led on the U.S. side by an assistant secretary of commerce, the Japanese government made public the restraint levels it was voluntarily applying to twenty items of cotton textile exported to the United States. In September 1956, negotiations began which led to a five-year voluntary agreement, providing for annual consultations with a view to adjusting the agreed restraint levels upward or downward.[36] During the course of this five-year agreement, Japan's exports of cotton manufactures to the United States declined from 55 percent of all such American imports in 1956 to 34 percent in 1961 (a low of 29 percent having been reached in 1960).

A substantial increase in imports from Hong Kong, however, offset to some extent the lessened imports from Japan and led the United States to exert pressure on Hong Kong to restrict imports, and, generally, to seek to widen the forum for actions restraining textile imports. This also necessitated framing the issue in more general terms, though textiles were quite clearly the immediate raison d'etre for the new exercise.

Market Disruption and the GATT

In 1959, Under Secretary of State Dillon suggested that GATT should adopt a multilateral approach to the problem of "sharp increases in imports, over a brief period of time and in a narrow range of commodities

---

35. Hunsberger, *Japan and the United States in World Trade*, p. 317 (quoting from a declaration by Secretary of State Dulles).
36. Ibid.

[which] can have serious economic, political and social repercussions in the importing countries."[37] He called for a study of the problem, thus broadening the issue from a Japanese to a worldwide basis. The ensuing GATT report detailed the various types of arrangements that had been made to discourage "market disruption"—a phrase often applied to attractively priced imports that consumers preferred to the higher priced domestic product. These arrangements included unilateral quotas and licensing schemes, and high rates of duty tailored to the competing article, as well as voluntary arrangements restraining exports.

Products then covered by unilateral or voluntary arrangements included "textiles and clothing, woolen gloves and other knitted hoods, suspenders, hoods and shapes for men's and boys' hats, casual footwear, stainless steel flatware, chinaware and glassware, clinical thermometers, aluminum foil, leather goods, plywood, plastic buttons, paint brushes, artists' watercolours in tubes, electric batteries, toilet combs, watches, lead and zinc, ceramics, optical goods, precision instruments, rubber shoes, toys, metal articles, chemical and pharmaceutical products, radio apparatus, sewing machines, discharge pipes, half capelines, graphite electrodes, zip fasteners, rubber hose, zinc-white, asbestos-cement products, tuna fish, umbrellas, paper cups, wood screws, iron pipe fittings and transistor radios."[38] Any idea that the United States was the only culprit must be dissipated by this list. Indeed Canada, the United Kingdom, and the EEC, to say nothing of the less developed countries, had been exercising similar restraints according to political exigencies.[39]

A GATT working party established to find solutions that would be "consistent with the principles and objectives of the GATT"—somewhat of a contradiction in terms—was able only to transmit the executive secretary's draft of a report. He described market disruption as situations that "generally contain the following elements in combination":

(i) a sharp and substantial increase or potential increase of imports of particular products from particular sources;

(ii) these products are offered at prices which are substantially below those prevailing for similar goods of comparable quality in the market of the importing country;

37. Press release, GATT, No. 59, Oct. 27, 1959, p. 222.
38. GATT Doc. L/1164, May 17, 1960.
39. Henry, "Voluntary Export Restraints," pp. 50–57. Less developed countries had been restricting imports to encourage domestic production.

(iii) there is serious damage to domestic producers or threat thereof;

(iv) the price differentials referred to in paragraph (ii) above do not arise from governmental intervention in the fixing or formation of prices or from dumping practices.[40]

With only one additional criterion—that the import be an article on which a concession had been granted—a perfectly valid escape clause action would have existed in any country party to GATT. Since by 1960 few articles had not been made the subject of concessions, this omission was of little importance. If, then, the escape clause was available, what function was served by this market disruption exercise? It seems clear that the "serious damage" criterion was meant to be only a very loose formulation of "loss of significant share of market." Quite clearly the search for a market disruption formula represented a tacit retreat from the Article XI prohibition of quotas, inviting all manner of ad hoc devices to curtail imports of politically sensitive commodities where escape clause action would not lie because its criteria—serious injury in consequence of concession-fed increased imports—could not be met.

No effort was made to relate market disruption to the capacity of the economy to adapt; there was no recognition that the prices of domestic goods that were undersold by imports might have been artificially set; there was no indication that domestic producers might be suffering from the effects of poor management far more than from imports. None of these ordinary facts of life, so well known to those who have listened to complaints about alleged injury due to imports, were adverted to in the executive secretary's report.

Indeed, market disruption raises the question of what constitutes normal competition. As Henry puts it, is competition normal only if foreign suppliers overprice their exports in terms of their own domestic prices? Why is trading at the lowest possible price abnormal? Or is abnormal foreign competition, through some xenophobic connotation, a more serious evil than abnormal internal competition?[41] (It has been estimated that the effects of the penetration of the U.S. textile market by low-priced imports have never come close to equaling the results of the displacement of textile production from the Northeast to the South.)[42]

40. GATT, *Basic Instruments and Selected Documents* (*BISD*), 9th Supp. (1961), pp. 1, 26.

41. Henry, "Voluntary Export Restraints."

42. Ibid.

It has been said of the European textile industry—and it is not off the mark for others—that it conceives of market disruption as the situation that prevails when the difference between import prices and domestic prices exceeds the fraction of value added that they are willing to forgo. In short, producers generally have an idea of the maximum price cut they would be prepared to make in order to meet competition from imports; if the difference between import prices and domestic prices exceeds that tolerable price cut, then they call the situation "market disruption" and hire lawyers and lobbyists in order to enlist the coercive efforts of their government to secure relief from the pressure on their profits of the "excessively competing import."[43]

Textiles since 1960

A sharp increase in imports of cotton textiles to the United States in 1959 and 1960 prompted President Kennedy to appoint a cabinet committee on textiles that recommended a conference of the principal textile importing and exporting countries "to seek international understanding which will provide a basis for trade that will avoid undue disruption of established industries."[44]

The United States arranged a meeting that was held, under GATT auspices, in July 1961. The sixteen participating countries agreed on a short-term arrangement (STA), to be submitted to the GATT contracting parties, to "secure from exporting countries, where necessary, a measure of restraint in their export policy so as to avoid disruptive effects in import markets."[45] It also sought to increase access to markets where imports were subject to quantitative restrictions and to maintain orderly access to markets not subject to such restrictions.

The STA was to last only a year, while a long-term solution to the problem of market disruption was being devised. The long-term arrangement (LTA) was quickly designed, being similar to the STA in all essentials. Entering into force on October 1, 1962, for a period of five years, it has been extended for three-year periods through September 30, 1973.

43. Ibid., p. 33.
44. Press release, White House, May 2, 1961. The Organization for European Economic Cooperation had similarly recommended negotiations in 1957 between European and Asian countries.
45. GATT, *BISD,* 10th Supp. (1962), pp. 18 ff.

The LTA aimed at "co-operative and constructive action . . . designed to facilitate economic expansion and promote the development of less-developed countries . . . by providing larger opportunities for increasing their exchange earnings from the sale in world markets of products which they can efficiently manufacture . . . provided that the development of this trade proceeds in a reasonable and orderly manner so as to avoid disruptive effects in individual markets and on individual lines of production in both importing and exporting countries."[46]

Any participating country whose unrestricted market was being disrupted, or was threatened with disruption, by imports was authorized to request the exporting countries concerned to initiate consultations with a view to removing or avoiding such disruption. It was to supply to the exporting country and to the Cotton Textiles Committee (the agent of the LTA) a "detailed, factual statement of the reasons and justification for the request." If no agreement materialized within sixty days after the request was made, then the requesting country was authorized to decline to accept imports from the exporting country beyond the level established in the twelve-month period ending three months before the receipt of the request. If, on the other hand, agreement could be reached, the details would be spelled out in a bilateral agreement, thus changing restraint levels into export quotas.

Countries experiencing domestic market disruption can thus impose import quotas where they are unable to reach bilateral agreements. Quotas cannot be lower than the level determined by procedures specified in the agreement; annual increases in quotas (usually 5 percent) are provided for if the restraints remain in force for additional twelve-month periods. Exports of participating countries cannot be restrained more severely than those of nonparticipants.

Over the life of the LTA, emphasis has shifted from the use of restraint actions on the part of the United States to increased use of bilateral agreements. For example, in the first year of the LTA the United States invoked unilateral restraints 115 times and arrived at only 4 bilateral agreements. During the second year, restraints decreased to 67, while bilateral agreements increased to 13. Since 1964 the number of unilateral restrictions has been insignificant; by 1971 the United States had entered into bilateral cotton textile agreements with 25 governments. Imports from these coun-

46. 12 U.S.T., pt. 2, 1675, T.I.A.S. No. 4884 (1961).

tries accounted for about 90 percent of total U.S. imports of cotton textiles during 1966.[47]

While imports of cotton textiles have increased markedly under the LTA—for example, from 1.1 billion equivalent square yards during 1960 to 1.8 billion during 1966—opponents have made clear that they would have increased much more without the arrangement. The less developed countries have criticized the LTA for having contributed only marginally to the solution of the problem of market disruption in importing countries and having failed to help solve the problem of market expansion facing exporting countries. They believe the agreement has been used as a charter of restriction granting carte blanche for imposing restrictive measures. While exporting countries have been required to restrain their exports, importing countries are permitted to intensify investment in their domestic textile industries (and avoid phasing out inefficient sectors) or to concentrate on higher priced goods, thus paving the way for more restrictions later on. Moreover, because of the lack of a proper definition of market disruption, importing countries tend to consider as disruptive most adverse changes that occur in their textile industries, even when such changes result partly from internal factors. The overall result of the LTA has been a continuous resort to restrictive measures, while "the general declarations about expanding trade opportunities still evoke a distant reality."[48]

Indeed, the ink was hardly dry on the LTA when the American textile industry commenced a campaign to limit the imports of manmade-fibered and woolen products. Since the 1950s, synthetics manufacturers in the United States had seen their share of consumption of all textile fibers increase rapidly; between 1961 and 1970 their share of total U.S. mill consumption rose from about 31 percent to 63 percent. Meantime, the share for cotton declined from 62 percent to 33 percent, and that for wool from 6 percent to about 4 percent. While total imports rose sharply during the period, the domestic textile producers, "by most broad measures, enjoyed a period of unparalleled growth."[49]

"By and large this growth is attributable to the sustained rise in the

47. U.S. Tariff Commission, *Report to the President on Textile and Apparel,* T.C. Pub. No. 226 (January 1968), p. C-14.

48. Henry, "Voluntary Export Restraints."

49. Thomas Bradford Curtis and John Robert Vastine, *The Kennedy Round and the Future of American Trade* (Praeger, 1971), p. 181.

level of economic activity in the U.S. economy," the Tariff Commission concluded at the end of 1967. Along with increased output, sales and employment in the textile and apparel industries had expanded. New investment in the industries was at the rate of about $1 billion per year in 1966 and 1967. "For the producers of textile mill products, profits as a percentage of net sales rose by 48 percent . . . for the producers of apparel and related products . . . 52 percent. The corresponding gain for all manufacturing operations over the same period [1960–68] was 21 percent."[50]

Increased imports obviously have not caused or threatened injury to the domestic textile and apparel industries. Any restraint of imports would penalize the American consumer, artificially increasing prices and intensifying the upward movement of domestic price levels, and would limit less developed countries' access to the American market, running counter to the oft-asserted American policy of easing access.[51]

Not only would extension of the LTA to include manmade fibers and woolen goods harm the public interest, but through the suppression of competition it would bring windfall profits to private interests that are in good health.

It would be most unusual for an American industry to attempt to secure a subsidy in that form at the expense of the public interest because of *domestic* competition. That the textile industry has done so because imports have increased, though without injuring the industry, and that the President of the United States should have been seeking actively, on pain of taking unilateral restrictive action through invocation of control provisions contained in the Trading with the Enemy Act, to secure the agreement of exporting countries to curtail their export of these additional textiles, is an indication of the extent to which the old, discredited protectionism persists despite GATT principles to which all the developed countries profess allegiance. By mid-1972 the United States had negotiated such agreements with major Far Eastern suppliers, including Japan, Korea, Taiwan, and the Philippines.

---

50. Tariff Commission, *Report on Textile and Apparel*, p. 7. Sales of the domestic textile industry increased by over 11 percent from 1967 to 1968, and sales of the apparel industry by more than 10 percent. In 1969 and 1970 there was a drop, coincident with the downward trend of economic activity. See *Survey of Current Business*, Vol. 51 (March 1971), p. S-38.

51. The United States has gone so far as to support proposals for tariff preferences for less developed countries.

Steel

The steel industry has been similarly successful in winning voluntary arrangements on its products. In negotiations led by the assistant secretary of state for economic affairs the steel industries of Japan and the EEC countries first agreed in 1969 to curtail their exports to the United States.

Those negotiations were preceded by agitation on the part of the domestic steel industry, joined by the United Steelworkers of America, for the curtailment of imports. Many believe that the marked increase in imports was a consequence of domestic prices administered at high levels by an oligopolistic industry; high demand caused by domestic economic growth; and efficiently produced foreign steel underselling the American industry. No independent investigation like the Tariff Commission's inquiry on textiles and apparel was made of the economic condition of the steel industry. The industry did not desire it, and neither the President nor an appropriate congressional committee was prepared to request it. Nor was the steel industry prepared to make out a case under the escape clause for relief from serious injury; indeed, it has never protested that it was being injured by imports, which reached a high of about 17 million tons in 1968, when American production was moving over 141 million tons.[52] Moreover, the industry has never attempted to make a case under the national security amendment.

In spite of this, the domestic steel industry secured the desired import curtailment through the official intervention of the U.S. government. The usual threats of an even worse fate should they be unwilling to curtail exports induced the foreign industry to succumb, as the communications from the Japanese and EEC industries make quite clear.[53] The nine leading companies in the Japanese industry, accounting for 85 percent of exports to the United States, "gave assurances" that their steel mill product shipments to the United States would not exceed 5.5 million metric tons in

52. Letters of December 1968 from Japan and the EEC to the United States, in American Iron and Steel Institute, Communications and National Affairs Coordinating Committee, *Steel Imports—A National Concern* (July 1970), p. 16. In 1970, production dropped to approximately 131.5 million tons although imports decreased to about 13 million tons and exports increased substantially. *Survey of Current Business,* Vol. 51 (March 1971), pp. S-31, S-32.

53. See *State Department Bulletin,* Feb. 3, 1969, pp. 93–94, for texts of the communications and of Secretary Rusk's transmittal to the chairmen of the House Ways and Means Committee and the Senate Finance Committee, sent at the President's request.

1968 and would be confined to 5.75 million tons in 1969 with a 5 percent increase each year through 1971, "depending upon demand in the United States market and the necessity to maintain orderly marketing therein." The Japanese conditioned their commitment on a 14-million-ton limit on all U.S. steel imports in 1969, with 5 percent increases in the two following years. They further assumed "that the United States will take no action, including increase of import duties, to restrict Japanese steel mill product exports to the United States" and "that the above action by the Japanese steel companies does not infringe upon any laws of the United States of America and that it conforms to international law."

The EEC steel industry, comprised of syndicates in each of the member countries, made an identical commitment, with the sole exception that it spelled out its assumption that the United States would not take such actions as quota systems, increase of import duties, or other restrictions. The negotiations concluded early in 1972 renewed the voluntary arrangements on a somewhat more restrictive basis for an additional 3-year period.

Prospects for Negotiations on Quotas and Voluntary Agreements

The area for successful negotiation of U.S. quantitative restrictions, the most potent nontariff barriers affecting agricultural goods, is practically nonexistent. Import quotas are a reflection of domestic agricultural policies limiting production or marketing or artificially supporting prices, or both. Accordingly, whether tailored to a particular commodity, as with meat quotas, or rather generally applied, as with dairy products, the import restraint is in effect the tail wagged by the domestic agricultural policy dog. This is equally as true of the EEC's agricultural import restraints as it is of the quotas and related barriers to agricultural imports imposed by the United States or any other country. Were countries to attempt international negotiation of their agricultural import quotas without being prepared to negotiate concerning their domestic policies, they would resemble actors attempting to perform *Hamlet* without the Dane.

When countries are ready to discuss international trade in agricultural products, the negotiation will not concern nontariff barriers such as quotas, but rather who will produce what quantity of a particular product, and at what price domestically as well as abroad. It is most likely to involve a group of related commodities, aiming at a rationalized world production and marketing of such commodities. Import restraints would be auxiliaries of the production and marketing schemes and supportive of them.

In the nonagricultural products area, there is more room for successful negotiation of unilaterally imposed quotas and voluntary agreements having equivalent trade-restraining effect. The area for successful negotiation appears to lie, however, in procedural reforms rather than in substantive matters; the prospect for domestic changes in law and practice also appears to be in the procedural area.

Quotas on Industrial Goods

As the 1960 effort to define *market disruption* in GATT discloses, there is no international agreement on the concept outside of the escape clause itself. To agree on criteria for imposing restraints on imports that are not causing or threatening serious injury but are nonetheless considered to be disrupting the market of the importing country would appear to be at least as difficult now as it has ever been. Countries may, of course, wish to retreat to managed levels of bilateral trade such as those tried in the prewar period as well as in the more distant past.

For the concept of noninjurious disruption implies nothing less than that when market penetration achieved through comparative advantage in the production and distribution of an article becomes too much or occurs too rapidly, the importing country should be permitted to restrict the importation; and it should be allowed to do so even though no socially countervailing objective, such as avoidance of serious injury to a domestic industry, is being frustrated through the increase in imports.

If the effort to achieve freer international trade on the basis of comparative advantage in production and distribution of goods—the fundamental GATT principle—is to persist, it must continue to be based on the facts of economic life within and between nations. These facts, in the era since the industrial revolution began, are rapid technological changes unevenly occurring within and between countries; accelerated but uneven change in the political, social, and educational environment within and between countries; and extremely volatile transportation and marketing techniques which affect seriously and unevenly the distribution of goods.

Efforts to stem increased imports, like those to thwart technological change —whether to protect blacksmiths or to suppress cotton ginning inventions—are in essence attempts to thwart the consequences of economic and social development in the interest of a temporary status quo which is inconsistent with the dynamics of the societal changes that brought them about.

Any new move to delimit market disruption would soon become a discussion of the amount of increase in imports within what time span would be deemed impermissible because disruptive of a domestic market, and the duration of any restraints allowed. Agreement on industrial imports in general would appear to be far more difficult than on a particular commodity. Recent failures to satisfy domestic industry with voluntary restraints in textiles and steel indicate the extreme difficulty, if not the impossibility, of securing international agreement on commodities, even when extreme pressures seriously affecting international cohesion are applied. There is no reason to believe a more ambitious effort could succeed.

Indeed, the latest U.S. effort to legislate standards for limiting import penetration underlines the practical impossibility of securing permanent protection for domestic industries in the guise of preventing market disruption. In 1970, in an upsurge of protectionist sentiment, the House of Representatives passed the so-called Trade Act of 1970. The bill was blocked in the Senate by twenty-two supporters of the liberal trade policy embodied in the trade agreements legislation first enacted in 1934. The bill would have imposed quantitative restrictions on manmade textiles and woolens and on shoes, which would have cut imports to the average 1967–69 import levels, or by approximately 25 percent. To protect the smaller and much less politically influential industries having no poorer case than textiles or shoes, Representative John Byrnes of Wisconsin proposed an additional injury determination in escape clause cases brought before the Tariff Commission.

Under the Byrnes Basket, if imports had constituted more than 15 percent of apparent U.S. consumption of an article in the year preceding an escape clause case, and the ratio of imports to consumption had increased at least 3 percentage points over the previous year, and the ratio for the latter year had increased at least 2 percentage points over the year before, quantitative restrictions were indicated if increased imports were substantially causing or threatening serious injury.[54] Thus on an

54. H.R. 18970, 91 Cong. 2 sess. (1970), sec. 301(b)(1)–(5).

escape clause proceeding brought in 1971, additional injury could be found if imports of widget A were 16 percent of apparent consumption in 1969 and had increased by 3 percent from 1968 to 1969 and by 2 percent from 1967 to 1968.

The impact of the formula was clear, even if its rationale was not. A confidential list of products prepared by the Tariff Commission disclosed that some 120 products were put at risk of quotas by the Byrnes Basket, ranging from various types of fish (swordfish, sardines, canned oysters), to leather and furs, to textiles, marble, tile and chinaware, bauxite, sewing machines, radios and television sets, and passenger cars.[55] The dollar value of imports into the United States of these articles in 1969 was more than $6.8 billion, and the articles were exported from practically every country with which the United States trades.

At no point was the choice of percentages or their supposed relevance to injury explained. Whether they were judged to amount to too much import penetration too fast, looked at separately, or whether they were arbitrarily selected simply to gain the largest spread in quotas is likely to remain an unanswered riddle. It would be foolish, nonetheless, to assume that the numbers had nothing to do with a judgment by the House of Representatives that no greater degree and spread of import penetration would be tolerated.

There is no resemblance between the concept underlying the Byrnes Basket formula—that the United States favors trade on the basis of comparative advantage only if in fact imports remain quite small compared to domestic production—and the liberal trade principles of the trade agreements program. Any practical coexistence, if not ideological compatibility, of the two principles would depend on a very different set of numbers. Conceivably it would be possible to create some tolerable, if short-run, benchmarks if the figures reflected some general sense of reality. But the widely varying degrees and speed of import penetration make agreement on the statistical degree of penetration that could trigger restrictions highly unlikely. Even a penetration figure as high as 50 percent automatically constrains U.S. aircraft exports to a number of countries and Japanese radio imports in the United States and would thus be difficult to accept.

It is this fact, of course, that makes the Byrnes Basket numbers important. For if they reveal anything of congressional sentiment, they dis-

55. See *National Journal,* Aug. 22, 1970, p. 1850.

close a set of figures wholly outside the realm of practical accommodation among major trading nations. Substantive negotiations on principles of permissible market disruption would be certain to founder on the rocks of what is "too much, too soon," or spell the end of the effort represented by GATT.

Procedural Agreements on Quotas

That substantive international negotiations on market disruption are simply unrealistic does not signify, however, that procedural negotiations are beyond achievement. There is no obstacle, legal or political, to a country's consulting its trading partners who could be affected adversely in advance of the adoption of quantitative restrictions or of an effort to press for voluntary restraints over their exports. No statute forbids it, no public opinion opposes such consultation, which would be accorded the same treatment as consultation concerning troop levels in Europe and other defense contributions to the North Atlantic Treaty Organization over the past twenty years. It could be achieved through a presidential agreement within the leeway of existing federal legislation.

Advance consultation should logically be conducted in the GATT forum, preferably within a new consultative organ. Such a consultative organ would prepare factual materials, based on submissions by the principal countries affected, and otherwise organize justification-and-answer discussions among the trading partners whose exports and imports would be mutually affected.

Consultation is of course no guarantee that restrictive trade measures will not ensue. But it offers a significant opportunity to prevent some and to lessen the severity of others. Advance consultation would be a distinct step forward toward freer trade. It is a legally and politically practical step. Nations should lose no time in adopting it by formal agreement and institutionalizing it within the GATT framework.

In the United States several necessary and, indeed, complementary measures should be taken to retard the imposition of quantitative restrictions on imports or voluntary restraints over exports. In a number of places, American domestic law provides for quotas on imports after an objective investigation of facts by a government agency. Thus, a reasoned governmental case that temporary restraints are necessary to prevent material interference with agricultural support programs, to remedy serious injury due to imports, and to avoid impairment of national security is required before unilateral quota action can be taken. The orderly marketing clause of the Trade Expansion Act requires such an objective investigation and finding of serious injury due to imports before the President may "negotiate international agreements with foreign governments limiting exports to the United States of goods causing serious injury," in lieu of establishing unilateral quotas or raising import duties.

Indeed, the only authority Congress has given the President to restrict imports without an objective factual investigation is to limit agricultural and textile products under the Agricultural Act of 1956. That authority, standing independently, is a mistake. International agreements limiting agricultural or textile imports should be authorized only in lieu of unilateral quotas imposed to support domestic production and marketing controls, and hence only after an affirmative finding of material interference with existing support programs.

Accordingly, the President should as a matter of policy refrain from negotiating agreements restraining imports of agricultural products, or of nonagricultural products and textiles, or inducing voluntary restraints by foreign governments or industry groups, unless there is a finding of material interference or serious injury. Such an investigation should be comprehensive, including specific information on the effect of any import curtailment on inflation, on consumers' welfare, and on the total national interest. The Agriculture Department and the Tariff Commission can develop adequately the economic facts. Neither has the talent or the expertise to assess the wider national interest. The President can be assisted in this task by the Office of Special Representative for Trade Negotiations and the interagency trade organization under it.

It follows that no international agreement should be negotiated, no voluntary restraint by foreign governments or foreign industry groups should be induced by the U.S. government, without a prior presidential determination, reasoned, public, and based on an objective factual appraisal with full opportunity for public participation. Under existing law, an independent factual appraisal is a sine qua non for any sort of presidential action liberalizing import restrictions. It is not too much to require such an investigation and appraisal before restrictive action is taken that harms American consumers, feeds inflation, and adversely affects the successful conduct of the foreign relations of the United States.

To summarize, in the quota and voluntary agreement area there are two approaches, one international, the other domestic, that offer promise of ameliorating the adverse effects on international trade caused by this trade barrier. The international approach is through agreement among nations to consult in advance of imposing quotas unilaterally or imposing pressure for voluntary agreements. On the part of the United States, this may be done by presidential agreement within the leeway of existing federal legislation. The second approach is through domestic legislation, or presidential action, or both, in the United States requiring that import restraints in the form of voluntary obligations assumed by foreign governments, trade associations, or companies not be induced by the United States in the absence of a prior presidential determination based on an objective and independent investigation.

CHAPTER SIX

Customs Valuation

THE UNITED STATES relies on two main types of duties on imported merchandise. It assesses duties at specific rates on weight, volume, or quantity (3 cents per pound, 2 cents per cubic foot), sometimes bringing value ranges into consideration (3 cents per pound if valued less than 90 cents per unit). The second category of U.S. duties, the ad valorem rate, is expressed as a percentage of the value of the imported merchandise. Like the value range method of applying specific rates, it requires an appraisement of the value of the goods. Sometimes an item will be subject to a combination of rates, a compound rate of duty—for example, 2 cents per pound plus 10 percent ad valorem.

Obviously, classification of merchandise for duty assessment is a critical first step in the import process. In its potential and some of its actual effects, customs valuation is perhaps the most important nontariff trade barrier in the United States. Not only tariffs, but some quotas, a number of other assessments, and even certain duty classifications depend on the assessed value of an imported product. Valuation is a barrier in part because of the uncertain and potentially arbitrary methods for determining dutiable value, and in part because determinations are made on substantially different bases than those used elsewhere.[1] Rather than reflecting the realities of international commerce, U.S. valuation bases are in some instances

1. See John Howard Jackson, *World Trade and the Law of GATT* (Bobbs-Merrill, 1969), p. 211; Robert E. Baldwin, *Nontariff Distortions of International Trade* (Brookings Institution, 1970), p. 137; Craig Mathews, "Non-Tariff Import Restrictions: Remedies Available in United States Law," *Michigan Law Review,* Vol. 62 (1964), pp. 1295, 1313.

clearly protectionist; and the U.S. valuation process and standards are more intricate, more confusing, and sometimes more inequitable than those of other major trading nations.

The Valuation Process

The intricacies of the entry process often add inconveniences and costs to the importation of goods. Furthermore, at various stages of the process, individual consular or customs officials can, through relatively hasty and arbitrary decisions, significantly affect the ability of merchandise to enter the United States, or to enter in a reasonable amount of time with a tariff or other assessment that is within the limits that Congress intended. In addition, the amount of duty the importer will be required to pay is often uncertain, not only because of valuation standards but because of the valuation process itself.

The entry process—a labyrinth of pitfalls that imported merchandise must survive before valuation standards are actually applied—falls into two stages, one when merchandise is being prepared for export and is exported, and the other when the merchandise is received in the United States, legally entered, appraised, and liquidated. Legislation with respect to both stages dates back to the nineteenth century.[2]

Exportation

A special customs invoice must normally be prepared at the port of exportation for merchandise being shipped to the United States. The invoice must contain a detailed description of the merchandise, including quantity and quality; a detailed description of the proposed import transaction (when and where the merchandise was or will be sold, by and to whom, the shipping point, the destination and port of entry); the purchase price, or the value of the goods if sold in the ordinary course of trade in the country of exportation; the currency in which value is stated; an itemization of all charges on the merchandise; an itemization of all drawbacks, rebates, or bounties on the merchandise; other information relevant to

2. For regulations governing the valuation process, see 19 C.F.R. pts. 8–16 (1970).

the appraisement and classification of the merchandise; and the origin and price of the merchandise if it is not shipped by the manufacturer. Each invoice may represent only one shipment of merchandise by one consignor to one consignee by one vessel or conveyance, with the exception of installment shipments arriving in the United States within seven days after the receipt of the invoice. In addition, each invoice must contain specific information called for by the classification in which the merchandise belongs.

Although the secretary of the treasury may require that the invoice be certified by a U.S. consular officer at the point of packaging or shipment, the person preparing the invoice normally proposes a classification and valuation based on his reading of the U.S. customs laws. The exporter retains a copy of the invoice and sends one to the carrier, to accompany the merchandise to the port of entry, and two to a U.S. consular officer, one for his files and the other for delivery to the collector of customs at the port of entry in the United States.

Importation

All merchandise imported into the United States must be entered unless specifically exempted (the main exemptions are merchandise valued in the country of shipment at less than $1, bona fide gifts received by one person in one day not exceeding $10 in aggregate value, certain packed packages, and certain mailed merchandise under $250 in value). In a normal commercial transaction, the consignee of the imported merchandise must enter it at a U.S. customs house within five days after its arrival at the port of entry. He must present a bill of lading, the invoice,[3] a declaration that the invoice and other documents are either true and correct or true and correct to the best of his knowledge and belief, and an entry form. The consignee may amend the invoice value upon entry.[4] Normally he deposits at this time the estimated duty payable on the imported merchandise; after final appraisal, differences are refunded or billed to the consignee.

---

3. The customs officer may require a verified statement of the cost of production from the manufacturer when he feels that such a statement is necessary to the appraisement of the merchandise.

4. Under certain narrowly construed circumstances, the customs collector can waive the invoice requirement.

The entry document is used for assessing duties, securing a proper examination and inspection of merchandise, classifying it, and appraising it. It varies, depending on such things as the purpose of entry, the dutiability of the merchandise, and the type of transaction involved. It must show the quantity of each class of merchandise; the claimed rate or rates of duty for each class; the aggregate of the entered value for each class (except for entry by appraisement); a description of the merchandise in terms of the claimed tariff classification; and the aggregate of the entered values of all merchandise on each invoice covered by the entry (gross value less the value of nondutiable items).

Appraisement

When the merchandise and its documentation are presented to the customs officer, he attaches a statement specifying the kinds and quantities of the merchandise and the value of the total quantity of each kind of article. For each invoice, he designates on a customs form the packages to be examined and the place where the examination is to be made. This order of appraisement must be applied to at least one in every ten packages. One exception to the rule is that "when deemed sufficient for the purposes, samples of merchandise may be used for examination and appraisement. Representative samples shall be selected by . . . an authorized customs officer from the merchandise or packages designated by the collector for examination, and shall be properly marked to insure identification and retained as long as the appraiser shall deem necessary."[5] The district director of customs is also given broad discretion to require samples from packages not designated for examination.

DUTIES OF DISTRICT DIRECTORS

The district director of customs is responsible for performing the appraisement functions. He must "appraise the merchandise in the unit of quantity in which the merchandise is usually bought and sold by ascertaining or estimating the value thereof by all reasonable ways and means in his power, any statement of cost or costs of production in any invoice, affidavit, declaration, or other document to the contrary notwithstanding."[6]

5. 19 C.F.R. sec. 14.3(g) (1970).
6. 19 U.S.C.A. sec. 1500 (1970).

He then determines the classification and rate of duty applicable, fixes the amount of duty and determines any amounts due or deposited in excess of the duty, liquidates the entry, and notifies the importer, his consignee, or agent.

The appraiser's performance, obviously, is crucial to the determination of the types and amounts of import restrictions imposed on imported merchandise.

POWERS OF CUSTOMS OFFICERS

Customs officers have very broad investigatory powers during the entry, classification, and appraisement processes. They may require "any owner, importer, consignee, agent or other person" to appear before them and be examined under oath "upon any matter or thing which they . . . deem material respecting any imported merchandise then under consideration or previously imported within one year, in ascertaining the classification or the value thereof or the rate or amount of duty." They may also "require the production of any letters, accounts, contracts, invoices, or other documents relating to said merchandise." At their discretion, appraisers and collectors may require any such evidence to be reduced to writing to "be given consideration in subsequent proceedings relating to such merchandise" (a reappraisement proceeding, or a criminal proceeding for improper statements as to value or nature of merchandise).[7] Failure to comply with such requests subjects the importer to criminal penalties.

Any appropriate customs officer, the secretary of the treasury, or the U.S. Customs Court may inspect the "books, papers, records, accounts, documents, or correspondence, pertaining to the value or classification of such [imported] merchandise" of "any person importing merchandise into the United States or dealing in imported merchandise."[8] If such inspections are refused, the secretary of the treasury is *required* to prohibit further importation of such merchandise into the United States by or for the account of such person, and to instruct the collectors to withhold delivery of such merchandise. If the failure continues for one year, the merchandise is forfeited.

VALUE DETERMINATIONS

The value of imported merchandise is determined in accordance with Section 402 of the Tariff Act of 1930. For some merchandise, customs

7. 19 U.S.C.A. sec. 1509 (1970).
8. 19 U.S.C.A. sec. 1511 (1970).

officers must decide whether the value falls within the scope of values on a final list of items given special treatment (Section 402a). If the decision is affirmative, the article must be classified and appraised by a different formula than that used for ordinary goods. Establishment of the date of exportation of the merchandise may be important, since it also affects valuation. Though the regulations provide that it is the date on which the merchandise actually leaves the country of exportation for the United States, there is considerable room for the exercise of the appraiser's discretion in making this and similar determinations.

The district director is also given very broad discretion to "determine the amount and dutiability of any costs, charges, and expenses which are incident to making the merchandise ready for shipment" to the United States. He has considerable discretion in determining whether "merchandise imported from one country, being the growth, production or manufacture of another country, . . . was destined for the United States at the time of original shipments";[9] on that decision depends which country's principal markets shall be used to establish the value of the merchandise. Although the district director must furnish the importer with the latest information he has as to the values of the merchandise, when the appraised value is higher than entered value, or when there is a classification change resulting from appraiser's value determination, or upon written request with cause, the procedural inconveniences in obtaining the information are so great that an importer is unlikely to object to a valuation at this early stage.

In addition, the district director has broad authority to review the entire transaction for errors, including errors in the construction of the law and errors adverse to the government as well as the importer. He may reliquidate on his own initiative within ninety days from the original notice of liquidation. Beyond this ninety-day period he may still act on the timely application of a party to review clerical errors and inadvertent or factual mistakes. This power is generally limited to one year and does not include authority to correct an error in the construction of the law.

The customs official liquidates the entry by calculating the duties on the imported merchandise. After the consignee pays any charges in excess of his deposit, the merchandise is released from customs custody; the release may be conditional, however, or subject to revision if new information as to value is found at a later date.

9. 19 C.F.R. sec. 14.3(d) (1970).

PROTEST OF APPRAISAL

Any importer, consignee, or person paying any charge may file a protest concerning the appraisal within ninety days of the liquidation or of the protested decision. The district director normally has a two-year period in which to make his review and take action; the importer, however, may request an accelerated disposition after ninety days, in which case the director must act within thirty days (failure to do so is deemed a denial of the claim).

A protesting party may seek a review by the commissioner of customs in lieu of the district director if he feels that the decision protested was inconsistent with a published ruling of the commissioner or with a decision made in any district on the same type merchandise, or that the question of law or fact involved has not been ruled on by the commissioner of customs or the Customs Court, or that, although the matter has been previously ruled on, new facts or legal arguments are now alleged. The importer's only recourse from denial of his protest by the commissioner is the bringing of civil suit in Customs Court.

In court the importer bears the burden of establishing that the classification and standard used by the appraising officer is erroneous, since the appraiser's actions are presumed correct[10] and hence prevail unless proven otherwise.[11] Thus, the government is required to prove the correctness of the appraised value only after the opposing party has made a showing that the appraisement is erroneous.[12]

When an American manufacturer, producer, or wholesaler believes that the appraised value of imported merchandise of a class or kind sold by him is too low, he may file a petition with the secretary of the treasury setting forth the value at which he believes the merchandise should be appraised and the facts on which he bases his belief. If the secretary finds the appraisal too low, he can determine the proper rate. If the secretary agrees with the original decision, the petitioner may contest the appraised value in Customs Court.

---

10. *Greb Industries, Ltd. v. United States,* 308 F. Supp. 88 (Cust. Ct. 1970) RD 11691; *Nomura (American) Corp. v. United States,* 299 F. Supp. 535 (Cust. Ct. 1969); *G. R. Bolton, Inc. v. United States,* 297 F. Supp. 1385 (Cust. Ct. 1969); *A. Zerkowitz and Co. v. United States,* 297 F. Supp. 350 (Cust. Ct. 1969).

11. *Ellis Silver Co. v. United States,* 308 F. Supp. 704 (Cust. Ct. 1969) RD 11688; *United States v. E. R. Squibb & Sons,* 42 C.C.P.A. 23 (1956).

12. *Frank P. Dow Co. v. United States,* 276 F. Supp. 1013 (Cust. Ct. 1967).

Valuation Standards

Dutiable value is a legal concept referring to the established base for the assessment of duties on imported goods. Customs valuation is a comprehensive act of relating a particular tariff rate to a duty value.

Duty valuation is figured from the basic cost of the goods; charges for finishing, packing, containers, transportation, insurance, subsidies, or abatements; the place where and the time when the goods are to be valued; and documentary evidence of these data.

Dutiable value is not solely related, however, to tariff imposition. It figures significantly in the determination of quantitative restrictions that limit the amount or value of goods that can be imported during a given period. Once the cut-off point is reached, no further goods may be imported under an absolute quota, or further imports may enter only at a higher tariff rate under a tariff quota. In either situation, dutiable value is the basis for applying the restriction.

The Tariff Act of 1930, as amended, establishes a primary, or basic, method of duty valuation and eight alternate standards that are triggered, in succession, when the prior method does not apply. The valuation standards for most imported merchandise (Section 402) are a revision of standards that applied prior to 1958. For a small amount of goods not included in the revision, the earlier valuation system continues to apply. These latter goods are specified on a "final list" drawn up by the secretary of the treasury in 1958 (Section 402a) that includes only items whose appraised value (based on the imports of fiscal 1954) would have fallen 5 percent or more under the revised standards.

The bases of value, under Section 402 of the Tariff Act of 1930, for the majority of imports are:

1. the export value, or
2. if the export value cannot be determined satisfactorily, then the United States value, or
3. if neither the export value nor the United States value can be determined satisfactorily, then the constructed value; except that, in the case of an imported article subject to a rate of duty based on the American selling price of a domestic article, such value shall be—
4. the American selling price of such domestic article.[13]

13. 19 U.S.C.A. sec. 1401a (1970).

The bases of value, under Section 402a of the act, for imports on the final list are:

1. the foreign value or the export value, whichever is higher;
2. if neither the foreign value nor the export value can be satisfactorily ascertained, then the United States value;
3. if neither the foreign value, nor the export value, nor the United States value can be satisfactorily ascertained, then the cost of production;
4. in the case of an imported article subject to a rate of duty based on the American selling price of a domestic article, such value shall be the American selling price of such domestic article.[14]

Ad valorem rates are based on the values determined by these priorities.

Export value

The primary standard of export value is "the price, at the time of exportation to the United States, at which the merchandise identical with imported or similar to the imported merchandise is freely sold or offered for sale in the usual wholesale quantities in the principal markets of the country of exportation for export to the United States, packed ready for shipment."[15]

This export market value need not be the same as other manufacturers' prices for the same or similar merchandise, although such other prices may be evidence of a fairly reflected export market value. The price is not synonymous with a negotiated or contract price; in determining the fairness of export prices, sales or offers to sell for home consumption as well as costs of production can properly be considered. Moreover, when the U.S. importer is an exclusive agent of the exporter or an affiliate or subsidiary, the prices at which the merchandise is freely offered for sale may suffice.

Determination of whether such charges as the cost of services, inland freight charges, taxes, and commissions should be included in the export value depends on whether or not the merchandise is ever sold or offered for sale at prices that do not include these additional charges. Charges

14. 19 U.S.C.A. sec. 1402 (1970).
15. U.S. Tariff Commission, *Report on Customs Valuation*, T.C. Pub. No. 180 (July 1966), p. 12; *Erb & Gray Scientific, Inc. v. United States*, 53 C.C.P.A. 46 (1966); *United States v. Continental Forwarding, Inc.*, 53 C.C.P.A. 105 (1966).

that accrue subsequent to the sale, however—inland freight, storage, and shipping insurance on merchandise priced ready for shipment to the United States either from the factory or from a specific destination loading point—are not included in the export value. Moreover, a buying commission is not deemed part of the export value, but a selling commission is includable. However, a buying commission is deemed part of the actual market value of goods when all ordinary sales include such a commission.

It is evident that a c.i.f. (cost, insurance, and freight) duty-paid delivered price is not what is meant by export value under the primary standard. Moreover, export value cannot be determined by deducting an arbitrary amount for post-export costs but must show that the deductions represent the actual charges.

Other factors that compound the exporter's difficulty in determining what duty he must pay are the terms *such or similar merchandise, freely offered for sale, usual wholesale quantities, principal markets,* and *ordinary course of trade.* They represent either legal prerequisites to the employment of export value as a standard or vital elements of the concept of export value. These imponderables, which make it almost impossible to ascertain in advance the amount of duty, or even more basically, to anticipate the valuation standard that will be used or the valuation basis or dutiable value on which the ad valorem rate will be computed, are a significant nontariff barrier to trade.

FREELY OFFERED OR SOLD

The term *freely offered or sold* has been included in the requirements for applying the export value standard in order to exclude the use of prices that are the result of a controlled market.[16]

The term "freely sold or, in the absence of sales, offered for sale" means sold or, in the absence of sales, offered—(a) to all purchasers at wholesale, or (b) in the ordinary course of trade to one or more selected purchasers at wholesale at a price which fairly reflects the market value of the merchandise, without restrictions as to the disposition or use of the merchandise by the purchaser, except restrictions as to such disposition or use which (i) are imposed or required by law, (ii) limit the price at which or the territory in which the mer-

---

16. A manufacturer who sells at different prices for home consumption and for export has been more rigorously required to explain his prices than one who sells only for export at a price different from that of his competitors. *United States v. Lockwood and Freidin,* 287 F. Supp. 283 (Cust. Ct. 1968).

chandise may be resold, or (iii) do not substantially affect the value of the merchandise to usual purchasers at wholesale.[17]

Merchandise like or similar to that imported must be freely offered to all purchasers, not just the greatest number or those of a particular class. *Freely offered or sold* refers to a price unrestricted by customer designations.

Where the merchandise is exclusively sold to a selected purchaser, however, the export value is the price at which such or similar merchandise is freely sold or offered in the ordinary course of trade to one or more selected purchasers at wholesale. Moreover, that price must fairly reflect market value of the merchandise. Should the price not fairly reflect market value, then the imports cannot be deemed freely sold and the export value standard cannot be applied.

SUCH OR SIMILAR MERCHANDISE

The term "such or similar merchandise" means merchandise in the first of the following categories in respect of which export value, United States value, or constructed value, as the case may be, can be satisfactorily determined:

(A) The merchandise undergoing appraisement and other merchandise which is identical in physical characteristics with, and was produced in the same country by the same person as, the merchandise undergoing appraisement.

(B) Merchandise which is identical in physical characteristics with, and was produced by another person in the same country as, the merchandise undergoing appraisement.

(C) Merchandise (i) produced in the same country and by the same person as the merchandise undergoing appraisement, (ii) like the merchandise undergoing appraisement in component material or materials and in the purposes for which used, and (iii) approximately equal in commercial value to the merchandise undergoing appraisement.

(D) Merchandise which satisfies all the requirements of subdivision (C) except that it was produced by another person.[18]

It has long been established that the words *such* and *similar* are distinctive and alternate terms, *such* meaning identical and having priority over *similar*. Similarity is recognized as similarity in construction, use of same materials; commercial interchangeability; or similarity in potential and actual use. Thus the price at which such or similar merchandise is freely sold in the ordinary course of trade *by others* may be used in the definition

17. 19 U.S.C.A. sec. 1401a (1970).
18. Ibid.

of export value for imported merchandise that is not itself freely sold. However, where the foreign manufacturer's selling prices do represent export value, such or similar merchandise produced by other manufacturers may be considered only to assure that the prices of the imported goods fairly reflect market value. Moreover, if export value has been ascertained for merchandise identical in physical characteristics with and produced in the same country by the same person as the merchandise undergoing appraisement, no other reference is necessary.

USUAL WHOLESALE QUANTITIES

The term "usual wholesale quantities," in any case in which the merchandise in respect of which value is being determined is sold in the market under consideration at different prices for different quantities, means the quantities in which such merchandise is there sold at the price or prices for one quantity in an aggregate volume which is greater than the aggregate volume sold at the price or prices for any other quantity.

The term "purchasers at wholesale" means purchasers who buy in the usual wholesale quantities for industrial use or for sale otherwise than at retail; or, if there are no such purchasers, then all other purchasers for resale who buy in the usual wholesale quantities; or, if there are not purchasers in either of the foregoing categories, then all other purchasers who buy in the usual wholesale quantities.[19]

Use of the quantity element to establish value recognizes that the basic unit price of merchandise is related, directly or indirectly, to the size of the purchase, reflecting the principle of economies of scale. The quantity terms are not arbitrarily tied to a specific transaction level, such as that of a wholesaler. Clearly, the term *purchasers at wholesale* relates merchandise sold at different prices depending on the quantity purchased to the volume of sales rather than the level at which the purchaser functions. However, comparative volume is immaterial where the price is the same regardless of quantity.

The price for *usual wholesale quantities* represents a basis of valuation irrespective of the particular quantity imported. It is a definitional term determined by that quantity most frequently sold in the export market. Thus the importer who finances large purchases at lower prices than the importer who deals in smaller quantities will not have a lower unit valuation, for the *usual wholesale quantity* is a constant of the particular export

19. Ibid.

market. Moreover, it is derived from all sales in the *quantity most fre-quently sold,* whether the purchaser be retailer or wholesaler.

ORDINARY COURSE OF TRADE

The term "ordinary course of trade" means the conditions and practices which, for a reasonable time prior to the exportation of the merchandise under-going appraisement, have been normal in the trade under consideration with respect to merchandise of the same class or kind as the merchandise under-going appraisement.[20]

The term *ordinary course of trade* is used to insure that a dutiable value basis is isolated that fairly reflects the nonnegotiated export market value of the goods imported. The term has no substantive significance peculiar to itself, but functions as a modifier of such terms as *usual wholesale quantities, freely offered for sale,* and *principal markets.*

PRINCIPAL MARKETS

The term *principal markets* is not specifically defined for purposes of determining export value. Moreover, the effect of this element may vary since there could be more than one principal market, and location may determine whether certain inland costs and charges, as well as services, are includable in the dutiable value basis. The principal markets are the main, leading, or chief places where goods are offered for export, as dis-tinguished from those places where the merchandise is manufactured or delivered.

United States Value

Fundamentally, U.S. value is a constructed export value that is arrived at by working backward from the selling price of the imported article in the U.S. market. It is

the price, at the time of exportation of the merchandise being valued, at which merchandise identical with or similar to the imported merchandise is freely sold or offered for sale in the usual wholesale quantities in the principal United States market, packed ready for delivery, less (a) the usual commissions or usual profit and general expenses on sales in the United States, (b) the usual cost of shipping it from the point of shipment in the foreign country to the

20. Ibid.

place of delivery in the United States, and (c) all customs duties and other Federal taxes applicable by reason of importation.[21]

The definitions of *such or similar merchandise, freely sold or offered for sale, usual wholesale quantities,* and *ordinary course of trade* are essentially the same for the U.S. value standard as for the export value standard. In determining the U.S. value it is necessary to isolate the principal U.S. market. Allowances for profits are based on the profits for such or similar merchandise, not on the profits for the firm or the industry as a whole. Generally, U.S. internal revenue taxes applicable to imports are included in the selling price in the United States and may not be deducted to arrive at the United States value.

The requirement that there be a freely offered price in the U.S. market on the date of exportation has been interpreted to mean a price based on a previous or prototype importation of such or similar merchandise that has been appraised on the basis of the cost-of-production standard. The deductions allowable in determining U.S. value are those incidental to the prototype import rather than to the goods under appraisement. The importer thus cannot use the price of the merchandise being imported to estimate the U.S. value. Nor can he predict the deductions that will be allowed for profits and general expenses.

Constructed Value

Constructed value is the basis for determining dutiable value when neither export nor U.S. value is applicable. It is

the sum, at a time sufficiently before the date of exportation to permit production, of the cost of producing the imported or similar merchandise and the usual general expenses and profit on sales of such merchandise made in the country of exportation, in the usual wholesale quantities for shipment to the United States, packed ready for shipping to this country.[22]

Constructed value is used for goods in process that are imported for assembly or completion by an affiliate or a subsidiary and for which there is no commercial transaction or normal selling price in the merchandise's imported condition. The constructed value process is used to establish a

21. Tariff Commission, *Report on Customs Valuation,* p. 13.
22. Ibid.

market price when a prototype is being employed in the U.S. valuation method.

In all events, the statutory standards for constructed value must be satisfied before this basis of valuation can be validly applied. These standards include the fixing of the cost of production, the usual expenses, and the profit which must be added to arrive at dutiable value. Items such as the cost of material, labor and processing, general expenses and expenses of packing, as well as the profit which is ordinarily added by manufacturers in the same country of the same class or kind of product are those elements that establish a prima facie showing of constructed value (cost-of-production value under Section 402a).

The elements of constructed value represent separate classes of cost whose additions roughly parallel those deductions allowed in computing U.S. value. The constructed value is a hypothetical export value computed by working forward from the basic costs of material and labor rather than backward from the selling price in the U.S. market.

American Selling Price

Four categories of articles—benzenoid chemicals (formerly coal-tar products), rubber-soled footwear, canned clams, and certain wool-knit gloves—are protected by the American selling price (ASP). It is

the price, at the time of exportation of the imported article to the United States, at which an article produced in the United States and packed ready for delivery is sold or offered for sale for consumption in the principal U.S. market in the usual wholesale quantities; or the price which a U.S. manufacturer would have received or was willing to receive for it when sold for consumption in the United States.[23]

The ad valorem rates of duty of most imports are applied to the wholesale price of the merchandise in the country of exportation (the export value). The rates for the highly protected articles that fall within the American selling price categories, however, are based on the *wholesale price of the U.S. domestic product that is like, similar to, or competitive with the foreign import, irrespective of its value.* The American manufacturer, allegedly for lack of competitive strength, is given the advantage of adjusting the level of the tariff protection against the foreign import

23. Ibid., pp. 13–14.

by determining the wholesale price at which he sells domestically. While both the U.S. value and the American selling price are based on wholesale prices in the United States, the U.S. value is predicated on the *price of the imported product,* the American selling price on *that of the competitive domestic product.*

For benzenoid chemicals where there is no competitive domestic product comparable to the imported product under appraisement, the U.S. value standard is used. If that value is not applicable, either constructed value or export value, whichever is higher, is used. For other products in the ASP categories that cannot be valued on the basis of like or similar domestic products, the conventional methods are employed and the rate of duty is applied to the value of the imported article itself.

No major trading country other than the United States maintains a valuation standard predicated on domestic prices of the importing country for nonagricultural products, although the variable levy of the European Community is similar in effect. Thus the ASP remains the most evident manifestation of a nontariff trade barrier in the customs valuation area.

Foreign Value

The most conspicuous difference in valuation criteria for the majority of imports and those on the *final list* is the addition of *foreign value* as a primary standard for the latter. It shares priority with export value. Foreign value is

the price, at the time of exportation to the United States, at which such or similar merchandise is freely offered for sale in the usual wholesale quantities for consumption in the exporting country to all purchasers in the principal markets in that country, plus the cost of packing the merchandise for shipment to the United States.[24]

This standard of foreign value represents a general market price, as contrasted with a specific or negotiated purchase price, of imported merchandise in the principal markets of the exporting country.

Foreign and export value must be determined independently of each other and separately considered as to such or similar merchandise in ascertaining dutiable value for final list goods. Foreign value focuses on prices of goods for home consumption in the foreign country, export value

24. Ibid., p. 14.

on prices of goods purposely designated for export. Export value more closely approximates actual transaction prices than does foreign value.[25]

Foreign value is applicable where it is higher than, or exists in the absence of, export value. Foreign value is most often higher because it includes taxes of the foreign government (customs, internal revenue, excise, production, consumption, and so forth) as well as other costs and charges generally applied to goods entering at wholesale into the foreign country's consumption; these expenses become substantive elements of dutiable value, even though they are not levied on the actual merchandise exported to the United States. Where export value is applicable, such expenses are inapplicable.

SPECIAL DEFINITIONS

Before 1956, foreign value was the primary standard for all imports. The necessity of investigating foreign value so complicated the process of appraisement and led to such unnecessary disputes with foreign governments that the Treasury Department advocated its abolishment. The Customs Simplification Act of 1956 was the result.

The change was made possible only by a compromise that accommodated opponents' claim that a new valuation system would lead to significant duty reductions on some products. The act separated from the main body of imports those products on which the valuation would decrease substantially more than an overall average of 2.5 percent. The secretary of the treasury compiled a list of all products that under the new law would be valued at 95 percent or less than their appraised value in 1954; it included 1,015 items.

On a casual reading, "foreign value or export value whichever is higher" —the standard for final list products—would appear to be identical for all practical purposes with the standards for all other products. There are significant distinctions between them, however. The two differ in their

25. Export value for final list merchandise "shall be the market value or the price, at the time of exportation of such merchandise to the United States, at which such or similar merchandise is freely offered for sale to all purchasers in the principal markets of the country from which exported, in the usual wholesale quantities and in the ordinary course of trade, for exportation to the United States, plus, when not included in such price the cost of all containers and coverings of whatever nature, and all other costs, charges, and expenses incident to placing the merchandise in condition, packed ready for shipment to the United States." 19 U.S.C. sec. 1402 (1970).

treatment of the amounts that may be deducted for commissions, profits, and general expenses to the importer. The maximum deductions for final list products are fixed percentages; for all other products the deductions are defined as the "usual commissions, profits, and expenses."

The meanings of terms that apply to foreign value have been established by administrative or judicial precedent over a long period of years; the same terms under the new valuation standard have been statutorily defined. Thus *usual wholesale quantities* for final list products means the price freely offered for quantities in which the largest number of sales are made, but for other products quantities in which the largest volume of sales is made. *Freely offered* on final list items is the highest price any industrial user or reseller other than retailer must pay for a usual wholesale quantity. Other distinctions in the meanings of common terms at times result in differences between the dutiable values on the two categories of goods.

Other Final List Variations

Another requirement peculiar to goods on the final list is that such or similar merchandise must be *offered for sale to all purchasers* in the principal markets whether for home consumption, for exportation to the United States, or for domestic consumption. Thus sales that are restricted to a particular group of purchasers cannot be used to determine foreign value, based on sales in the home country; export value, based on sales for export to the United States; or U.S. value or American selling price, both based on prices in the domestic U.S. market. Likewise, the cost-of-production standard, which corresponds to the constructed value standard, approximates the market price in the home country for such merchandise.[26]

A Change in Standards

As the valuation system now stands, it is neither realistic nor manageable. A sensible change would be to increase emphasis on actual import transaction prices as a reflection of true value. Except where the trans-

26. The cost-of-production standard for final list items sets minimum levels of profit (8 percent) and of general expenses (10 percent) to be included. On constructed value the "usual profits and expenses" are allowed.

action is suspected of being used to avoid payment of duties rather than for normal commercial motives, there seems no reason for not using the invoice value. This, of course, would entail eliminating the foreign value provisions for final list items. Such an elimination would probably have little if any effect on revenue but would greatly reduce the workload of shippers and customs officials alike.

Valuation Standards and the GATT

The General Agreement on Tariffs and Trade (GATT) prohibits a contracting party from altering its method of determining dutiable value so as to impair the value of its tariff concessions (Art. II[3]). This negative obligation recognizes the potentiality for destructive use of customs valuation standards. For example, should the ad valorem rate of duty on an article valued at $1.00 be negotiated from 50 percent down to 25 percent, the tariff concession would result in a reduction of duty from 50 cents to 25 cents. But should the valuation standard be changed so as to increase the dutiable value basis to $2.00, the tariff concession would be a sham, for the new 25 percent rate would not lower the duty from the original 50 cents.

The GATT goes on to impose five affirmative obligations on the contracting parties. They are required to recognize the validity of the GATT valuation principles and to implement them in their domestic laws (Art. VII[1]). Each party agrees to review, at the request of another contracting party, the operation of its customs valuation standards (Art. VII[1]). Each must subscribe to a method of valuation that does not exceed the outer limits of actual value, as prescribed by GATT, or its nearest ascertainable equivalent (Art. VII[2]). Where the valuation requires foreign currencies to be converted into the importing country's currency, the conversion must be conducted under the exchange rate rules of the International Monetary Fund or comparable rules (Art. VII[4]). Each contracting party is required to publicize its standards of valuation and its administrative methods thereunder in order to assure a reasonable degree of certainty in transactions (Art. VII[5]).

In establishing valuation standards, GATT requires that "the value for customs purposes of imported merchandise should be based on the actual value of the imported merchandise on which duty is assessed, or of like merchandise, and should not be based on the value of merchandise of national origin or on arbitrary or fictitious values" (Art. VII[2][a]). Actual value is defined as "the price at which, at a time and place determined by the legislation of the country of importation, such or like merchandise is sold or offered for sale in the ordinary course of trade under fully competitive conditions" (Art. VII[2][b]). This definition recognizes the constant, recurring elements in any valuation standard: price, time, place, quantity, transaction level, and competition.

Where quantity is a factor in determining price, "the price to be considered should uniformly be related to either (i) comparable quantities, or (ii) quantities not less favourable to importers than those in which the greater volume of the merchandise is sold in the trade between the countries of exportation and importation" (Art. VII[2][b]). Though the transaction level is not specifically referred to, it is necessarily implied since it is one of the elements that conditions the factors of quantity and price.

The GATT attempts to work toward common principles on customs valuation, taking into account the variations and practices among the world trading partners. It begins with the premise that a tariff is the only permissible form of trade barrier and that any customs duty must bear a reasonable relation to the actual value of the imported merchandise. Any valuation basis, such as American selling price, predicated on the domestic market structure of the importing country is therefore fictitious or arbitrary. However, where such standards antedate the GATT, they do not constitute a violation of GATT because of the grandfather clause in the Protocol of Provisional Application of GATT.

To achieve a measure of certainty and yet accord latitude in the administration of customs laws, each country is required to set the time and place of importation, thereby fixing the point at which dutiable value is considered. This minimal requirement permits nations to subscribe to either an f.o.b. basis, referring to prices paid in the country of origin, or a c.i.f. basis, referring to prices paid in the country of importation.

The basis of dutiable value may not include any exempted or recoverable internal tax applicable within either the country of export or import, but may include "any non-included charges for legitimate costs which are proper elements of 'actual value' and plus any abnormal discount or other reduction from the ordinary competitive price."[27] Moreover, the

27. GATT, Annex I, art. VII(3), par. 1.

GATT recognizes that actual value may be represented by the invoice price, thus accommodating the Brussels Tariff Nomenclature (BTN) preference for this basis for a finding of normal price.

It allows dutiable value to be predicated "uniformly either (1) on the basis of a particular exporter's prices of the imported merchandise, or (2) on the basis of the general price level of like merchandise."[28]

One index of dutiable value is current domestic value, the price at which goods comparable with the exported merchandise are sold in the internal markets of the exporting country. This basis would include species of foreign value (goods offered or sold in the exporting country for home consumption) and export value (goods offered or sold in the exporting country for export) and constructed or cost-of-production standards.

Another index, transaction value, is the price at which the imported merchandise is sold from the exporting country to the importing country. This basis would include species of landed, c.i.f. values as evidenced by the invoice price. A third index, import market value, is the price at which merchandise comparable with the imported goods is sold in the markets of the importing country. This basis would include species of landed, c.i.f. values, but would not be restricted to the actual exporter's prices manifested in the invoice. Rather, it would recognize the general price level of imports in the country of importation. The U.S. value standard falls within this category of import market value. This basis is not fictitious or arbitrary, for the price is that of comparable domestically produced merchandise in the country of exportation.[29]

In recognition of the competition element of any definition of dutiable value, GATT permits a contracting party to exclude "any transaction wherein the buyer and seller are not independent of each other and price is not the sole consideration."[30] Moreover, because price is determined by that prevalent in the ordinary course of trade *under fully competitive conditions,* "prices involving special discounts limited to exclusive agents" may be excluded from consideration.[31] Each contracting party may decide for itself whether transactions of "associated houses" partake sufficiently of the competitive quality of an "at arm's length" transaction.[32]

28. Ibid., art. VII(2)(a and b), par. 4.
29. See "Report of the Working Party for the Ninth (Review) Session," in GATT, *Basic Instruments and Selected Documents,* ed. Supp. (1955), p. 104.
30. GATT, Annex I, art. VII(2), par. 2.
31. Ibid., par. 2.
32. Jackson, *World Trade and the Law of GATT* (1969), pp. 451–52.

The use of the standard of *such or like merchandise* injects another variable into the determination of dutiable value. It incorporates the problems of identifying product similarities and of classifying or determining when two physical entities bear such a relationship to each other as to permit the attachment of legal consequences to that association.

Correlation of Dutiable Value Definitions

Under GATT, the contracting parties must give effect to the principles of valuation "in respect of all products subject to duties or other charges or restrictions on importations and exportations based upon or regulated in any manner by value." The Brussels Tariff Nomenclature (BTN) recommends that "the concept of value . . . be employed for the valuing of all goods subject to customs declaration." The United States in its customs laws provides that the basis for the assessment of duties shall be the appraised value of the goods as determined by the applicable standard of valuation set forth in the statute. Thus, the GATT, the BTN, and U.S. law all postulate the imposition of tariffs on a concept of value.

The GATT basis of actual value is embodied in the Brussels definition of normal price. The U.S. counterpart is found in the standards of export value, U.S. value, constructed or cost-of-production value, and foreign value. Standards based on the "value of merchandise of national origin" are outlawed by GATT. The Brussels definition precludes such valuation by requiring that the value be that of the merchandise actually imported. The American selling price is the only U.S. standard of valuation that does not meet the GATT requirements.[33]

Valuation standards, according to GATT, must specify the time, place, quantity, and competitive conditions before duties may be imposed. The Brussels definition fixes the time as the time when the duty becomes payable; the United States as the time of exportation of the imported merchandise.

The place for determining the price is fixed under the BTN definition as the port or place of introduction of the merchandise into the country of importation; the United States specifies the place as the principal market in the exporting country for the standards of export, foreign, and con-

---

33. Any domestic valuation standard that imposes a duty on the value of comparable domestically produced goods, and not on the value of the imported merchandise, conflicts with the GATT standard.

structed (or cost-of-production) value, and as the principal market for the imports in the United States in determining U.S. value (place is ignored under the American selling price).

The GATT requires that where quantity influences the price, the actual value should be determined in relation to either comparable quantities or quantities not less favorable to importers than those in which the greater volume of the merchandise is sold in the trade between the countries of exportation and importation. The Brussels definition of normal price follows the GATT option of comparable quantities, providing that where value is dependent on the quantity element, it is necessary to assume that the sale is a sale of quantity to be valued. The U.S. specification of "usual wholesale quantities" is a variation of the two GATT options. For the majority of imports, it refers to an aggregate volume of trade between the exporting and the importing countries, but for items on the final list it refers to the greatest number of sales made in the exporting country of like or similar merchandise. Under the GATT both the volume and the number of sales standards in the second option are tied to the volume of trade between the two countries, which is a reference point distinct from the volume of trade in the markets of the exporting country itself. Moreover, the use of the term *wholesale* in the U.S. definitions of value signifies not so much a level of transaction (within the chain of distribution) as a reinforcement of the aggregate volume quantity concept.

The GATT definition of actual value—the price at which such or like merchandise is sold or offered for sale in the ordinary course of trade under fully competitive conditions—is comparable to the BTN definition of normal price—the price which the imported goods would fetch on a sale in the open market between buyer and seller independent of each other—and the phrases explaining competitive level are regarded as identical in meaning. The U.S. definition must be gleaned indirectly from the use of the terms "such or similar merchandise is *freely* sold or, in the absence of sales, offered for sale . . . in the ordinary course of trade," which have been interpreted to refer to a competitive market that is not controlled by a party to the transaction.

GATT provides for an alternate standard of valuation based on the nearest ascertainable equivalent of actual value, and the United States employs the alternate secondary standards of U.S. value and constructed or cost-of-production value which are constructs of its primary standard of export value or of foreign value. The BTN, which is uniformly applicable to all imports, requires that the dutiable value basis be the nearest ascertainable equivalent to the normal price. Where the price cannot be ascertained, the normal price will be the price that the imported goods *would fetch* on a sale. This *would-fetch* basis necessarily implies a factually corroborated value basis, comparable in spirit to the actual value requirement of the GATT.[34]

GATT requires that the rates of the International Monetary Fund be used when the value of the import must be converted to that of the country of importation. The Brussels definition specifies that when the value of the imports depends on factors expressed in a currency other than that of the country of importation, conversion is to be made at the official rate of exchange applied by the country of importation to the currency of the exporting country. Prior to 1971, both the United States and the BTN countries adhered to rates of exchange generally corresponding to those established in conformity with the requirements of the International Monetary Fund.

The United States and the BTN countries comply with the GATT obligations that the bases and methods of determining value be stable and that publicity be sufficient to permit traders to estimate beforehand the value for customs duties. Both publish tariff schedules and standards of valuation, the BTN through the Permanent Nomenclature Committee of the Customs Cooperation Council, and the United States through the secretary of the treasury, who is charged with disseminating such information as is necessary to secure a just, impartial, and uniform appraisement of imported merchandise and the classification and assessment of duties.

The world trading countries clearly satisfy the GATT valuation standards except where value is based on prices of goods produced in the importing country. The GATT objective of uniformity is unrealistic, however, because of basic differences that arise from the use of f.o.b. and c.i.f. standards.[35] In order to achieve true uniformity, GATT would have to eliminate the optional time–place requirement for valuation and specify either a c.i.f. or an f.o.b. basis. If this were done, upward or downward

---

34. See Brussels Tariff Nomenclature, Interpretative Note 5 to Article I.

35. F.o.b. (free on board) represents a price that includes all costs up to a certain point of departure or stage of delivery including transportation, packing, and insurance. C.i.f. (cost, insurance, and freight) represents a price that includes the cost of the merchandise, the freight charges to a specific destination, and the insurance on the shipment of goods.

rate adjustments would be in order, since tariff rates were set initially, and later negotiated, on the basis of differing standards.

If the actual value requirement of GATT is an attempt to reflect an objective value of goods in a competitive, open market, an f.o.b. standard appears to embody the proper approach. A c.i.f. standard permits greater variation of costs since the components of insurance and freight vary from shipment to shipment, depending not only on the type of transportation used (air freight being more expensive than sea freight) but also on the destination in the country of importation and that country's very location in relation to the country of exportation. As these variables add to the complexity of the valuation system or standard, they detract from the objective of uniformity. Ultimately a c.i.f. standard may result in an exporter's merchandise being accorded different dutiable values in different ports of entry in a single importing country. Moreover, insofar as the GATT represents the collective desire of countries to minimize their tariff barriers, the c.i.f. standard is less compatible than the f.o.b. standard, for it includes expenses up to the arrival of the merchandise in the port of entry in the country of importation and generally results in a higher dutiable value basis.

The breadth of the standards of valuation sanctioned by GATT leaves no country in the position of finding its valuation system as a whole inconsistent with the international requirements. In an effort to bring about more uniformity, a GATT working group has suggested that all countries accept the following principles:

(a) An acceptable valuation system should be neutral in its effect and in no case be used as a disguised means of offering additional protection over and above that provided by rates of customs duties either regularly, with respect to all shipments of particular kinds of goods, or in special cases when dumping was suspected, or to penalize imports from competitive sources.

(b) An acceptable system should be non-discriminatory as between different countries of supply.

(c) Valuation systems should be simple and in no case use arbitrary or fictitious values.

(d) Administration of valuation systems should take into account:

    (i) the need for advance certainty to traders as to which method of valuation would apply to particular classes of goods and types of shipment;

    (ii) full publicity to the bases on which value would be calculated under the method applicable (covering factors such as time, place, quantities, level of distribution to be considered);

(iii) expeditiousness of the procedure;
(iv) the safeguarding of business secrets;
(v) an adequate appeals procedure, carried out by agents independent of those making initial decision.[36]

While these principles deal explicitly with the trade barrier potential of valuation standards, they do not attack the lack of uniformity brought on by the basic difference in the f.o.b. and c.i.f. standards.

Moreover, these suggestions do not aid an importer who must decide from a multiplicity of statutory standards, as in the United States, which standard is applicable to his particular transaction. The greater the uncertainty facing the importer, the greater is the measure of protection accorded the domestic industry.

Postwar Attempts to Change the U.S. System

Many of the U.S. importation and valuation procedures and standards are, arguably, trade-distorting—some more so than others. Matters that have caused particular concern in other countries are the complexity of the U.S. standards (nine possibilities) in comparison with those of the BTN countries; the added complication of a system based on f.o.b. value rather than the commonly used c.i.f. value; the unreasonable ASP standard that bases value on competitive U.S. products whose prices are artificially determined by U.S. manufacturers; and the discriminatory standard of foreign value for final list items that includes charges omitted in the other standards.

It has been argued, on the other hand, that the inequities of the U.S. system are minimal when it is compared with most other countries' valuation systems. For example, it has been suggested that a changeover to the BTN system, though it might bring uniformity, would not solve the significant problems that already exist of nonuniform application among the BTN countries; in other words, de facto, not de jure, uniformity must be insured before a complete overhaul of the Tariff Schedule of the United States (TSUS) could be justified.[37] Similar arguments have been made against changing from the U.S. system of f.o.b. values to the c.i.f. values

36. *Report of Working Group 2 on Non-Tariff Barriers*, GATT Spec. 70 (April 10, 1970), p. 3.
37. Baldwin, *Nontariff Distortions*, p. 138.

of most of the rest of the world. Serious attempts have been made since 1947, however, to alleviate other effects of the U.S. system in tacit admission of their inequity. This has been particularly true with regard to *American selling price,* which is the most blatantly unreasonable barrier, and to a lesser extent with regard to the *final list* and *foreign value.* In addition, there have been various attempts to simplify the complexities of the valuation process.

Customs Simplification Act of 1956

Foreign value as a basis for appraisement became an issue in the United States in the early 1950s, when it was found to be a hindrance to the entry of foreign goods.[38] The move to eliminate that valuation base and bring others into conformity with current trade practices resulted in the Customs Simplification Act of 1956. Objections of certain industries threatened by lowered tariff barriers led to retention of the foreign value base of items designated on the secretary of the treasury's final list.

The final list was intended to include only those products whose appraised value would drop at least 5 percent under the new provisions. By 1965, the Bureau of Customs found, the listed products averaged only 2.1 percent lower by foreign value than they would on export value, and for several products the appraised values would be higher if the final list were terminated. The passage of time, in effect, had nullified the final list. The 2.1 percent average difference is, in fact, less than the 2.5 percent average that had applied across the board to all ad valorem products in 1956 when the list was drawn up. Today the final list is really nothing more than a group of ad valorem commodities subject to a special appraisement. Having lost its intended purpose, it is now an administrative burden and a source of delay and irritation for those engaged in international trade.

One of the administrative problems arises in the determination of export value. If the importer has the option of buying merchandise at the price prevailing at the factory or at the price including shipping and handling charges to the port of shipment, the merchandise is appraised at the ex-factory price; inland shipping charges are not part of the dutiable value. However, if the importer can only buy at a price including de-

38. *Compendium of Papers on Legislative Oversight: Review of U.S. Trade Policies,* Senate Committee on Finance, 90 Cong. 2 sess. (1968), p. 23.

livery costs to the port of shipment, the merchandise is appraised at the f.o.b. price and the charges become a part of the dutiable value. Determining which of these conditions exists at times requires extensive investigation in the country of exportation.

The vexation caused by complexity of administration is not easily measured, but it is not necessary to look far for concrete evidence of the unfairness caused by the final list. A recent example is the treatment of vacuum tubes from Japan. The marketing system in Japan is such that the Customs Bureau found no large-scale sales that could be taken as the basis for foreign value. However, Customs did find sales at a wholesale house in Tokyo at a price much higher than the normal factory price for the domestic market. Though many of the wholesale house's sales were closer to retail than to a normal wholesale price, its values were adopted by Customs and sustained by the Court of Customs and Patent Appeals.[39] Importers often are faced with duties assessed on values considerably higher than the prices they actually paid.

In American selling price valuations the arbitrariness and unfairness are inherent in the method of valuation. For most imports, the factors controlling foreign or export value can be affected by the terms of transactions between exporters and importers. With ASP goods, it is offers by the American producers—the competitors of the importers—that can be arbitrarily controlled to affect the import duty. In consequence, appraisers may be compelled to disregard terms of transactions at which 90 percent of U.S. products are sold in order to find a price that meets the statutory standards (as is the case with rubber-soled footwear).

The Kennedy Round Agreements on ASP

One of the Kennedy Round agreements signed in 1967 was a pledge by the United States to seek legislation eliminating the ASP standard with respect to benzenoid chemicals on condition that further chemical cuts and other concessions be made by other countries. Duties on coal-tar chemicals were to be converted to export value rates and the resulting duties cut by as much as 50 percent. In return, the European Economic Community, Switzerland, and the United Kingdom would reduce certain barriers, after which the United States would agree to further staged re-

39. *Daystrom, Inc. v. United States,* C.A.D. 920 (1967).

duction in certain non-coal-tar chemicals. A separate agreement was written with Japan with respect to canned clams and wool-knit gloves. The ASP on footwear was not covered by an agreement.

In the trade bill of 1970 the administration not only sought to implement the Kennedy Round ASP agreements but asked for prior authorization to make agreements to convert the ASP rates on footwear.

The House Committee on Ways and Means stated its clear intention "that the President may proclaim the 1967 agreements on chemicals, canned clams, and wool-knit gloves if he determine[s] that they fully compensate for concessions to be granted thereunder by the U.S."[40]

The Senate Finance Committee, however, refused to agree to repeal of ASP on chemicals. Though the bill failed on other grounds, no fair test was made of the ability of the chemical industry to block the ASP repealer. A 1971 bill, with the same kinds of stipulations on ASP as the 1970 bill, was never actively considered.

Outlook for Customs Valuation Negotiations

Several characteristics of the U.S. valuation process and standards control the effectiveness with which the United States can negotiate regarding impediments significant enough to be called nontariff barriers to trade. Both procedures and standards are regulated by existing legislation, and that legislation is drawn quite narrowly, particularly as far as valuation standards are concerned. The U.S. ability to negotiate effectively under existing law is therefore, in practical terms, nonexistent.

There is no clear authority to negotiate on valuation under existing law. Consequently, the President, if exercising his independent constitutional power over foreign affairs, would either have to negotiate an agreement ad referendum or secure congressional authority in advance. Existing legislation on valuation, and particularly on standards, is so detailed that without congressional approval any attempt even to make the valuation process uniform would be virtually impossible, unless the standard of uniformity were the current U.S. process.

The impediment to the effectuation of the 1967 agreements that would eliminate ASP on all but rubber-soled footwear is the need for imple-

40. *Trade Act of 1970*, H. Rept. 1435, 91 Cong. 2 sess. (1970).

menting measures from Congress. The administration in its 1973 trade proposals sought congressional authority to conclude agreements eliminating the ASP method of valuation without referring the agreements to Congress for possible disapproval. The House Ways and Means Committee reported a revised administration bill in October, but not including the specific authority sought concerning ASP.[41]

Whether new agreements on the valuation process and standards, and perhaps on universal uniformity, would be well received is a different question. There is no authority to conclude them without referring them to Congress, thereby risking disapproval. Since, presumptively, all countries are complying with the GATT criteria, specific changes would need to be justified as intrinsically sound in terms of national objectives. To change the U.S. f.o.b. basis of valuation for the c.i.f. basis would *not* appear to qualify on this score.

Future efforts in the valuation area should be directed, therefore, at effectuation of the ASP agreement and at internal changes in American law designed to simplify current valuation standards. Further international negotiation efforts, either specific or general, should be given low priority, for they are likely to be either unproductive or retrograde.

41. H.R. 10710, accompanied by *Trade Reform Act of 1973*, H. Rept. 571, 93 Cong. 1 sess. (1973). The bill did authorize conversion of ASP rates to ad valorem rates in trade agreements to be submitted to Congress for possible disapproval (sec. 102[g]).

CHAPTER SEVEN

Industrial Standards

INDUSTRIAL STANDARDS—what are normally called engineering and manufacturing standards—comprise the criteria that, when reduced to writing and accepted by one or more manufacturers in an industry, describe a product to be produced, how it will be produced, and how it will be serviced.

Industrial standards include dimensional specifications that are essential to the functioning of a product or system. The distance between rails (gauge) and between wheels in a railroad, for example, must conform to a standard if the railroad is to function. In addition, standards may be essential to assure interchangeability of parts, within an industry or a particular firm. For instance, automobile tires are interchangeable on an industry-wide basis, whereas the wheels on which they are mounted are generally interchangeable only on vehicles produced by a single company, since the number and spacing of the bolt holes in wheels have not been standardized. Quality and performance specifications assure a quality level that is adequate for the required service and uniformity in quality from one item to another. Quality is the dominant factor in safety standards—for example, in seat belt standards and in specifications for steel forgings for pressure vessel shells. Methods of test provide a common basis for evaluating materials and products, offering standardized procedures for determining critical dimensions or product quality. They are essential for determining compliance of a product with specifications, as in the mechanical testing of steel products. Descriptive standards include codes, symbols, sampling and other statistical practices, terminology, format for engineering drawings, and common engineering techniques. Typical are small scale estimations of the average quality of a lot or process, color coding of electronic components, codes for highway signs, identification colors for pipes conveying gases and liquids, and the nuclear energy glossary. A particular standard may be drawn from one of these categories or from all of them.[1]

Industrial standards can also be categorized as mandatory, voluntary, or hybrid.[2] Mandatory standards are those that are governmentally formulated and imposed, at either the national or local level, by statute or regulation; they can easily be affected by international agreement. Voluntary standards are formulated by private groups and industries—trade associations, or groups created specifically for the purpose of formulating standards—and adopted voluntarily by individual firms or industries that feel it is in their best interests to do so, rather than because of governmental statute or regulation; such voluntary standards are more difficult than mandatory standards to affect by international agreement. A hybrid standard is one that has been formulated and adopted voluntarily, by private groups, but has subsequently been made mandatory by governmental legislation or regulation either for the class of persons for whom it was originally intended or for others. Hybrid regulations often appear as legitimately motivated health or safety regulations.

Another distinction among industrial standards is in their various units and methods of measurement. The U.S. Bureau of Standards estimates that no more than 25 percent of industrial standards problems are affected or caused by differences in units of measurement.[3] While the percentage is far smaller than some had thought, adoption of a uniform measurement language such as the metric system by all countries, including the United States, would be quite helpful.

Standards Formulation

Basically the international industrial standards problem is twofold: one of formulating standards and another of enforcing or certifying the standards. Industrial standards are needed to insure that manufactured products are uniform in type. When use of one product depends on another

1. See U.S. Department of Commerce, National Bureau of Standards, *U.S. Metric Study Report: International Standards* (1970), pp. 54–56.

2. Interview with William B. Kelly, Economic Consultant, Special Representative for Trade Negotiations, Washington, June 6, 1971.

3. *U.S. Metric Study,* p. 56. Only standards in the dimensional specifications category would be adversely affected by measurement differences.

product, produced perhaps by another manufacturer, then both manufacturers need standards in order to insure marketability of their products.
Consumer demand, reflected in marketability, controls somewhat the
nature of and need for standards. Among the numerous benefits of standards is their usefulness as a basis for technological development and
improvement in product lines.

The existence of compatible standards in a given economic area, in
short, enhances trade within that area. As the relatively limited economic
areas of interest in international trade have broadened, the need for international standards has become more widely recognized. Among the forces
responsible for the change in attitude are the worldwide expansion of the
technological revolution, the huge expansion of world trade, the development of the multinational corporation, and certain standards harmonization efforts. Technological interdependence has brought into sharp focus
some of the problems created by the narrow-market view. For example,
standards peculiar to national production in many instances result in limiting the products they affect to the national market. If sold elsewhere, the
products cannot be easily maintained, perhaps not even operated. Differing mandatory standards in two countries may be tantamount to a zero
import quota and will at the very least cause some difficulties and additional costs for foreign articles. Standards formulated without consideration of the interests of consumers or dependent producers beyond national
boundaries tend to limit the flow of trade outside those boundaries.

The need for more and better international standards has recently been
studied by international organizations as well as many national governments, but little of substance has been developed. Some progress has been
made by voluntary standards groups, which have recommended 1,500
international standards since the 1920s; over 85 percent of these have
been issued in just the last ten years. The United States, by comparison,
has an estimated 20,000 national standards. Such diversity in industrial
standards is likely to have adverse effects on international trade and, in
consequence, become an increasingly important nontariff barrier.

Standards Certification

Once the proper ingredients have been combined to produce an adequate standard for a product, how will the various countries of the world
determine that a given product meets that standard? Will each be forced

to establish a testing procedure within its borders and subject each imported product to this certification process, or will all agree that if the product is tested and certified in one country, that certification will be sufficient evidence in all countries that the product in fact does comply with the standard? Should such intergovernmental agreements be a "closed club" or open to nations willing and able to fulfill the requirements of membership? Such questions of certification will remain to be dealt with even though international standards may be formulated. The current system of competing and conflicting national and local standards makes their resolution the more complicated, for there is no agreement on the essential bases for certification.

National and local certification and testing requirements can act as significant nontariff barriers. They can effectively block out foreign products that have not been inspected and certified abroad, even though they are of high quality; and they can cause needless delays and administrative hindrances for goods that have been tested and certified but whose foreign certification is not recognized by the importing country. As more local and national standards are developed, there is greater likelihood that their certification will have increasingly important effects on world trade.

The International System

Nearly all industrially developed countries have either a national office, often with agency status, or an officially sanctioned and funded national private group that oversees the formulation and certification of national industrial standards and represents those interests in international standards organizations. The amount of government aid received by these groups ranges from 100 percent in the Soviet Union to about 75 percent in France, 50 percent in the United Kingdom, and about 9 percent in Germany. The national organ also oversees the development of local, regional, or individual organization standards into national standards. Most of these national bodies are private except in state trading countries such as the USSR, and most standards consequently are voluntary rather than mandatory.

The presence of a recognized national standards representative that can serve various interest groups, including the government, has assisted most countries in the formulation and certification of both national and international standards. It also affords a ready count and description of the national standards that exist within a country. Of course there is in all countries a large body of mandatory laws and regulations totally unconcerned with international trade that significantly affects industrial standards formulation and certification.

Numerous regional groups currently are working on or experimenting with solutions to the need for international standards formulation and certification. Some are treaty groups, based on international agreements; some are private. The common goal of all of these groups is to formulate standards and certification procedures that will facilitate the movement of goods and services within their geographic markets. Each of them takes into account, however, less than the world market, and their activities thus contribute pro tanto to adverse trade effects, though not nearly so much as do national or local standards that are based on an even narrower market view.

Of most concern to the United States are the activities of the Committee for the Coordination of European Standards in the Electrical Field (CENEL).[4] This treaty group was formed in 1960 to assist in harmonization of standards within and between the European Economic Community (EEC) and the European Free Trade Association (EFTA). In 1966 the United Kingdom, France, and Germany formed a committee to accelerate the harmonization among CENEL countries, and in 1970, CENEL agreed to implement the committee's Harmonized System of Quality Assessment for Electronic Components. The system provides for compatible standards and mutual recognition of certification and testing of electronic components that could place U.S. products at a competitive disadvantage because they would have to undergo local testing in each country and, in addition, might not qualify for official procurement in CENEL countries.

4. The most important nontreaty, private regional group is the Pan American Standards Committee (COPANT) which was formed in 1956 and began functioning in 1961; its region includes all of the Americas. The International Exchange of Authenticated Performance Test Data (EXACY) was recently formed by the Scandinavian countries and Austria. Other European treaty groups include the International Commission on Rules for the Approval of Electrical Equipment (CEE) which operates a certification body that is making considerable progress in reciprocal acceptance of tests on electrical devices and appliances of West European countries and six other nations; the International Special Committee on Radio Interference (CISPR); and the Economic Commission for Europe (ECE). Such regional groups as the Economic Commission for Asia and the Far East (ECAFE), the Organization for Economic Cooperation and Development (OECD), and the North Atlantic Treaty Organization (NATO) also have standards study groups.

The most significant standards groups with worldwide objectives are private, nontreaty groups. The two key private groups are the International Organization for Standardization (ISO) and the International Electrotechnical Commission (IEC), formed in the first years of this century.[5] Their memberships consist of the national standardization bodies of fifty-four participating countries, some of which are governmentally controlled. They operate through committees of experts from member countries, each headed by a secretariat held by one of the member organizations. Standards are proposed by the committees and adopted by the whole organization. Their status is merely recommendatory, however; members are under no obligation to adopt or encourage their adoption among domestic industries. Nevertheless, ISO- and IEC-recommended standards are persuasive. The substantial markets that compliance may open up make it important that the national standards organization adequately represent the interests of the industries of a given country. If a U.S. standard, for example, is recommended for international adoption by the ISO or IEC, U.S. industries already in compliance with that standard may have a substantial head start on noncomplying competitors for the markets that adopt the standards.

In the last decade, activities of the ISO and IEC have accelerated rapidly, and the prospect is that the acceleration will continue. The IEC, for example, issued 432 recommendations (and revised 94) between 1950 and 1969, but 272 of the recommendations (and 42 of the revisions) were made between 1965 and 1969. The ISO in that twenty-year period issued 1,206 recommendations (and 37 revisions), with 786 (and 36) occurring in the final five years. Though the sole function of these organizations has been standards formulation, both have begun to consider what role they can and should play in standards certification.

The United States System

The dominant characteristic of the U.S. system of standards formulation and certification is an extreme lack of systemization. Partly as a result of this, no one knows very much about it.

5. Other international organizations, whose standards work has been primarily investigatory or in a specialized area, are the World Health Organization, the International Labor Organization, the International Telecommunications Union, and the International Atomic Energy Agency.

The confusing U.S. approach reflects the extent to which both state and federal governments have left standards formulation and, to a lesser extent, standards certification in private hands. The system has been described as being unique in its absence of government involvement. In place of government, a myriad of private groups—most of them quite producer-oriented—has taken up the slack. Some have been national in scope, some local; some have been concerned exclusively with standardization, others only peripherally; some have represented a single industry or economic sector, others have cut across industries and economic sectors.

This is not to say that there has been no government involvement, or that such involvement does not have an adverse effect on international trade. In fact, with the growth of government activity at all levels since World War II, government has become increasingly involved in standardization activities, albeit often without cognizance of their potential effects on international trade. Governmental concern over the trade effects of standardization, including not only formulation and certification but the language of standards (that is, the metrication movement), did not really begin to bud until the 1960s. Studies instigated by the CENEL harmonization movement indicated that U.S. participation in international standards formulation through ISO and IEC was woefully inadequate and that the U.S. system differed substantially from that of the rest of the world.[6] They also raised questions whether the general public's interests were adequately represented in standards formulation and certification.

Just how significant standards formulation, certification, and measurement are as a barrier to trade is difficult to measure. Only occasionally do state statutes expressly bar the use of foreign-made articles. At the federal level, the definition of standards is relatively fluid and a great variety of legislation could arguably affect standards. A vast network of private groups affects standards and certification in a variety of ways. No calculations have been made of the trade impact of standards activities in either government or the private sector. That reflects the absence of an official body authorized to act on behalf of the federal government in negotiations

6. See *International Commercial Standards Activities,* Hearings before the Ad Hoc Subcommittee of the House Committee on Science and Astronautics, 89 Cong. 2 sess. (1966), especially pp. 77–84 and 8–27.

with other countries or in actions affecting domestic or international standards organizations.

Private Voluntary Groups

It has been estimated that there are over 400 private standards formulating or certifying groups in the United States; they have issued over 20,000 industrial standards (some of them duplications), considerably more than have been issued in other countries.[7] This number does not include government mandatory standards or standards that are effectively established by virtue of government procurement specifications.

Private standards groups in the United States fall into five categories: voluntary standards writing and promulgating bodies; professional societies; trade associations; listing bodies; and scientific bodies.[8] The writing and promulgating bodies are unique because their activities are exclusively concerned with standards and standardization. They produced about a third of the voluntary standards currently in effect, and they annually write over a thousand consensus standards in a great variety of technical areas. Most of these, however, are industrial market product standards including many test methods for specific quantities and materials. The American National Standards Institute (ANSI) serves as the coordinating organization for the system, promulgating standards submitted by other organizations as "American national standards." It is ANSI that represents the United States on ISO and IEC committees and provides funds for

7. *U.S. Metric Study*, p. 54. France has an estimated 7,000 national standards, Great Britain 5,500, Germany 11,000, Italy 6,000, the Soviet Union 13,000, India 5,000, and Japan 7,000.

8. *International Voluntary Standards Cooperation Act of 1971*, Hearings before the Subcommittee on Foreign Commerce and Tourism of the Senate Committee on Commerce, 92 Cong. 2 sess. (1971). The professional societies include such groups as the Institute of Electrical and Electronic Engineers (IEEE), the Instrument Society of America (ISA), the Society of Automotive Engineers (SAE), the American Society of Heating, Refrigerating and Air Conditioning Engineers (ASHRAE), and the American Society of Mechanical Engineers (ASME); the trade associations include the Aerospace Industries Association of America (AIAA), the American Gear Manufacturers Association (AGMA), the Electronic Industries Association (EIA), and the National Electrical Manufacturers Association (NEMA); the listing bodies include the Underwriters' Laboratories (UL) and Factory Mutual Engineering Corporation (FMEC); and the scientific bodies include the American Chemical Society (ACS) and the International Union of Pure and Applied Chemistry (IUPAC).

these standards activities. ANSI originated in 1928 as the American Standards Association. Since 1966 it has been quite active in increasing U.S. participation on the IEC: from 10 technical committee secretariats in 1966 to 17 in 1971; from spotty participation in committees to representation on virtually all committees. The ANSI membership consists of approximately 160 technical, professional, and trade organizations and some 1,000 individual companies. Standards developed by members are reviewed by ANSI and, if approved, become American national standards. Of the 20,000 voluntary standards in the United States, approximately 4,000 have been submitted and approved as American national standards.[9] Other standards bodies in the United States are the original sources of the remainder of the voluntary standards.

The most active and productive standards-writing organization is the American Society for Testing and Materials (ASTM), founded in 1898 for "the promotion of knowledge of the materials of engineering, and the standardization of specifications and the methods of testing."[10] Through more than 100 technical committees the ASTM has developed approximately 4,000 widely used standards. On its committees, producers may not outnumber nonproducers (including consumers, consulting engineers, educational institutions, and government agencies that are not consumer agencies). Its diversified membership includes 10,000 individuals, 1,000 institutions, 3,000 companies, trade associations, and research institutes.[11] On behalf of ANSI and the United States, it participates on a substantial number of ISO and IEC committees.

Federal Government

The federal government participates in the standards system through technical contributions of the National Bureau of Standards and other offices in the Department of Commerce; through mandatory, legislatively-based standards formulation, certification, or measurement; and through federal procurement specifications. The Bureau of Standards has since 1921 provided nonfinancial, technical assistance to the private sector in developing standards. The bureau has developed and published standards independently for certain commodities and has done so in cooperation with industry for many products. Its personnel have served on technical

9. Ibid.
10. *International Commercial Standards Activities,* Hearings, p. 85.
11. Ibid., p. 86.

committees of domestic standardization bodies and a few international committees. Through the Office of Commodity Standards of the Department of Commerce it is directly involved in domestic voluntary standards development for some 80–100 industries.[12]

Because the federal government is the largest consumer in the United States, if not the world, its desires as to type and style of product carry substantial weight in the marketplace. Government procurement specifications are probably the key influence in creating standards for a substantial number of products. The Department of Defense alone is estimated to be responsible for the creation of some 35,000 procurement specifications, many of which serve as the basis of production for nongovernment consumers as well.[13] Other federal agencies, notably the General Services Administration, play similar roles. Of course many of these standards or specifications differ somewhat from and overlap with standards that have been developed privately.

With the increasing legislative interest in consumer and environmental protection, the number of standards required by law has mushroomed. It is difficult to decide whether some mandatory legislation should be considered standard-creating or more appropriately standard-influencing. Most such standards are established in the "public interest" to protect health, safety, welfare, or the national security, although their trade effects —both domestically and internationally—may be substantial and adverse. For example, automobile exhaust emission standards inspired by concern for the ill effects of polluted air, and eyeglass material and thickness standards to guard against shattering lenses may have a significant adverse effect on foreign manufacturers and exporters to the United States. Though little has been done to catalog such effects, an Interagency Committee for Standards Policy is responsible for overseeing these areas of federal standards activity.

State Standards

State and local governments participate in the standards system in much the same way as the federal government, although there is no focal

---

12. Ibid., p. 67. It has been estimated that these standards amount to only some 3 percent of all standards in the United States and that they do not give as much voice to nonproducer interests as voluntary groups. Ibid., p. 81 (testimony of Mr. LaQue).

13. *U.S. Metric Study,* p. 59.

point like the Department of Commerce for technical assistance in standards development. Their most important impact on trade is through legislation and regulations pertaining to such things as building codes and requiring compliance with a broad assortment of voluntary standards and standards certification schemes that often are peculiar to a limited area. The intent of the legislation and regulations is normally to protect or promote the public interest. In the construction industry, for example, each of some 6,000 jurisdictions has its own building code. The code is essentially an assembly of standards relating to parts, materials, and finished structures unique to the local area. Items not common to all codes must be manufactured on a small scale or more expensively fabricated by hand. The cost of housing is increased accordingly.

U.S. Participation in International Standardization

Participation by the United States in international standardization has fluctuated over the years.[14] At the end of the nineteenth century there were many U.S. members of the International Association for Testing Materials (IATM). Out of their interest the American Society for Testing and Materials (ASTM) was incorporated in 1902. The International Electrotechnical Commission (IEC), founded in 1906, was another outgrowth of U.S. interest. By the beginning of World War I, more than 20 percent of IATM members were in the United States. Specifications for steel products were published in four languages by ASTM in 1913, and the U.S. Department of Commerce subsequently translated ASTM standards having an important bearing on export trade and distributed them to consular offices throughout the world.

International standardization efforts disintegrated with World War I, but U.S. societies maintained informal contact with other nations' organizations. New international organizations founded in the late 1920s failed to revive the prewar interest, and they ceased to function when World War II started.

During World War II the allied nations formed the United Nations Standards Coordinating Committee, which led to the establishment in 1946 of the International Organization for Standardization (ISO). Meantime, the IEC had survived both wars. These two organizations have

14. See ibid., pp. 60–62.

become predominant in international standardization. The United States is represented in them by ANSI, which has recently become a very active participant. The United States is the secretariat for one of the three most active ISO committees. Some of the committees it is especially active on represent industries particularly sensitive to the base measurement units— for example, aircraft and space vehicles, and textile machinery.

Other countries have developed similar interest. Germany and Japan are now translating many of their standards into foreign languages, just as the United States did between 1913 and 1930. Indeed, Japan's success since 1945 in establishing standards for high-quality products, implemented by quality control and certification programs, has spurred similar programs now being developed among European countries.

The United States and the Metric System

In 1968 Congress authorized the National Bureau of Standards to study in depth the effects on the United States of the worldwide movement toward adoption of the metric system of measurement. The movement toward metrication has since then so accelerated that the United States may soon stand alone in its failure to adopt the metric system. One of the last bastions of the nonmetric system, Canada, in 1970 declared that it had adopted "conversion as a definite objective of Canadian policy. . . . Accumulated investments around the older system increase with time, and opportunities for conversion are missed as obsolete assets are replaced. . . . There would need to be increased participation in standards development if the long-run trade advantages of conversion are to be secured."[15] A year and a half later the Bureau of Standards recommended that the United States undertake a deliberate change to the metric system over a ten-year period.[16]

Even immediate adoption of the recommended program would leave the United States years behind the rest of the world. The Bureau of Standards estimates that 25 percent of all industrial standards would be adversely affected by international measurement differences. In terms of trade, this means that either manufacturers must confine themselves to production for *either* the U.S. market *or* the rest of the world, or else they

15. Ibid., p. 13.
16. U.S. Department of Commerce, National Bureau of Standards, *Report to Congress: A Metric America* (1971).

must adopt two sets of standards—thereby increasing their production costs and, ultimately, the cost to the consumer. Because of the size of the U.S. market, the latter might be the alternative for many manufacturers— but not all, and in all likelihood for a diminishing number as the metric movement outside the United States matures. On the other hand, in a change to the metric system, U.S. manufacturers' standards would have to change, thereby presumably increasing their short-run costs and putting them at a short-term disadvantage in competition with manufacturers of products whose industrial standards already have a metric base.

Congressional Interest in Standardization

Serious, but unsuccessful, attempts have been made within the Congress to support U.S. participation in the development of international standards. In 1966 several bills sought "to promote and support adequate representation for United States interests in voluntary international commercial standardization activities and to authorize the establishment and support of appropriate central information clearinghouses for commercial or procurement standards and standards activities for the benefit of producers, distributors, users, consumers, and the general public."[17] The only action on the bills was three days of hearings held by an ad hoc House subcommittee; in 1967 no action at all was taken.

Annually from 1965 to 1969 the National Bureau of Standards espoused legislation to promote greater U.S. involvement in international standards activities. In 1968 the bureau proposed that a concurrent resolution express the sense of the Congress that the United States should participate vigorously in international standardization activities to promote the compatibility of voluntary international standards and standards followed in this country, thereby to facilitate broad domestic access to international trade. The proposal has never been submitted to the Congress.

In 1970 the House Ways and Means Committee, reporting favorably on the trade bill that did not become law, called for

full cooperation and coordination between government and industry in standards matters. . . . In particular, this will require adequate funding of U.S.

17. Ibid., p. 19.

participation in international standards writing and ensuring that the United States possesses the institutional facilities necessary to take part in testing and certification arrangements. The Department of Commerce is the logical agency within the U.S. Government to initiate and coordinate these efforts as they relate to industrial products.[18]

Clearly, the interest in standards of both the executive and legislative branches of government is growing. A 1971 bill introduced on behalf of the Department of Commerce sought to vest in the secretary of commerce authority to promote international standardization activities, in part by issuing grants to private nonprofit organizations for the development of international standards, and to promote the adoption of appropriate standards in the United States.[19] More attention would be given to the public interest—that is, to consumers and small firms, and to U.S. foreign antitrust and environmental policy. The secretary would be guided by an interagency committee for standards policy and would act as a clearinghouse for listing of and information concerning international standards. The authority would cover standards certification as well as formulation. The intent of the legislation was to maintain a voluntary standards system, with the public interest protected but the private sector retaining priority, and with the active participation of the secretary of commerce. The legislation has not yet been enacted.

Trade Effects of the U.S. System

Most U.S. interest in the ill effects of standards has focused on the internationalization movement, and particularly on the threat that regional schemes such as CENEL pose for U.S. exports. There has been no systematic study of the extent to which the U.S. system for standards formulation, certification, and measurement acts as a trade barrier to foreign imports. Nor have foreign businessmen complained about the effects of U.S. standards except in an antitrust context. Nonetheless, various examples of trade effects of standards application demonstrate that the standards system is potentially, if not already, an important nontariff barrier.

18. Carl J. Gilbert, "Standards as Nontariff Barriers," *Materials Research and Standards,* Vol. 11, No. 3 (1970), p. 11.
19. S. 1798, 92 Cong. 1 sess. (1971).

Standards Formulation and Measurement

Basically the adverse trade effects arise from a lack of uniformity between U.S. and other standards, and a dearth of information about standards that can be readily communicated across national boundaries.

In the 1960s, U.S. manufacturers complained that differences between European and American standards for the depth and thread of lamp sockets and lamp bases were detrimental to their exports;[20] European manufacturers would have found the same problem in their exports to the U.S. market. About the same time, one of Canada's trading partners proposed standards for pig aluminum that would have effectively prevented the export of Canadian aluminum.[21] Both cases prove the point that "where one country has certain gauges of steel and another country has a different size drill, or where different countries have different shapes and sizes of screw threads," the incompatibility caused by lack of uniformity has an adverse trade effect.[22]

Where governments impose mandatory standards, no matter what their intent, trade problems may also arise. The recently enacted federal laws regarding automobile design and construction and engine exhaust emission controls have been imposed to protect the public health and welfare; their negative side effect is the burden placed on manufacturers, domestic and foreign, to meet the new requirements.

In order to comply with the National Emission Standards Act, manufacturers must submit a test engine to the secretary of health, education, and welfare. The foreign manufacturer must await acceptance of his test vehicle before beginning shipments and must declare that each vehicle subsequently imported is in all material respects like the test vehicle.[23] Manufacturers also must guarantee the emission control systems for 50,000 miles. The trade consequences of these standards can be severe, effectively embargoing an entire make or model of a car for as long as it takes to meet the requirement. The Simca, a French import, was denied entry for a twelve-month period because of inability to meet exhaust emis-

20. *International Commercial Standards Activities,* Hearings, p. 4.
21. Ibid., p. 78.
22. Ibid., p. 53.
23. 42 U.S.C. sec. 1857(f)(5) (Supp. V, 1970); see also 45 C.F.R. secs. 85.50–53, 85.200–03 (1970), and 19 C.F.R. sec. 12.73 (1970).

sion criteria.[24] The president of Volkswagen of America feared that incompatibility of the popular "Beetle" design with bumper requirements might drive that model from the American market.[25] Significantly, Volkswagen sells more cars in the United States than in Germany.[26] For manufacturers whose sales in the United States are less than 50,000 a year, the prohibitive costs of design alteration may close the U.S. market.[27]

A regulatory action of the Food and Drug Administration (FDA) brought strong protests from foreign manufacturers and U.S. importers in 1970. In October the FDA proposed that all eyeglasses and sunglasses sold in the United States meet certain impact and thickness standards.[28] Trouble quickly arose. The thickness requirements would have demanded a wholly new design for fashion sunglasses and retooling of the industry's machinery. The FDA had asked for replies within thirty days in order that promulgation could be expedited, claiming that the regulation had been drafted with the aid of the eyeglass trade, professional associations, and optical manufacturers.[29] Neither the foreign sunglass manufacturers nor their U.S. importers had been consulted, however, and approximately half of the fashion sunglasses sold in the United States came from Western Europe.[30]

The importers were concerned because of the large inventories they had on hand, the foreign manufacturers for the loss of their large American market. The proposed regulation was not, however, a complete surprise to them. Portents of stricter controls had been in the air for as much as two years. At least two states (Connecticut and Alaska) had similar, if not more stringent, standards. The industry, moreover, had planned to introduce in their sunglasses for the 1971–72 season the glass specified in the FDA proposal[31] and would have had to begin production not long after the notice was issued.

24. Telephone interview with M. Macaire, chief, Economic Study Department, French Commercial Counselor, Washington, Feb. 19, 1971.
25. *New York Times,* Jan. 19, 1971, p. 75.
26. Ibid.
27. Ibid.
28. 35 Fed. Reg. 15402 (1970).
29. Press release, U.S. Department of Health, Education, and Welfare—Food and Drug Administration, Sept. 30, 1970.
30. See 35 Fed. Reg. 15402 (1970).
31. Ibid.

The degree of damage to the imported sunglass industry caused by the October 1970 notice is difficult to determine. Claims were made that the proposal resulted in drastic cuts in activity and in employee layoffs. However, at a meeting of European manufacturers and American importers shortly after issuance of the proposal, the parties were instructed to exaggerate to FDA the potential effects of the proposal.[32]

Nonetheless, both the proposed regulation and the manner in which it was introduced are disconcerting. If European sunglass sales on the U.S. market have been increasing as fast as indicated,[33] and if the allegation that the domestic competitors can adapt to the new standards more quickly is true,[34] then the U.S. manufacturers may be able to recapture much of the American market share that they have lost over the last few years.

To alleviate the ill effects of the regulation, the FDA extended the deadline for replies by three months to allow fuller consideration of the issue. The deadline for compliance was set fifteen months after the original proposal and applied only to the *manufacture* of lenses.[35] Thus, sunglasses manufactured before that date and not in compliance with the standard could still be sold in the United States.

Standards Certification and Approval

The requirement that a foreign exporter obtain for his products a certificate or mark of conformity will normally necessitate either submission of a sample of his production to a body in the importing country for inspection or visits by inspectors from the importing country to inspect and test the product in his factory. Even if the fees for inspections and tests are not deliberately discriminatory, the exporter may be placed at a competitive disadvantage compared with domestic manufacturers, with a resultant distortion of competition. A trade barrier may also be erected if the body responsible for certification and approval acts in such a way as to prevent or hamper the access of foreign goods to the country in which

32. Minutes of meeting held at Milan, Italy, Oct. 11, 1970.
33. One company claims that 95 percent of its production is sold in the United States and that sales in 1968 amounted to $480,000; in 1969, $800,000; and the first six months of 1970, $520,000. Letter from Occhialeric TAL di Tabacchi Alessandro to FDA commissioner, Oct. 12, 1970.
34. 35 Fed. Reg. 15402 (1970). Moreover, the American manufacturers allegedly knew of the proposal in advance and had an opportunity to begin the switch earlier.
35. 35 Fed. Reg. 17116 (1970).

it operates. For example, the certifying body may simply refuse to certify foreign products, it may apply prohibitive fees for testing and inspecting foreign products, or it may deliberately delay the granting of its certificate or mark of conformity.[36]

Certification problems may arise from voluntary or mandatory actions, or both. For example, a U.S. manufacturer might decide as a matter of internal policy that it would buy a certain part only if it were tested and approved by a particular domestic firm. If the testing firm chose not to accept foreign samples, or imposed unreasonable fees or requirements on foreign samples, or otherwise favored U.S. over foreign parts in its decisions of what, when, and how to test, foreign parts manufacturers would feel an adverse trade effect occasioned wholly by voluntary means. If either the prime manufacturer or the testing firm or both were enforcing a federal, state, or local law or regulation that established the same requirements for foreign parts, the trade effect would be the same but the means would be mandatory.

Perhaps one of the most flagrant U.S. abuses in the standards certification field has been in the certification of boilers and pressure vessels. The certification practices have resulted in a virtual embargo on all like products originating outside North America.

The standards were imposed years ago because of recurrent explosions of boilers and pressure vessels. To ensure that future design and construction would minimize this hazard, the American Society of Mechanical Engineers (ASME), an incorporated group of professional mechanical engineers, adopted a Boiler and Pressure Vessel Code. A National Board of Boiler and Pressure Vessel Inspectors, an unincorporated association comprised mainly of chief inspectors of various states, was created to implement the code.

The board provided for the testing and certification of inspectors who inspected the products individually for conformity to code standards. Products that passed the test were granted a code symbol by the ASME.

The symbol soon became commercially very valuable, and bid specifications often demanded products bearing it. Many states have turned the voluntary standards of ASME into compulsory standards. Some thirty-nine states and thirty-nine counties and cities require the code symbol in all sales within their jurisdiction. Some statutes specifically require adop-

36. R. W. Middleton, "Technical Specifications—A Case Study of Non-Tariff Barriers to Trade," *EFTA Bulletin,* March and April 1971, pp. 3, 6.

tion of the ASME code, with supervision by the national board, whereas others achieve the same result with less demanding language.

The difficulties that arose for foreign manufacturers under the ASME procedures were indeed formidable. The code symbol was granted only to products inspected and approved by inspectors certified by the national board. But the ASME and the national board by agreement refused to inspect the products of or grant the code symbol to manufacturers outside North America whether or not their product were good![37] The Department of Justice in 1970 filed suit against the ASME for arbitrarily refusing to issue the code symbol to qualifying foreign manufacturers and against the national board for refusing to register foreign boilers and pressure vessels that had been approved by one state and used in another.[38] The government further alleged that in 1969 a majority of ASME's executive committee were officers or employees of domestic boiler and pressure vessel manufacturers. On September 11, 1972 a consent judgment was entered in the case enjoining ASME from treating foreign manufacturers or foreign-made boilers or pressure vessels differently from domestic producers or products with respect to issuance of symbol stamps or certificates of authorization, authority to use National Board stamping, registration of manufacturer's data reports, or commissioning of inspectors of such products.[39]

A seemingly innocuous federal law that has been in existence for nearly seventy years has in its implementation become an artificial barrier to international trade. The law requires that all instruments, machines, and equipment used in lifesaving apparatus on a steam vessel flying the U.S. flag be approved by the commandant of the Coast Guard. The goals of this measure reflect a legitimate interest in protecting the safety and welfare of seamen and passengers by seeking to ensure that escape from a potential disaster will be as safe as possible.

The adverse effect on international trade arises not from the purpose of the act, but from its administration. The elaborate procedures for inspecting lifesaving equipment require that inspection take place *during the manufacturing process,* and, upon approval, that a Coast Guard stamp

37. Statement of American Importers Association, in *Foreign Trade and Tariff Proposals,* Hearings before the House Committee on Ways and Means, 90 Cong. 2 sess. (1968), Pt. 3, p. 847.

38. *United States v. American Society of Mechanical Engineers, Inc. and National Board of Boiler and Pressure Vessel Inspectors,* Civil No. 70 CIV 3141 (S.D. N.Y., filed July 22, 1970).

39. Ibid.

be affixed on each item.[40] Nowhere in the regulations is there any provision for inspection of foreign-made equipment. Should a foreign manufacturer wish the Coast Guard inspector to service him, he would have to bear the cost, which would be quite onerous. The result is that foreign lifesaving equipment is effectively barred from purchase by owners of U.S. flag vessels. Complaints to that effect have been made.[41]

Benefits and Detriments of Standards

Are all of the various methods by which imports to the United States are put at a disadvantage by either voluntary or mandatory standards formulation, measurement, or certification schemes undesirable? It is clear that neither the United States nor any other country is prepared to answer in the affirmative. The question then is how to weigh the benefits to the public against the disadvantages to imported products, where such disadvantages are quantitatively substantial, and how to arrive at an equitable solution—in short, how to effectuate a trade-off between the benefits and detriments of particular standards. For example, with respect to automotive emission standards, the need for protection of U.S. citizens' health from air pollution must be balanced against the adverse trade effects on Volkswagen and Simca, and an accommodation found. This might ultimately be done only by relatively inexpensive design changes in the smaller model automobiles. The Environmental Protection Agency, however, might well assist in this process by taking into consideration smaller-car problems and foreign-manufacturer problems in the formulation of their standards and regulations, and by providing technical assistance toward the development of an adequate emission control device.

Four factors seem to be involved in the trade-off process, once adverse trade effects are identified. All need to be carefully investigated and weighed in arriving at solutions. First, the need for the standard must be examined. If the need is important, then the importance must be balanced against other factors in arriving at a solution. Second, the quantity, both actual and probable, of the adverse trade effects must be considered. If these effects are substantial, then there are two competing needs—for example, the need for cleaner air and the need to permit U.S. consumers

40. 46 C.F.R. secs. 33.01–25 (1970).
41. Written Statement and Other Material Submitted by Administration Witnesses, in *Inventory of Alleged United States Nontariff Barriers*, House Committee on Ways and Means, 91 Cong. 2 sess. (1970), p. 181.

the price advantages of competition. Third, the means used to effect the result must be examined to determine whether they are reasonable, and whether alternative means might better accommodate both of the needs. Fourth, the legality of the standard, including procedural fairness in its adoption, must be examined.

The main legal controls over voluntary standardization schemes in the United States are antitrust laws. Unfortunately, these laws have not been applied stringently—a situation common throughout the world. Mandatory standardization schemes have been subject to virtually no controls.

Internationally, standardization schemes have been discussed and studied by the GATT. Although there is no consensus as to which articles of the GATT are most apt to apply to restrict standardization schemes or what types of restrictions they impose,[42] there appears to be an increasing recognition that the restrictions are presently inadequate.

It is clear that, thus far, there has been inadequate systematic investigation of the factors involved in balancing the social considerations behind the creation and administration of industrial standards in the United States. No doubt this is due in great measure to the dominance of the voluntary sector in the U.S. system and the continuing emphasis given it. In addition, however, the failure of governments at all levels to consider adequately the harmful trade effects of mandatory legislation in the standards area has played an important role. This is correctable. Whether the correction can or should be made through international agreement is another question.

Outlook for Negotiations on Industrial Standards

A multitude of factors make negotiation of international agreements on systems of industrial standards formulation and certification difficult: many industrial standards are voluntary; mandatory standards often are imposed by local rather than federal law; identification of existing standards is incomplete; those identifiable number in the thousands and are extremely varied; almost all have seemingly quite benign public health

42. For example, some consider that Articles I, III, and XXI anticipatorily prohibit such limited membership regional schemes as CENEL while others feel that only Articles XXII and XXIII can be used against CENEL, and that consequently an actual and substantial adverse trade effect must be shown.

and welfare purposes and are not intended to be protectionist; and their adverse trade effects are extremely difficult not only to identify and quantify, but to weigh against their benefits. These circumstances militate strongly against overall solutions to the trade barrier effects that the growth of industrial standardization has created.

While detailed international agreements regulating the creation and enforcement of industrial standards are obviously not now possible, there are several areas in which agreement is feasible, both politically and legally.

The United States should be able to enter an international agreement along the following lines: The parties (such as the GATT contracting parties) would agree to support financially and technically the work of voluntary organizations (the IEC and the ISO) in formulating international standards and gaining recognition of testing and certification schemes. They would agree to consider—and have their political subdivisions consider—the adverse effects on international trade of any mandatory action they may take with respect to industrial standards, and to seek to mitigate or eliminate such effects. They would agree to establish immediately an international clearinghouse for information concerning industrial standards and certification schemes, and to undertake to establish national clearinghouses to the same end. They would agree to seek removal or change of unreasonably discriminatory standards or enforcement thereof. The parties would agree that unreasonably discriminatory standards or enforcement thereof are measures that can nullify or impair the benefits of the GATT, under Article XXIII thereof, and, in consequence, can lead to consultation and the other remedial measures provided for therein.[43]

The President's authority to negotiate such an agreement would be quite clear once his trade agreements legislative authority is renewed. Even in the absence thereof, his constitutional authority alone would permit the undertaking with no substantial risk of congressional repudiation, since such an agreement would be well within the leeway of existing federal legislation.

43. While technically the contracting parties to GATT may interpret Article XXIII to cover such measures in a particular complaint, it has been more usual for GATT to proceed by rule-making—that is, by a special resolution stating that henceforth a given measure will be deemed to be a nullification or impairment within the meaning of Article XXIII, when it has not been generally so considered prior thereto.

CHAPTER EIGHT

Governmental Aids to Industry

THE GOAL of free trade is a worldwide flow of goods, unimpeded by artificially created obstacles, that allows the most efficient producer to assume the role of the principal supplier.[1] To the extent that governments adopt measures to assist their domestic industries the goal cannot be reached. It matters little whether the aid is direct or indirect. The ability to obtain a federally sponsored capital improvement loan at lower than normal interest rates (an indirect subsidy) may permit a company to recognize a saving in costs. The effect on international trade will be indistinguishable from the effects of a direct grant of equal value from the government to the producer. All such governmental action could be broadly characterized as a subsidization of the affected industry.[2] Only a few assistance programs, however, have a clearly recognizable impact on imports. The number of such programs in the United States, in marked contrast with many other industrial nations, is relatively limited.

Subsidies for U.S. Shipping

Probably the single most conspicuous example of direct subsidization of an industry within the United States is the assistance provided the

1. See Charles Poor Kindleberger, *International Economics,* 3d ed. (Irwin, 1963), pp. 310–11.
2. John Howard Jackson, *World Trade and the Law of GATT* (Bobbs-Merrill, 1969), p. 366.

shipping industry. The Merchant Marine Act of 1936, as amended,[3] allows any U.S. citizen or U.S. shipyard to apply for a construction-differential subsidy in order to offset the uncompetitively high costs of domestic shipbuilding. Basically, as long as it can be shown that the planned ship will meet requirements of U.S. foreign commerce, will help promote the development of that commerce, and will be suitable for military use in time of national emergency, it will be eligible for the government aid. The subsidy may equal the excess of the bid for construction over the estimated cost of constructing the same type vessel in a foreign yard, though it may not represent more than 50 percent of the total cost. To the furthest extent possible, U.S. materials must be used in constructing the subsidized vessel. Once completed, the ship must remain engaged in foreign trade or the owner must face repayment of the subsidy to the government.

Also, the Maritime Commission may insure mortgages and loans made by private lending institutions for the construction, reconstruction, or reconditioning of vessels owned by U.S. citizens. In addition, war risk insurance, when not obtainable from regular insurers at reasonable rates, can be provided by the federal government.

Government aid is not limited to construction and insurance, however. Once a ship is ready for operation, the U.S. owner can avail himself of an operating-differential subsidy in an amount that the secretary of commerce determines is necessary in order that he can meet foreign flag competition. This assistance is designed to offset the competitive advantage that foreign carriers secure through lower wage scales, maintenance costs, and insurance rates.

Shipowners also benefit significantly from legislative acts requiring that all coastwise shipping be by U.S. built, owned, and operated vessels and that 50 percent of all U.S. government financed cargo must be shipped in U.S. vessels.

The history of U.S. programs to aid shipping extends back through the Merchant Marine Acts of 1928 and 1920. It has long been believed, particularly by the shipping industry, that the maintenance of a strong U.S. merchant fleet and a viable shipbuilding industry are essential to ensure national security. Because of the policy established by congressional acts, and the still strongly argued national security justification for existing subsidies, hope for fruitful negotiation in the near future on the removal or substantial diminution of these programs would be quite unwarranted.

3. 46 U.S.C. secs. 1101–1294, as amended.

Aid for U.S. Aviation

In a somewhat different manner the U.S. aviation industry has been the recipient of substantial government aid. Until recently, neither the U.S. international air carriers nor the civilian sector of the aircraft construction industry were receiving direct government assistance. A move toward direct subsidization may, however, have begun. The effort to obtain government financial support for the construction of a supersonic transport, though defeated in Congress in 1971, might well be revived should the foreign versions of the aircraft prove economically practical and ecologically benign.

The government has provided guarantees on loans made by commercial lending institutions to the Lockheed Corporation, albeit by a narrow margin of approval in the House and Senate. In spite of all-out support by the President and an extensive lobbying effort by interests as diverse as organized labor and Wall Street financiers, the congressional opposition to the Lockheed bailout was surprisingly strong and broadly based.[4] For this reason it would be premature to divine a trend. It could well be that the $250 million Lockheed loan guarantee represents an anomaly rather than a precedent-setting event.

If U.S. commercial aviation has had little history of direct subsidization, it has benefited substantially from government expenditures made in the development of *military* aviation. Design and development breakthroughs in the military aircraft field have enabled the domestic producers to achieve great success in the marketing of civilian transports. For example, the Boeing 707, one of the most widely used planes in the history of commercial aviation, was an outgrowth of defense expenditures on manned bombers. By utilizing engines that had been developed for the Air Force and had undergone considerable testing and refinement in day-to-day operation, the civilian segment of the industry was able to avoid the high risks and costs normally associated with the design of aircraft engines.[5]

4. The legislation passed the House of Representatives 192 to 189 and the Senate 49 to 48—by less than 1 percent of the aggregate votes cast. Senator Marlow Cook (Republican of Kentucky), who broke the Senate tie, said that he was opposed in principle but was too disturbed over the state of the economy to vote against a bill that the President said was necessary to save 60,000 jobs. *Aviation Week and Space Technology*, Aug. 9, 1971, p. 24.

5. By contrast, the aircraft industry developed wide-body jets without prior mili-

The high point of military aircraft development in the United States was reached during the 1950s and 1960s. Emphasis has since then switched to development of missiles and other types of defense weaponry, and the competitive advantage of the civilian aircraft manufacturers has been dwindling rapidly. Conversely, the subsidy programs that other countries had adopted as a means of equalizing the advantages that the U.S. defense program provided to the U.S. civilian aircraft industry—such as the British and French support of the Concorde—are becoming much more significant to international civil air transport.

This shift in American defense priorities has accomplished what would never have been possible through international negotiations. Since military aviation is considered essential to overall U.S. defense policy and any benefits bestowed on the civilian aviation sector are regarded as a by-product, it would have been useless to attempt international negotiation to minimize the latter if, as appears probable, this could only have been accomplished by subjecting military construction to international restraints.

If the United States should ever resort to direct subsidization of the civilian aircraft industry in an attempt to prevent foreign manufacturers from capturing an inequitable share of the markets through their own countries' assistance programs, an argument put forth in the debates over the merits of government funding of the supersonic transport plane, the question of control and reduction of the assistance programs might well become a proper topic for international discussion. At present, however, there appears to be no substantial problem.

General Research and Development

Government-sponsored research and development can provide assistance to other kinds of domestic industry in much the same manner as military aircraft requirements have resulted in substantial benefits to the

---

tary development. The Boeing 747, the first of these new passenger planes, employs engines that were designed and developed specifically for this plane. The plane encountered delivery delays, and its operating costs during the first few months were well in excess of what had been expected. Development of engines for the Lockheed Tristar caused even more significant problems. Rolls-Royce's failure in the production of the Tristar's engines resulted in bankruptcy for Rolls and contributed greatly to the poor financial position of Lockheed.

civilian aircraft industry. While government-funded research and development is considerably more extensive in the United States than in other
countries, most of the expenditures are funneled into nuclear, space, and
defense technological research and can only be indirectly and indiffer-
ently translated into the economic end product of consumer goods and
services that affect international trade. In many other industrialized countries on the other hand, a much greater percentage of the gross national
product represents governmental research directed toward purely domestic economic ends that can affect trade across national boundaries.[6]
The same considerations that militate against international agreement
concerning aid to the aircraft industry appear, however, to apply here.

Tax Relief Measures

The U.S. oil industry is the recipient of yet another type of government
aid, this one in the form of extremely generous tax treatment. The oil
depletion allowance, along with the ability to write off most of the costs
incurred in drilling a well, results in a government aid to the industry just
as significant as an outright compensation payment. It has been estimated
that the removal of the depletion allowance alone could cause a 20 percent
jump in the price of domestic petroleum.[7] As long as imports of oil were
restricted by quotas, the liberal tax treatment available to the domestic
producer had little actual impact on imports. With the quota system eliminated, however, the depletion allowance and other lucrative tax exemptions could have a significant restrictive effect on the domestic demand
for foreign oil were there no physical shortages.[8]

---

6. The U.S. government's expenditures on research and development (R&D)
equal 2.2 percent of the gross national product (GNP), but only 0.05 percent is
devoted to such economic ends as industry, agriculture, transportation, and construction. By contrast, France spends 1 percent of the GNP on R&D projects but
0.24 percent on the economic sector, and the United Kingdom 1.2 percent on R&D
but 0.27 percent on the economic sector. Japan spends only 0.04 percent of her
total GNP on this type of activity. Robert E. Baldwin, *Nontariff Distortions of
International Trade* (Brookings Institution, 1970), pp. 123–24.

7. Ibid., p. 116.

8. The depletion allowances are not limited to oil. Almost all firms involved in
the recovery of natural resources are able to benefit from these provisions.

Other forms of tax relief such as investment tax credits and accelerated depreciation of capital assets provide substantial benefits to many U.S. businesses. The sheer number of industries enjoying these advantages makes it virtually impossible to measure their distorting effect on imports. Since almost all other industrialized nations provide for capital investment write-offs at a more rapid rate than does the United States,[9] it is reasonable to assume that in general imports into the United States are not more unreasonably restricted as a result of these tax measures than are imports into other countries employing similar devices.

A number of provisions of the Internal Revenue Code were clearly intended from their inception to influence foreign trade. For example, the Western Hemisphere Trade Corporation Act, which enables American companies to take advantage of preferentially low rates of taxation on business outside the United States but within the hemisphere, provides significant tax relief for export sales from the United States.[10]

A variety of measures of indirect assistance to enterprises that could have side effects on imports do not appear to have resulted in harmful effects thus far. Adjustment assistance in the form of tax-loss benefits, technical assistance, and low-interest loans for firms injured by increased imports caused by trade agreement concessions could have such a result. So too could low-interest loans to small businesses, or special technical and other assistance to depressed areas. These types of measures thus far, however, do not appear to have affected imports adversely.

9. Richard N. Cooper, "National Economic Policy in an Interdependent World Economy," *Yale Law Journal,* Vol. 76 (1967), pp. 1273, 1288.

10. Peter Buck Feller, "Mutiny Against the Bounty: An Examination of Subsidies, Border Tax Adjustments, and the Resurgence of the Countervailing Duty Law," *Law and Policy in International Business,* Vol. 1 (1969), pp. 17, 44–45. Another tax-subsidy measure was proposed in the 1970 trade bill that failed to gain congressional approval. The bill provided for the establishment of domestic international sales corporations which, although designed to improve U.S. balance of payments, in effect virtually exempted U.S. exporters from U.S. taxation by inviting them to set up dummy corporations to receive income from their foreign sales. Like foreign corporations, these shell corporations would not be subject to tax so long as they met the technical requirements, and shareholders would be entitled to defer half their earnings indefinitely for tax purposes. These accumulated untaxed profits then would be available to the parent as intracompany low-interest loans. This measure, revived as part of President Nixon's new economic policies, found its way in a modified form into the *1971 Revenue Act,* Pub. L. 92-178, 85 Stat. 536.

The Negligible Trade Impact of Aid

In general, U.S. aid to domestic industry has had a small impact on foreign trade. While indirect aid has given significant competitive advantages to the aircraft industry, a gradual shift in the direction of government development programs has greatly diminished the importance to the civilian aviation industry. Shipbuilding and ship operation subsidies, on the other hand, continue to offer substantial competitive advantages to domestic producers, with no change in sight.

Even if there were a recognizable international need to reduce these types of subsidies, the United States' ability to negotiate effectively concerning them would be severely restricted. Congressional approval would be required for any practical accord on removal of such subsidies. Negotiation of a presidential agreement within the leeway of existing federal legislation would thus be unavailable. The relationship between the existing domestic aid programs and considerations of national defense and security, and the deep entrenchment of these programs in U.S. economic policy, make it highly unlikely that Congress would act favorably to effectuate any agreement that the President might negotiate under his independent powers, or to authorize such an agreement on its own.

In light of these considerations, the United States is not in a position to negotiate effectively on the reduction of its relatively limited governmental aid to domestic industries. Indeed, because the scope of current subsidy programs is so limited, their continuance by the United States government, while undoubtedly posing some problems for the foreign competitors of subsidized American industries, does not constitute a matter of crucial concern when viewed from a total world trade perspective.

CHAPTER NINE

Prospects for
U.S. Negotiations

THE UNITED STATES is in a position to negotiate successfully for the reduction or elimination of certain of the six American nontariff barriers considered in this study while serious difficulties still inhibit such negotiation of others. There are appropriate strategies for conducting those negotiations that are feasible and some that are unwise. Certain kinds of agreements hold promise of successful negotiation and some do not.

The chief executive of any country, and particularly the United States, has greater power—fewer constraints on his ability to act alone—in the area of foreign political policy than he does in dealing with foreign economic policy. Recognition of a foreign government and the choice whether to enter into or sever diplomatic relations are clearly executive decisions that will be constrained primarily by adverse public opinion. In the main, the forces most responsible for affecting public sentiment are unwilling to interfere with the President's right to decide these questions as his informed discretion dictates.

Not so with the great bulk of foreign economic policy questions. Here, issues are rarely new. Usually contention among competing interest groups within the country has been resolved in legislative enactments. At any given time the President is confronted with existing law—be it the Tariff Act of 1909 or 1913 or 1930—governing the rates of duty on imports. Regardless of his desires to reduce or raise these rates, he is unable to do

223

so alone. Whatever leeway he has must be found within the legislative enactment itself.

Nor are duties the only important constraint on foreign economic policies. Almost every aspect of trade in goods is the subject of legislation, whether it be customs valuation standards and procedures, such regulation of international trade practices as antidumping and countervailing duties, or the purchase of imports for governmental use.

Indeed, as legislation responds to social needs, the new constraints can affect imports even though imposed without particular reference to them. Industrial standards or specifications imposed for health or safety reasons can and often do affect imports, as the automobile safety regulations of recent years attest. Domestic subsidy measures to prop up ailing industries such as shipbuilding, or even relatively healthy ones such as agriculture, inevitably have as their consequence restraints on imports that can render ineffective both the subsidy and the objective it sought.

In all these areas of trade, as well as in questions of foreign financial affairs involving loans and grants to foreign countries and enterprises, the legislature speaks in the form of statutes and the chief executive acts within the limitations—the amounts available and the conditions of expenditures—laid down therein.

Thus if the adverse effects of nontariff barriers on international trade are to be eliminated or moderated, there must be collaboration between the President and the Congress. That collaboration can take the form of advance authorization by Congress of presidential agreements with foreign nations eliminating or moderating nontariff barriers, subject to specified limitations; of a policy resolution of Congress calling for negotiation, with subsequent legislative approval of the agreements; of subsequent approval of overall agreements without a prior policy resolution by Congress; or of presidential agreements without the advance authorization or subsequent approval of Congress but within the leeway permitted by a fair construction of existing legislation. This last method can fairly be said to represent a presidential-congressional collaborative effort even though the two branches act at different times. The intent of Congress expressed in an enactment containing latitude for presidential discretion continues until the legislation is changed. A presidential agreement that remains within that statutory leeway—conforming with the continuing congressional intention—is the culmination of a truly collaborative effort.

Reliance on Congressional Authorization or Approval

The political balances between protectionist and liberal trade forces often make quite impractical any plan to secure advance authorization by the Congress of presidential agreements eliminating or reducing nontariff barriers affecting trade adversely. This appears to be particularly true in the early 1970s, which have witnessed a burgeoning of protectionist sentiment that favors raising, not lowering, domestic trade barriers.

A policy resolution by Congress, with later legislative approval of the ensuing agreements, puts the President in no better position than the alternative of simply securing subsequent approval of agreements. Moreover, there is a substantial risk that a policy resolution will make exceptions for certain notariff barriers that could otherwise be negotiated in a presidential agreement kept within the confines of existing legislation. Even authorization to negotiate agreements subject to their being disapproved by either house of Congress by simple majority of those present and voting is a shaky foundation for negotiation. Surely, the bitter experience of the American selling price (ASP) agreement will make foreign governments wary of negotiating seriously on such a basis.

It has been suggested that, with the strongest kind of presidential prodding, Congress might give subsequent approval to, or withhold disapproval from, a balanced package of nontariff barrier relaxations in which each benefiting country compensates for the relaxations of its trading partners. But the ASP package in the Kennedy Round was such a balance; it was not approved because the American beneficiaries of reduced European road taxes were industries other than the American chemical industry, which feared the repeal of ASP that would have benefited the Europeans.[1] It will almost always be thus in balancing nontariff barriers—the domestic forces opposed to the relaxation of a particular nontariff barrier will care more, and fight harder and more successfully, than the domestic beneficiaries of another barrier's relaxation by a reciprocating country.

The very concept of a balance among nontariff barriers assumes that benefits are quantitatively commensurable. But if the benefits to be derived

1. For an interesting discussion of the ASP package, see Rehm, "The Kennedy Round of Trade Negotiations," *American Journal of International Law,* Vol. 62 (1968), p. 403.

from the elimination of nontariff barriers cannot be quantified with some precision, the concept is unworkable—true reciprocity is impossible. There is little evidence that such balancing of advantage can be accomplished.

Indeed, even in the relatively simple bargaining of ordinary tariffs, reciprocity in quantitative terms has always had in it large elements of fiction. Thus, the press release at the close of a tariff bargaining round may declare solemnly that the United States granted concessions—rate reductions and bindings of already low rates—covering $1 billion of French imports in 1970, while France granted similar concessions to American imports—including rate reductions in whatever degree and bindings of whatever nature—amounting to $980 million, and that this constituted reciprocity. Reciprocity has never been taken any further than that. The precise content of the concessions in terms of their trade effects has never been investigated. Depending as they do on many variables, the trade effects of tariff bargaining have been considered to be statistically unknowable. Since this is true of ordinary tariff bargaining, the much more difficult task of determining commensurability between various relaxations of nontariff barriers is even less likely to be successful.

Yet another difficulty of a package of reciprocal relaxations is its scope; it would sweep up in an agreement that required legislative approval many components that might well fall within the leeway of existing legislation and therefore not need such approval. If the package agreement then failed to secure legislative approval, a pall would be cast over any subsequent breakout of its components for independent activation and application.

The most unlikely negotiating possibility is a major political effort by the President to put across a balanced package of negotiated reductions or eliminations of important nontariff barriers. There have been three major, successful moves in the direction of freer trade in the United States during the past four decades. Each has followed an event affecting U.S. trade interests that could be described to the people and the Congress as necessitating a change in the overall foreign policy strategy in the national interest. In 1934 the trade agreements program was adopted as part of a strategy to lift the United States out of a depression by reviving her foreign trade.

This trade had fallen drastically; U.S. losses were much greater proportionately than those suffered by other countries during the Great Depression. The sharp decline had followed the enactment of the infamous Smoot-Hawley Tariff Act of 1930, which had raised American tariffs to the highest levels in American history. In consequence, the stage was set for a major breakthrough to new ground—reciprocal tariff reductions through international agreement, with reductions as deep as 50 percent of the existing rates.

The bilateral trade agreements flowing from the 1934 act only moderately allayed unilateral economic moves during the 1930s. Each country before World War II sought through these moves to export its unemployment. The postwar planners envisioned a world requiring increased international cooperation in the trade and financial areas—no less than one-world political principles, and organizations to support them. The United Nations Charter, the Bretton Woods institutions, the General Agreement on Tariffs and Trade (GATT), and the International Trade Organization Charter (the last of which failed to come into being) were to be the political and economic framework for a new and better world of international cooperation. The Roosevelt administration put forward, and Congress enacted, the 1945 Trade Agreements Extension Act in response to this conception. It authorized 50 percent tariff reductions in reciprocal international agreements, but this time negotiated multilaterally; it established an overriding rule of most-favored-nation treatment or nondiscrimination in trade, as well as other important trade rules.

The third forceful move in the direction of freer trade was also triggered by politico-economic circumstances and opportunities. When, in 1962, the Kennedy administration put forward a bold proposal for a 50 percent tariff-cutting authority, a sharply tightened escape clause, adjustment assistance to firms and workers, and special added authority to cut tariffs if England joined the European Economic Community (EEC),[2] it was to maintain American exports to the burgeoning Community, which was dismantling its internal tariff and other barriers. It was believed that a major tariff reduction by the United States, reciprocated in the common external tariff rates of the EEC, could go a long distance toward reducing the otherwise adverse impact of the Common Market on American exports. A major response was believed to be required to a major politico-

2. See ibid.

economic phenomenon, the EEC. Congress responded with the Trade Expansion Act of 1962, making possible the most successful tariff negotiating session ever held, the Kennedy Round.

What are the chances, realistically assessed, of anything like those watershed events occurring in the near future in the nontariff barrier area? Obviously, they are not good. The ink was barely dry on the Kennedy Round agreements of June 30, 1967, when Congress felt the first tremors of a still ominous protectionist movement. The favorable balance of trade of the United States disappeared and is only now beginning to reappear. Rising and persistent inflation, consequent on many factors, particularly a long and costly involvement in a Southeast Asian war without an initial accompanying increase in taxes, sucked in foreign products ranging from textiles and shoes to steel. These are among the factors that have fueled the current drive to curtail imports. Its high-water mark, the nearly-enacted trade bill of 1970, would have resulted in a serious curtailment of U.S. trade, putting at risk more than $7 billion of imports, and heralding a drastic change in U.S. trade policy from that pursued since the 1934 Trade Agreements Act.[3]

With divided counsel from the Nixon administration—the State Department opposing the bill, the Commerce Department lobbying in favor of its passage, and the White House taking no position—the House of Representatives passed the bill by a vote of 216 to 165, a smaller margin than had been expected, and one that might well have evaporated altogether had there been vigorous presidential opposition to the measure. The determination of a small group of senators resulted in the death of the bill at the close of the second session of the Ninety-first Congress. Hard-fought, rear-guard defenses of the advocates of liberal trade avoided a rout by protectionist forces. Substantial gains have been made, however, by the protectionists during the past several years. Voluntary restrictions on imports of steel, textiles, and shoes have been forced through pressure from the government, acting at the behest of domestic industries desiring to cut back competitive imports.

These protectionist advances are not proof that the United States has embarked on a course that will lead unmistakably to the reversal of its trade policies of the past four decades. The forces, protectionist and freer trade, are at present too closely balanced to suggest that a rout is immi-

3. See Stanley D. Metzger, "The Mills Bill," *Journal of World Trade Law,* Vol. 5 (1971), p. 235.

nent. Nonetheless, the protectionists, augmented in recent years by the defection of organized labor from their freer trade policies of the past thirty years, have grown stronger and there is little to suggest that freer trade forces will be strong enough in the near future to mount a major offensive. Yet this is precisely what would be called for if a determined chief executive bent on vigorous pursuit of liberal trade objectives were to urge forcefully on Congress an overall nontariff barrier elimination-or-modification agreement.

Everything conspires against such an occurrence. An administration concerned with protecting against excessive imports while not giving up the liberal trade franchise, a Congress hesitant to offend domestic protectionist forces—these facts of life are inconsistent with any near-term freer-trade breakthrough. The terms of the 1973 trade reform bill, as reported by the House of Representatives in October 1973, appear to support amply this assessment.

Moreover, the external circumstances are not nearly as conducive to a bold new forward trade move as those that attended the three earlier advances. The EEC has just acquired three new member countries. Japan is attempting to scale down its huge trade surplus—which requires a wide opening of its market after twenty years of deficits and the attendant efforts to expand its export trade. The EEC has a particularly acute political and economic agricultural problem, which sorely tests U.S. goodwill as the common agricultural policy poses a threat to America's traditional agricultural export market in Europe. And as Japan slows its vigorous export expansion, the less developed countries hope to accelerate their exports, through tariff preferences and other measures. The mood of Americans tends now to be one of watching and considering carefully future policies, rather than striking ambitiously for major removals of trade barriers that curtail imports. In short, current political and economic circumstances conspire against congressional approval following negotiation of an overall nontariff barrier agreement.

This pessimistic appraisal is, of course, based on current realities. Should the heads of government of the United States, the enlarged European Community, and Japan decide that a major effort to integrate the economies of their countries was essential to forestall further division into competing economic and political blocs, legislative authority might be given to enable U.S. participation. National leaders might decide, for instance, that they must press for a free trade area in industrial goods within a ten year period, with specific staged reductions in tariffs and quotas during the period, that they should harmonize their agricultural production and distribution so as to avoid or severely limit export subsidies and import restrictions,[4] and that major nontariff barrier reduction should be otherwise essayed.

Authorization for agreements in the nontariff barrier area that would alter inconsistent domestic legislation, if not disapproved by either house of Congress within ninety days after the President had laid the agreement on the table of Congress, could eventuate.[5] It would be imprudent to suppose, however, that such authority would be utilized in any important degree when protectionist sentiment militates against relaxation of nontariff barrier legislation that is protective in effect, and one house of Congress by simple majority of those present and voting can upset any agreement purporting to change domestic laws having such effect.

Reliance on Existing Legislation

The one method of negotiation that does not rely on congressional action is the presidential agreement within the leeway of existing legislation. This method carries with it certain clear implications for the content and timing of nontariff barrier negotiations that appear to be consistent with, not antagonistic to, existing political realities.

Each major nontariff barrier identified as important to trade among developed countries, or between them and less developed countries, must be examined in detail, to determine whether negotiating leeway exists, and what the boundaries are.

If no leeway seems to exist for a particular nontariff barrier, it should be consigned to a stand-by, lower priority, position—put in the "future" book of barriers that must await a better day for international action. Antidumping duties and countervailing duties (for developed country exports), substantive agreements on quantitative restrictions, government aids to industry (such as shipbuilding subsidies), and customs valuation (other than ASP) fall within this area, where none of the negotiating methods appear to be feasible.

4. As suggested in *Reshaping the International Economic Order*, A Tripartite Report by Twelve Economists from North America, the European Community, and Japan (Brookings Institution, 1972), p. 12.

5. H.R. 10710, reported by the House Ways and Means Committee in October 1973, so provides.

If substantial latitude is apparent for a particular nontariff barrier, it should qualify as a high-priority item for negotiation in the near term. Buy-national laws and policies, the procedural aspects of quantitative restrictions and voluntary agreements, and industrial standards fall in this category.

The Unpromising Candidates

The antidumping statute is being administered in a manner that is inconsistent with U.S. obligations under the International Antidumping Code of 1967. The countervailing duty statute is inconsistent with the GATT requirement that a duty be imposed to offset subsidization only after a finding of injury; it is saved from being a violation only by the grandfather clause of the GATT's Protocol of Provisional Application. Were the Antidumping Code of 1967 to be applied, so that dumping duties would be assessed only where sales at less than fair value were the principal cause of serious injury to the domestic industry—judged by such normal criteria as serious loss of sales, profits, and employment—countries would have gone a fair distance toward containing the potential trade-distorting effects of antidumping laws. The difficulty, however, is that neither U.S. law nor its administration is consistent with the code. The need here is for domestic legal and administrative change to bring American law and administration into conformity with the code, not for more international agreement.

In the countervailing duty area, the immediate need is for domestic legal changes to bring the statutes into conformity with GATT by providing that subsidized imports must cause material injury to a domestic industry before the duty may be imposed, and to grant the President discretion to refrain from countervailing such imports when he deems it important to the national interest, a discretion that is now not accorded. While international agreement on what constitutes a *subsidy* would be useful, the many years of effort in that direction do not augur well for renewed efforts. Moreover, further definition is less important than action limiting the use of subsidies that are not in definitional dispute.

Agricultural subsidies, practiced by all trading nations, are the most important of these acknowledged subsidies. It seems clear that it will only be possible to limit them through comprehensive agreements relating to production and marketing policies, not agreements relating to subsidies alone. Direct subsidization of industrial goods has not been a major trade problem for some time among developed countries. Here the problem has been indirect subsidies to exports through concessional government financing, which again is not a definitional problem but one of curtailing use of this means of augmenting export earnings. Negotiations looking toward such curtailment cannot be viewed as promising in the light of stepped-up employment of such devices in the United States and elsewhere.

Substantive agreements on quantitative restrictions also look unpromising for productive negotiations in the near future. Negotiations on international trade in agricultural products, for instance, must be concerned not only with external barriers such as quotas but also with who should produce how much wheat, or other products, and market it at what price, domestically as well as abroad. This kind of negotiation would of course involve such matters as quotas; but dealing separately with agricultural quotas, as such, would be fruitless in light of their intimate connection with domestice price-support and other subsidy schemes.

Substantive negotiations appear to be equally unpromising in the near future on industrial goods quotas. Past efforts to define *market disruption* in international negotiations have proved to be singularly unproductive, since general criteria for determining whether "too many" imports are occurring "too soon" have eluded agreement. Such events as the near enactment of the 1970 trade bill, with its definition of "too much" as more than 15 percent import penetration and "too soon" as 3 percent plus 2 percent in successive years, indicate that any renewed effort would founder on the attempt to reach general agreement.

Aid to industry that has an adverse impact on imports—while being relatively little practiced by the United States—appears to be far too stubborn in those areas where it is employed to warrant optimism about its being subjected to an international negotiating process. Shipbuilding and ship operating subsidies, and exclusionary laws affecting coasting trade, all designed to encourage the relatively uneconomic American shipbuilding industry and U.S. flag-carrier fleet, show no signs of diminishing. Indeed, recent support for a three-hundred-ship building program over a ten year period demonstrates that the United States is less disposed than ever to negotiate away from the use of such subsidies in the limited area in which this means of support for domestic industries has been employed.

The statutory system of customs valuation (other than ASP) practiced by the United States—cumbersome, complex, and often arbitrary—is embedded in legislation that cannot be changed by the President's acting on his own authority. Neither advance authorization nor subsequent approval without such authorization can be expected from the Congress. On ASP, which Congress has indicated some willingness to eliminate, action depends on the fate of the 1973 trade bill.[6] Domestic action directed at amelioration of the antidumping and countervailing duty statutes— such as adding an injury requirement to the countervailing duty law and changing the Antidumping Act to conform with the code—is clearly in order, even though its immediate prospect is not bright. Indeed, efforts will be required in the next few years to resist protectionist attempts, exemplified in certain provisions of the 1973 trade bill, to make these barriers even more effective and onerous than they already are.

The Promising Candidates

Those nontariff barriers that are capable of effective and successful negotiation under the President's authority to act alone should have highest priority on any agenda for negotiations. Efforts should be made to create separate regimes within the agreement on each nontariff barrier, with reciprocal, mutually beneficial commitments among the negotiating countries. Thus, each participating country would benefit from the relaxation by its trading partner of a particular barrier affecting it adversely in exchange for its own relaxation of that barrier.

The prognosis for productive negotiations on buy-national laws and policies appears to be quite favorable so far as the United States is concerned. Despite the existence of federal and state buy-American laws, a presidential agreement within the leeway of existing federal legislation is feasible. The federal statute contains no minimum percentage of preference, and specifically refrains from endorsing preferences that would require that governments pay "unreasonable" prices. From time to time the President has applied preferences ranging from 6 percent (including duty) to 50 percent. He could enter into an international agreement sharply limiting the margin of preference to a level that would not be a significant deterrent to international trade—say, to 6 percent, thereby satisfying a basic objection to buy-American legislation. In doing so, he should eliminate the possibility of reinstitution of a higher margin of preference through the invocation of a balance of payments exception. This should

6. H.R. 10710 authorizes conversion of ASP to ad valorem rates in trade agreements. Ibid.

not raise great difficulties because he could also require reciprocity from other major trading nations, through a comparable reduction in the impact of their buy-national policies, which are even harsher than those of the United States; the balance of payments effects of such an agreement would be largely neutralized. While escapes or exceptions would doubtless be necessary, for national security reasons or to protect domestic bidders in labor-surplus areas, indiscriminate and frequent use of these provisions could be forestalled by a requirement of consultation with affected parties prior to a deviation from the agreement.

A buy-national agreement should be self-executing in terms, overriding inconsistent state legislation, and it should provide for a consultative organ —a committee of the GATT, perhaps. Such an organ, with a small staff charged with administering the advance consultations required for escapes as well as those necessitated by complaints of failure to comply with the agreement, could also be useful in administering other nontariff barrier agreements that might be negotiated from time to time. The director of the consultative organ could quite usefully be clothed with the informal investigative functions of an ombudsman.

The procedural aspects of quantitative restrictions or voluntary agreements curtailing specified exports can also be treated in presidential agreements within the leeway of existing federal legislation. There is no obstacle, legal or political, to countries consulting their trading partners who could be affected adversely in advance of the adoption of quantative restrictions or the exertion of pressure for the adoption of voluntary restraints over their exports. No statute forbids, no public opinion opposes such consultation, which would be like the consultation on troop levels and other contributions to the North Atlantic Treaty Organization that the United States has engaged in over the past twenty years. The consultative organ could prepare any necessary factual materials, based on submissions by the principal countries affected, and otherwise organize justification-and-answer discussions among the exporting and importing countries whose trade would be affected by the proposed measures. Consultations in advance of restrictive trade measures are, of course, no guarantee that the restrictions will not ensue. But they offer a significant opportunity for avoiding some trade restrictions and for lessening the severity of others and would thus be a distinct step toward freer trade.

Additionally, the United States should take parallel domestic procedural measures. Under existing law, an independent factual appraisal by a public body is a sine qua non for any sort of presidential action liberalizing import restrictions. It is not too much to require such an investigation and appraisal before restrictive action is taken that harms American consumers, feeds inflation, and adversely affects the successful conduct of the foreign relations of the United States. It follows that no international agreement should be negotiated and no voluntary restraint arrangement by foreign governments or foreign industry groups (such as the restrictions on steel exports with no independent factual appraisal) should be induced by the U.S. government without a prior presidential determination, reasoned, public, and based on an anterior, governmental, factual appraisal with full opportunity for public participation.

The facts that many industrial standards are voluntary, and not imposed by law; that they are extremely varied and number in the thousands; that a number have been imposed by governments for benign reasons of public health and welfare and not for protectionist reasons; and that the adverse trade effects of existing standards are extremely difficult to identify and quantify militate strongly against overall solutions to the trade barrier problems that standardization has created. But while specific international agreements regulating in detail the creation and enforcement of industrial standards are premature, there are several areas in which an agreement is wholly feasible.

An international agreement along the following lines, concluded by the President within the leeway of existing federal legislation, should be perfectly possible for the United States: The parties (such as the GATT contracting parties) would agree to support financially and technically the work done by voluntary organizations with respect to the formulation of international standards and the mutual recognition of voluntary testing and certification schemes. The parties would agree to consider—and to have their political subdivisions consider—the adverse effects on international trade of any mandatory action they may take with respect to industrial standards and to seek to mitigate or eliminate such effects. They would agree to establish immediately an international clearinghouse for information concerning industrial standards and certification schemes and to undertake to establish national clearinghouses to the same end. They would agree to seek removal or change of unreasonably discriminatory standards or enforcement thereof to the extent feasible; moreover, they would agree that these are measures that can nullify or impair the benefits of the GATT and that can, in consequence, lead to consultation and the other remedial measures provided for under Article XXIII.

The Quality of Negotiation

Of course, it may not be possible to create fully reciprocal regimes within a negotiation on a single nontariff barrier. Under an agreement to reduce preferences for domestic products in government procurement, for instance, two countries might not be able to increase their exports to each other in equal amounts simply because one enjoys a comparative advantage in the production of the types of goods that bulk large in modern government procurement. This kind of circumstance would no doubt lead to moves to widen negotiations on nontariff barriers so that a package balanced in terms of the trade impact on the negotiating countries could be arrived at.

Nontariff barriers being incommensurate and very uneven in their trade effects, however, such widening should be undertaken with care lest it become a search for an elusive reciprocity in numbers.

What would probably, though not necessarily, eventuate from international negotiation to ameliorate the trade effects of nontariff trade barriers that are within the leeway of existing U.S. federal legislation is a series of negotiations on individual barriers, or relatively small groups of them, over a span of several years. The results could be put into effect piecemeal or as a package. In neither event would legislative reference be necessary for the United States, for by definition agreement on each nontariff barrier would be within the leeway of domestic legislation. It would be wise, however, to put into effect each agreement as its negotiation is completed. In that way each country could reap the benefits of increased trade earlier than if all barrier relaxations or removals had to await the last one achieved. And as each negotiation resulted in improvement of access to each other's market, without horrendous destructive effects on local industries, the successful negotiation of those agreements that followed would become easier.

The negotiating strategy suggested in this study indicates that it would be most useful, if not essential, that negotiations be under the auspices of a consultative organ on nontariff barriers which should be created within the GATT (or possibly the Organization for Economic Cooperation and Development if there developed any special GATT problems). Under effective leadership, this consultative organ could prepare for negotiations, initiate nontariff barrier studies in aid of negotiations, assist negotiations, and through such activity prepare itself to follow through as the organ for handling disputes and consultations and otherwise assisting to administer the agreements arrived at. In terms of effectuation of agreements arrived at, it would be well to establish a special ombudsman as part of the consultative organ in order to follow the workings of the agreement in signatory countries.

The same paucity of strong leadership may appear to threaten these modest freer trade policies that render more ambitious initiatives highly unlikely. But not as much leadership and not as much expenditure of political capital are required to carry out a program that is kept within the leeway of domestic legislation as would be necessary in the employment of those methods of achieving reduction or elimination of important nontariff barriers adversely affecting international trade that require congressional concurrence. The course of action proposed in this study appears to fall within the leeway of political realities, as well as law.

APPENDIX A

Buy American Act

41 U.S.C. 10a
American materials required for public use

Notwithstanding any other provision of law, and unless the head of the department or independent establishment concerned shall determine it to be inconsistent with the public interest, or the cost to be unreasonable, only such unmanufactured articles, materials, and supplies as have been mined or produced in the United States, and only such manufactured articles, materials, and supplies as have been manufactured in the United States substantially all from articles, materials, or supplies mined, produced, or manufactured, as the case may be, in the United States, shall be acquired for public use. This section shall not apply with respect to articles, materials, or supplies for use outside the United States, or if articles, materials, or supplies of the class or kind to be used or the articles, materials, or supplies from which they are manufactured are not mined, produced, or manufactured, as the case may be, in the United States in sufficient and reasonably available commercial quantities and of a satisfactory quality. (Mar. 3, 1933, ch. 212, title III, Sec. 2, 47 Stat. 1520.)

41 U.S.C. 10b
Contracts for public works; specification for use of American materials; blacklisting contractors violating requirements.

(a) Every contract for the construction, alteration, or repair of any public building or public work in the United States growing out of an appropriation heretofore made or hereafter to be made shall contain a provision that in the performance of the work of the contractor, subcontractors, material men, or suppliers, shall use only such unmanufactured articles, materials, and supplies as have been mined or produced in the United States, and only such manufactured articles, materials, and supplies as have been manufactured in the United States substantially all from articles, materials, or supplies mined, pro-

238

duced, or manufactured, as the case may be, in the United States except as provided in section 10a of this title: Provided, however, That if the head of the department or independent establishment making the contract shall find that in respect to some particular articles, materials, or supplies it is impracticable to make such requirement or that it would unreasonably increase the cost, an exception shall be noted in the specifications as to that particular article, material, or supply, and a public record made of the findings which justified the exception.

(b) If the head of a department, bureau, agency, or independent establishment which has made any contract containing the provision required by subsection (a) finds that in the performance of such contract there has been a failure to comply with such provisions, he shall make public his findings, including therein the name of the contractor obligated under such contract, and no other contract for the construction, alteration, or repair of any public building or public work in the United States or elsewhere shall be awarded to such contractor, subcontractors, material men, or suppliers with which such contractor is associated or affiliated, within a period of three years after finding is made public. (Mar. 3, 1933, ch. 212, title III, Sec. 3, 47 Stat. 1520.)

41 U.S.C. 10c
Definition of terms used in sections 10a and 10b.

When used in sections 10a and 10b of this title—

(a) The term "United States," when used in a geographical sense, includes the United States and any place subject to the jurisdiction thereof;

(b) The terms "public use," "public building," and "public work" shall mean use by, public building of, and public work of, the United States, the District of Columbia, Hawaii, Alaska, Puerto Rico, American Samoa, the Canal Zone, and the Virgin Islands. (Mar. 3, 1933, ch. 212, title III, Sec. 1, 47 Stat. 1520; 1946 Proc. No. 2695, eff. July 4, 1946, 11 Fed. Reg. 7517, 60 Stat. 1352.)

41 U.S.C. 10d
Clarification of Congressional intent regarding sections 10a and 10b (a).

In order to clarify the original intent of Congress, hereafter, section 10a of this title and that part of section 10b (a) of this title preceding the words "Provided, however," shall be regarded as requiring the purchase, for public use within the United States, of articles, materials, or supplies manufactured in the United States in sufficient and reasonably available commercial quantities and of a satisfactory quality, unless the head of the department or independent establishment concerned shall determine their purchase to be inconsistent with the public interest or their cost to be unreasonable. (Oct. 29, 1949, ch. 787, title VI, Sec. 633, 63 Stat. 1024.)

Executive Order 10582 of December 17, 1954

C.F.R. (1954 Supp.) 96, 19 Fed. Reg. 8723, 41 U.S.C.A. 10d
Uniform Procedures for Determinations

Section 1. As used in this order (a) the term "materials" includes articles and supplies, (b) the term "executive agency" includes executive department, independent establishment, and other instrumentality of the executive branch of the Government, and (c) the term "bid or offered price of materials of foreign origin" means the bid or offered price of such materials delivered at the place specified in the invitation to bid including applicable duty and all costs incurred after arrival in the United States.

Section 2. (a) For the purpose of this order materials shall be considered to be of foreign origin if the cost of the foreign products used in such materials constitutes fifty per centum or more of the cost of all the products used in such materials.

(b) For the purposes of the said act of March 3, 1933 [Sections 10a–10c of this title], and the other laws referred to in the first paragraph of the preamble of this order, the bid or offered price of materials of domestic origin shall be deemed to be unreasonable, or the purchase of such materials shall be deemed to be inconsistent with the public interest, if the bid or offered price thereof exceeds the sum of the bid or offered price of like materials of foreign origin and a differential computed as provided in subsection (c) of this section.

(c) The executive agency concerned shall in each instance determine the amount of the differential referred to in subsection (b) of this section on the basis of one of the following-described formulas, subject to the terms thereof:

(1) The sum determined by computing six per centum of the bid or offered price of materials of foreign origin.

(2) The sum determined by computing ten per centum of the bid or offered price of materials of foreign origin exclusive of applicable duty and all costs incurred after arrival in the United States: provided that when the bid or

offered price of materials of foreign origin amounts to less than $25,000, the sum shall be determined by computing ten per centum of such price exclusive only of applicable duty.

Section 3. Nothing in this order shall affect the authority or responsibility of an executive agency:

(a) To reject any bid or offer for reasons of the national interest not described or referred to in this order; or

(b) To place a fair proportion of the total purchases with small business concerns in accordance with section 302(b) of the Federal Property and Administrative Services Act of 1949, as amended [sections 252(b) of this title], section 2(b) of the Armed Services Procurement Act of 1947, as amended [repealed; now covered by sections 2301, 2303–2305 of Title 10], and section 202 of the Small Business Act of 1953 [section 631 of Title 15]; or

(c) To reject a bid or offer to furnish materials of foreign origin in any situation in which the domestic supplier offering the lowest price for furnishing the desired materials undertakes to produce substantially all of such materials in areas of substantial unemployment, as determined by the Secretary of Labor in accordance with such appropriate regulations as he may establish and during such period as the President may determine that it is in the national interest to provide to such areas preference in the award of Government contracts: Provided, that nothing in this section shall prevent the rejection of a bid or offered price which is excessive; or

(d) To reject any bid or offer for materials of foreign origin if such rejection is necessary to protect essential national-security interests after receiving advice with respect thereto from the President or from any officer of the Government designated by the President to furnish such advice.

Section 4. The head of each executive agency shall issue such regulations as may be necessary to insure that procurement practices under his jurisdiction conform to the provisions of this order.

Section 5. This order shall apply only to contracts entered into after the date hereof. In any case in which the head of an executive agency proposing to purchase domestic materials determines that a greater differential than that provided in this order between the cost of such materials of domestic origin and materials of foreign origin is not unreasonable or that the purchase of materials of domestic origin is not inconsistent with the public interest, this order shall not apply. A written report of the facts of each case in which such a determination is made shall be submitted to the President through the Director of the Bureau of the Budget by the official making the determination within 30 days thereafter.

DWIGHT D. EISENHOWER

Index

243